FROM FARM TO FIRM: RURAL DIVERSIFICATION IN THE ASIAN COUNTRYSIDE

*For Elisabeth, Charlotte and Katie
who have spent many hours
so patiently*

From Farm to Firm: Rural Diversification in the Asian Countryside

RICHARD SLATER

Development Administration Group
University of Birmingham

Avebury

Aldershot · Brookfield USA · Hong Kong · Singapore · Sydney

Published by

Avebury
Academic Publishing Group,
Gower House, Croft Road, Aldershot,
Hants. GU11 3HR, England

Gower Publishing Company
Old Post Road, Brookfield, Vermont 05036
USA

ISBN 1 85628 006 3

Printed and Bound in Great Britain by
Athenaeum Press Ltd., Newcastle upon Tyne.

Contents

List of tables

1 Introduction: agricultural intensification and the off-farm economy

Off-farm opportunities offer an important source of occupational diversification for many rural households. This is particularly the case under land scarce, labour surplus conditions or where sub optimal agro–climatic environments place a real constraint on increasing the productivity of agricultural land. In these situations off–farm potential is often the key to economic advancement and yet our understanding of the off–farm sector is still rather limited.

The expression 'farm to firm' is used in this book in an inferential sense to denote the increasing importance of employment and income diversification in the rural sector. Here, full time farm employment is giving way to part time farm and off–farm activity in the rural firm. The latter could range from a conventionally structured capitalist or micro capitalist firm to a household enterprise. In this sense, the defining 'partnership' element of the firm might be of a formal or informal (family) nature. It is interesting to point out that as the traditional family farm gradually adopts a diversified employment and income generating strategy there is a concomitant increase in the complexity of the reproduction process relating to labour deployment, technology, investment and marketing. Obviously, those households that depend on off–farm employment rather than self–employment will not be involved in all aspects of decision making that govern an enterprise. They will, nevertheless, be confronted by a range of work decisions that are distinct from those in agriculture. As the traditional farm household begins to engage in nonfarm activity there is a change in its production and consumption behaviour. For

1

some households this shift contains a degree of continuity in the size and scale of production, the use of family labour and high exposure to risk where the small farm and the small firm embody similar characteristics. Indeed, many households may be in the process of undertaking both farm and nonfarm activity simultaneously. For those households which become more fully integrated into the off-farm sector via regular waged or salaried employment, the farm to firm shift represents a straightforward change in emphasis from agricultural to non agricultural employment, although many may continue to perceive themselves as semi-agricultural retaining small plots for cultivation.

In formulating the central theoretical problem to which this study is addressed, it will be essential to outline some of the previous theoretical attempts to explain the nature of rural transition in newly industrialising and less developed countries. In so doing, the emphasis will be on sketching the development of the argument that has provided the main inspirational source of this study, focusing in particular on the more recent debate over the capitalist dissolution and replacement of non capitalist forms of production. As Long (1984) contends drawing on the views of Goodman and Redclift the 'basic difficulty, of course, with this type of debate is that arguments are frequently posed in terms of either/or propositions in search of some universal validity. What we now know of agrarian transitions suggests that the issues involved are highly complex and require careful specification of the articulation of capitalist and non capitalist forms placed within a broader analysis of the processes of economic and political incorporation' (Long 1984: 1).

The main theoretical problem to which this study is addressed is that concerning the debate over the development of capitalism in the countryside, and the more recent reformulation of this debate in terms of the failure of conventional capitalist production relations to become more widely generalised. By conducting a comparative investigation into the dynamics of the smallholder rice farming it is hoped that some light will be shed on the inadequately conceptualised nature of rural transition in monsoon Asia. In this way the findings may supplement the substantial amount of technical farm management material already in existence. The expansion of technology and artificial inputs in agriculture throughout much of monsoon Asia has inspired a good deal of literature on the main social and technical changes associated with rice cultivation (see for example Farmer 1977, Hansen 1981, Harriss 1982, Bayliss-Smith 1984 etc) which makes the re-examination of agrarian production relations of particular contemporary significance.

Bray (1986) argues that the particular physical and technical characteristics of wet rice cultivation have meant that substantial progress in output and yield has been made possible by low cost labour intensive innovation rather than high cost capital intensive transformation. This pattern of development, which is seen throughout much of South and Southeast Asia, has tended to reinforce a smallholder agricultural structure with a high degree of off-farm diversification. The exact nature and form of this diversification will depend

2

on a number of political and economic factors outside the realm of agriculture and it is important to recognise that while certain technical factors might favour a particular type of farm structure, the process is by no means exclusively technologically determined. As Moore (1985) has shown in the case of Sri Lanka, the particular nature of the smallholder farm structure has much to do with State policy and public intervention.

From a theoretical standpoint, it is hoped that this study may contribute towards the re-evaluation of processes of rural change. In particular this study will take issue with Structural Marxism which is seen as being rather too deterministic in its characterisation of agrarian change where agricultural transition is seen in terms of a Western oriented universal definition. As Kahn and Llobera (1980) have pointed out such definitions are often based upon idealist notions of historical materialism where social totality is seen as a structure of the 'hierarchy of instances'. In sympathy with Kahn and Llobera's rejection of the atomism implied in Structural Marxism, the approach adopted in this study will be to focus on both comparative case studies and concrete empirical analysis which may result in questioning the adequacy of much existing theory to account for change in all circumstances. At the same time this approach may serve to add to some of the more abstract anthropological accounts of social and economic change. For example, it has been argued with reference to Sri Lanka that the findings of anthropological field research can be somewhat platitudinous. Black-Michaud (1981) has argued that this is often the result of attempts to substantiate evidence within a framework that incorporates only limited theoretical innovation whilst simultaneously tending to be over complex in terms of the rather simple nature of the base material that is drawn upon. In addition, he has argued, with reference to Sri Lanka, that the anthropological concern for revealing basic 'themes' of village life which often depends upon a descriptive account of a particular community, tends to result in an uninspiring comparison with some previously detailed account of a composite model of a traditional peasantry (Black-Michaud 1981: 69-70).

Chapter two is concerned with the theoretical debate on the nature of rural transition in the light of increasing rural diversification. In this chapter an attempt is first made to place the theoretical debate in an historical context by examining the background to current transition theories through a brief discussion of neoclassical and neomarxist approaches. An attempt is then made to characterise the emerging forms of rural production which are seen as distinct from conventional notions of agrarian capitalism or pre capitalism and embody complex labour and capital strategies which extend beyond the family farm. Finally, an alternative interpretation is suggested which focuses on the concept of the means of living rather than the mode of production in order to encompass the complex mix of economic relations at the local level.

Chapter three examines the nature and extent of off-farm diversification in a comparative context. After an initial review of the data across a selection of developing countries attention is focused on Southeast Asia generally and Taiwan and the Philippines in particular. Two cases are then explored in more detail representing rice economies at opposite ends of the development and income spectrum. The first is a study of the evolution of the off-farm sector in Japan, which demonstrates considerable rural diversification in the context of substantial agricultural intensification alongside rapid industrial growth. The second is a study of the contemporary rural economy in Kerala in Southwest India which displays a high degree of off-farm diversification within the context of declining levels of farm intensification and a poorly developed industrial sector, although considerable welfare expenditures have ensured impressive physical quality of life indicators.

Chapters four and five extend this analysis of rural diversification through a detailed empirical study at village level in Sri Lanka as a means of identifying the specific nature of the farm to firm interaction in a precarious smallholder rice farming environment. This micro study sets out to analyse the nature of agrarian production relations within a rice farming community in the Kurunegala district of Sri Lanka. It is argued here that an understanding of agrarian transition in this context can only be achieved with reference to the regional economic and political setting and the links that are struck up between villagers and the wider economy. This study was undertaken during 1983-84 before the dramatic escalation in civil disorder that followed the Indo-Sri Lanka accord of 1987. Although it has not been possible to study the impact of the 1987-90 period on the village economy and wider political setting it has been reported that many of the tendencies identified in the following pages have been reinforced during this period of more widespread violence. This issue is discussed again under the heading 'village study methodology' below. The main question that is raised in these chapters relates to the nature and form of agrarian transition as expressed in the diversified smallholder economy within a less than stable political and economic environment.

The main focus in chapter four is on smallholder paddy cultivation where the household forms the primary economic unit. Attention is initially centred on the form of ownership and control of the means of production focusing on land distribution, tenancy and transmission through sale, mortgage and inheritance. Examination of the organisation of labour and overall employment characteristics along with the pattern of agricultural investment and exchange relations in the form of agricultural distribution, marketing and credit, all assist in the characterisation of agrarian relations.

Chapter five examines the nature and extent of diversification into off-farm activity and the impact this has had on production relations in the village. The process of diversification is seen to have fused certain elements of traditional practice and discourse with new modes of behaviour and social interaction deriving from a new regional economy and polity. This is seen to have eroded the traditional organisation of the community but at the same time has set

4

specific limits on forms of agrarian differentiation, based on increasing polarisation between landed and landless classes, which might be seen to follow from the logic of an ideal model of capitalist development in agriculture. The changing political structure of the village is an important area of concern and is examined in terms of emerging patterns of stratification and conflict alongside regional and national political incorporation up to 1984. The methodological approach also highlights changing consumption patterns and the extent to which consumerist trends in the regional and national economy were successful in penetrating the village economy. In the process of identifying dominant agrarian relations and emerging patterns of stratification, relations between households and different groups within the village, as well as between villagers and other sections of society, are all emphasised. In this way it is hoped that apart from providing a contribution to the general theoretical debate on rural transition based upon concrete historical analysis within the context of a precarious Asian rice economy.

Chapter six seeks to draw the main threads of the argument together by firstly considering the various forms of off-farm development that have manifested themselves in different economies in Asia. These range from the stable and fast growing economies of East and Southeast Asia (Japan and Taiwan) to the less developed (Kerala) and precarious economies (Sri Lanka) of South Asia. At the same time the chapter considers the implications of some of the more detailed information at village level in Sri Lanka derived from empirical data and direct (participant) observation during 1983-84. The second part of the chapter then examines the policy implications of promoting off-farm employment and small enterprise through a variety of public and private initiatives at macro and micro level. These include fiscal incentives, different forms of concessional finance and operational support as well as different small industry structures and organisational forms. This analysis examines both the existence of actual policy initiatives in a variety of countries that have taken concrete steps to promote rural employment through small and self-employed enterprise and at the same time identifies specific modifications and innovations that could be usefully adopted in the drive to increase rural income and expand employment in the off-farm sector.

Nomenclature, definition and measurement

The term 'household enterprise' is taken to signify a hybrid economic and social entity combining aspects of the traditional family farm, the main activities of which are examined below in relation to a fairly typical smallholder rice environment, and the family firm as represented by the wider economic activities in the off-farm sector. Suffice to say at this stage that the farm enterprise will be taken to include all agricultural, horticultural and animal husbandry activity. The term rural diversification will consequently

5

refer to a diversion of labour time from farm to off-farm activity and will not be taken to mean an extension or expansion of farm based activity from food grain cultivation, for example, into cash crops or animal husbandry.

Off-farm activity will be taken to include all secondary and tertiary sector employment of both a permanent and casual nature. This sector is by its very nature heterogeneous comprising the self-employed or own account operators of a marginal status, those engaged in micro enterprises with more capital and technology and those with formal employment in both the public and private sectors. The problem of analysis, as Smith (1969) points out, relates to the scattered, widely varied nature and changing form of off-farm activity all of which makes it extremely difficult to assess the proportion of population engaged in it and the level of income generated from it. Since activity in this area is quite diverse it is not surprising to find a number of different terms used in the literature to refer to off-farm employment. A common term is that of rural industrialisation as a counterpart to agriculture but this appears rather inadequate on account of the fact that much activity is not strictly of an industrial nature but of a service orientation. Others use the term rural enterprise which is seen to have a sufficient nonfarm connotation but once again this term appears rather limited since these characteristics are not exclusive to nonfarm activity. In chapter one it is argued, for example, that the combination of farm and off-farm activity has emerged as a hybrid form of household enterprise.

This study will therefore use the term off-farm when referring to those activities which are not related to the process of cultivation or animal husbandry and are carried on outside the sphere of farming as defined above. The term off-farm was widely used in the 1983 Bangkok conference on diversification in rural Asia. For our purposes, the term will not exclude processing activity which is closely related to the farm nor will it exclude other secondary or tertiary activity carried out on or around the household plot. A final point worth mentioning is that the term off-farm implies off any farm and not simply off one's own operated holding and will thus exclude income from wage employment in agriculture.

In these circumstances it is immediately obvious that many traditional demarcations may no longer be of relevance. Some households may work exclusively in the rural area while others may work exclusively in a neighbouring urban area and others still may work in both. Similarly, some may be engaged solely in agriculture while others are engaged solely in non agriculture and others still, may be engaged in both. One of the main difficulties in interpreting the nature of the household enterprise so constituted, arises from the fact that one is not examining a single category but as Anderson and Leiserson (1980) point out, a combination of forms that lie on the boundary of the conventional categories of rural-urban or agriculture and industry with no single dividing line.

6

One of the important aspects of this examination of rural diversification will be to identify a trend towards off-farm earnings for households which once relied almost exclusively on earnings from agriculture. This necessitates taking a broad view of off-farm employment covering households which obtain the majority of their income from this source through to those which are involved in off-farm employment but remain predominantly agricultural. Obviously, this presents a number of problems from the point of view of measurement. Some studies of the nonfarm sector have only included those households which derive their main source of livelihood from within this sector. This is most commonly the case in the official census data which tends to categorise households by primary occupation.

Another problem that arises from time to time concerns the precise definition of the term rural. The conventional definition relates to the size and/or density of the population contained within a single administrative unit. This may be supplemented by an occupational criterion relating to the proportion of the total population directly concerned with agriculture or the level of public services in the form of street lighting, refuse collection etc. Although the United Nations has taken 20,000 population as the cut-off point to distinguish urban from rural settlements many national studies of rural off-farm employment have restricted their sample frame to exclude all small or medium towns located in rural areas. In India, for example, any settlement with a population of more than 10,000 is considered to be urban. Over and above this there are three categories of municipality. Towns with a population of up to 15,00 are then classified as C class municipalities; those with a population of between 15,000 to 35,000 are B class municipalities; those with a population of 35,000 to around 100,000 (i lakh) are A class municipalities; above this are corporations. Many of the urban settlements and smaller market towns which have a primary agro-processing and marketing function are therefore excluded from the analysis.

Since the main interest in this study is to examine the changing nature of the farm-off-farm relationship, our primary focus will be on households residing in settlements of a distinctly rural character and thus many of the boundary problems mentioned above will not prove to be of such an issue. The main exception to this will be with regard to the place of work. Those residing in rural settlements but working in neighbouring urban areas will be seen as contributing to the process of rural diversification whereas those who have migrated to urban centres will not be included, unless they form part of a statistical analysis which encompasses the total population of a broadly defined rural area including small local towns.

Many of these definitional inconsistencies have led to problems with the measurement of off-farm employment and income and estimates of the overall size and extent of the sector. An immediate problem in this regard relates to the limited published data on the sector and the even more limited empirical material arising out of field studies conducted at the micro level.

This contrasts with the abundant literature on the urban informal sector at both a macro and micro level, much of it arising out of Latin America where the informal labour force accounts for between one fourth and one third of the total urban labour force. During the 1980s the share of the informal sector in non-agricultural employment in Latin America rose from around 24 percent to over 29 percent and the fact that the informal labour market is largely populated by the poor has meant that government and researchers are beginning to take a renewed interest in the sector.

The size, composition and character of the off-farm sector has not been clearly elucidated for a number of reasons over and above those already mentioned. Most of the estimates at an aggregate level are drawn from census data or employment surveys which not only tend to focus on primary employment and primary source of income but may not encourage the enumerator to collect detailed information on secondary, part time or additional activity. This emphasis on primary occupation results in a serious under estimation of secondary and tertiary activity in the local economy. In some cases these subsidiary activities may contribute to a greater share of total household income than the primary occupation itself. In other cases off-farm earnings may again exceed farm income although the head of the household may work exclusively in agriculture. There are many further variations on this theme where, for example, more family members are engaged in some form of agriculture than in off-farm work, although off-farm income might be higher or where the number of hours working off-farm throughout the year exceeds the number of hours of farm work during the cultivation season. In all these scenarios off-farm income or employment could be more important than farming yet the symbolic nature of farming in many cultures often results in its apparent dominance in interpretations of the local economy. Misawa (1970) shows that original Ministry of Agriculture statistics in pre war Japan did not clearly define part time farming and thus in 1938 estimated that it accounted for 33 percent of all farming. In the same year the statistics were revised providing a clearer definition of part time farming and the estimates of part time farming rose to 54 percent.

Other problems relating to the reliability of the estimates are concerned with the nature of data collection. The closed questionnaire format does not invite answers to questions that have not been posed and in these circumstances household members may not disclose the full range of activities that they engage throughout the year. Furthermore, many households are reluctant to disclose off-farm earnings for fear of incurring additional taxes or other costs. Some activities in this category are performed within the black economy where there is a strong preference for them to remain unreported and unrecorded.

The Japanese survey data shows that reporting on agriculture tends to be more complete than for non agriculture. Off-farm employment offers wider possibilities of non reporting since, as Smith (1969) argues, its forms, times and places of production are more varied and private minimising the chance of detection. One of the outcomes of this situation reflected in some Japanese surveys has been the anomaly of a large amount of nonfarm income apparently generated from a small proportion of nonfarm earners even after adjustments allowing for the under reporting of farm income by generous 25 percent (Smith 1969).

A final problem that has not been dealt with in a satisfactory way and which is likely to continue to cloud the whole debate on off-farm employment is that of household based activity which is located outside the market. This includes all work which generates a product which is consumed by the household or exchanged with other households and does not have a direct monetary value attached to it. This is particularly relevant when considering the role of women in the household enterprise. Since most data has tended either to discount labour engaged in this way on the basis that it does not contribute in a financial sense to household income or to simply ignore its existence, on the assumption that the necessary information is too complex to collect or too widespread to document, it will be an impossible task to begin to inject estimates of this form of activity on a case by case basis. One can only hope that this lacuna is addressed in future case studies and analyses of off-farm activity.

Field study environment and methodology

An empirical analysis of smallholder production relations and off-farm employment at village level outlined in chapters four and five is based upon fieldwork conducted in Sri Lanka in 1983–84. This period represents the early phase of the post 1983 ethnic conflict. In fact communal tension and civil unrest has long been a feature of political life in Sri Lanka with intermittent outbreaks of violence dating back to 1958 (see Slater 1985). However, it was not until the outbreak of violence in mid 1983 that the situation took a drastic turn. Initially, the conflict was contained to the Tamil populated northern and eastern regions of the country and it was during this period that fieldwork was undertaken. At this time a number of political and economic features came to dominate life at village level. These included the penetration of a free market economy based largely on imported goods coupled to a tightening of local political control (see Manor 1984) over many aspects of an expanding off-farm (service based) sector. The escalation of violence following the signing of the Indo-Sri Lanka accord in 1987 and the arrival of the Indian peace keeping force (IPKF) which led to a radical Sinhalese backlash orchestrated by the Janatha Vimukthi Peramuna (JVP), had a marked effect on many parts of the country including those outside the main conflict areas which by this time spread to the South and later the hill areas in the Southwest. The period 1987–90 was characterised by widespread killings and disruption. During this period the JVP are said to have killed 6,500 people in the South while Government security forces have been accused of as many as 50,000 deaths (British Refugee Council 1990).

It is difficult to estimate the precise impact that this has had on the diversified smallholder economy since 1983-84 but initial evidence points to the reinforcing of a number of characteristics identified in this study such as the dominance of local political control. It is likely that a tightening of the civil budget has depressed sectors of the off-farm economy but households will, nevertheless, have been anxious to adopt and strengthen diversified economic strategies to ensure their survival in a precarious economic and political setting. The case of Sri Lanka thus demonstrates, through a detailed micro study, the specific characteristics of the off-farm economy in a less than stable free market economy at the lower end of the income spectrum. Any subsequent research of this subject in Sri Lanka will be able to extend this analysis by examining the role of off-farm diversification in a political and economic setting under considerable stress.

The field study was undertaken as part of a doctoral dissertation which was concerned with the changing nature of production relations and social institutions in a smallholder farming economy. Fieldwork was based a village approximately ten miles northeast of Kurunegala town in the intermediate zone of Kurunegala district. The name of the village and individuals mentioned in the text have been changed in order to observe a modest level of confidentiality. Initial quantitative data was collected in the form of a simple household census after mapping the area to help establish the parameters of the village, a spatial appreciation of the settlement pattern and a basic land use survey. The census was designed to establish household name, size and structure, kinship relations, caste and ethnic origin, education, occupation and land holding pattern. After this initial census had been conducted, household records held at the office of the Grama Sevaka (village officer) and the Agrarian Service Centre were examined for additional information and/or discrepancies.

A more detailed household schedule was then drawn up in consultation with a number of key informants in the village. This was specifically designed to gather quantitative data on farming operations, sources of income and expenditure, material assets and credit status. Farm data encompassed land ownership, tenurial relations, land transmission, organisation of labour for each stage of cultivation, use and extent of inputs and credit, ownership of equipment, livestock, water management and crop yield. This data was accompanied by a series of open ended questions on a range of social and political and local power relations. All survey schedules were administered by the author and a research assistant.

Statistical data in the text on land ownership, labour use, employment categories, income sources and productivity returns, refers to the total census population or the total population of a specified subset. Numerical data on ownership of consumer items, plot distribution, marriage forms, input use,

10

tractor use, extension and credit, income distribution and average earnings, refers to various population sizes which are specified in each case. These population sizes do not represent statistical samples and are used descriptively. Variation in population sizes between different tables and case studies is partly due to incomplete responses and inaccuracies in responses which were only discovered during later analysis. In the case of income data (income distribution and average earnings) which was complete for all households, the data has been weighted according to basic occupational criteria relating to land operation, landless labouring and off-farm employment categories. In the case of credit, data is drawn only from those cases where responses of debtors could be checked with those of creditors and in the case of input use, where informants could reliably estimate the quantity used during a particular season. Finally it is important to note that given the small total population (153 households) of the village study, one would have to be a little cautious about extrapolating robust statistical conclusions in every case. Finally, the village data generated from this series of questionnaires, informal interviews, discussions and participant observation over a nine month period between 1983–84, has been compared and contrasted as far as possible with other studies conducted in and around the locality.

Agricultural intensification: the pre-condition of diversification

The trend towards rural diversification and off-farm employment is particularly marked in parts of Asia where the topographical and climatic conditions have favoured agricultural intensification. This has been largely based on the deployment of considerable cultivation skills and divisible technologies which have raised land productivity within a smallholder farming structure. The maintenance of this structure has meant that families have been able to attend to the family farm at the same time as securing off-farm employment of both a seasonal and permanent nature.

The following section describes certain features associated with a typical pattern of smallholder rice farming in contemporary Asia and may help to identify the nature of small farm intensification which has provided the basis of rural diversification and the rise of the part time farm phenomenon. The account below describes a pattern of farming found in an intermediate agro-climatic zone in South Asia where monsoon paddy is cultivated on a rainfed and irrigated basis. The latter is undertaken within a minor irrigation system which has facilitated the introduction of double cropping and a considerable rise in yield and output especially during the drier northeast monsoon period. For the purposes of this chapter little need be added to our understanding of the family farm which has been extensively treated in rural development literature elsewhere in both theoretical and descriptive terms.

11

Paddy cultivation

One of the major factors behind the parcelisation of productive land into numerous small plots is the physical limit on land extension under conditions of wet rice farming which requires the careful levelling and terracing of land to ensure uniform levels of water. Furthermore, as Bray (1986) demonstrates, wet rice fields enjoy the enormous advantage of gaining fertility over years of use as the soil structure and composition are altered in a process known as podzolisation. This is brought about by the constant percolation of water and its interaction with various organic acids which affect the subsoil. This maintenance of an optimal level of fertility as a result of continuous cultivation coupled to the enormous levelling effort required to bring new land under cultivation has meant that intensive rather than extensive methods of cultivation tend to be preferred. The obvious result of this in the context of a rising rural population has been an increase in land fragmentation and the diminution of plot size. Just as the construction of paddy fields have traditionally required substantial labour inputs so much of the routine field preparation work is labour intensive. A great deal of routine field work, for example, is concerned with the construction and repair of field bunds which help to conserve moisture and prevent erosion. Before ploughing, each plot is levelled to ensure that the necessary degree of water retention is maintained.

Farmers cultivate paddy during the wet and dry seasons, the latter depending on actual rainfall and available storage water. The reduced effectiveness of the monsoon during the dry cultivation season means that the second crop is much less certain than the main crop and can result in crop failure. The existence of a minor irrigation system, however, means that for many farmers, cultivation can be attempted over most of the paddy land and that labour intensity during this season has risen sharply. By the mid 1980s farmers were typically reporting yields of 1,500–2,000 kgs per acre compared to around 700 kgs prior to irrigation and the intensive use of inputs. Under former conditions farmers rarely applied anything approaching the correct level of inputs and associated labour and cultivation was fairly non intensive.

Traditional rice varieties have been gradually replaced over the years by high yielding varieties such as H.4 and H.7 which have, in turn, been replaced with new indigenous varieties often better suited to local conditions. Bray has shown that rice is a relatively high yielding crop even under adverse conditions with a high yield to seed ratio. Fast maturing varieties are capable of producing up to three crops a year, providing there is sufficient water, even without the use of biochemical inputs. 'This means that once rice cultivation is established in a region it will sustain population growth almost indefinitely. No other crop has such a great population–carrying capacity, and this is one of the factors to which we can attribute the success and popularity of rice' (Bray 1986: 26).

The introduction of dwarf and semi-dwarf hybrids has had a major impact on yields. These new varieties are shorter in stem and able to convert more dry matter to grain than straw with a reduced tendency to lodge. Being less photoperiod sensitive than many traditional varieties they are capable of maturing in a shorter period and can thus be planted later and allow for multiple-cropping on a given plot of land. These new varieties are often sown in a separate seed bed before being transplanted out in straight lines under conditions of careful water control and the application of fertiliser. Frequent weeding is undertaken throughout the growing season although water control helps to limit this problem. The widespread adoption of new varieties has meant that traditional disease and pest control practices have tended to give way to the frequent application of herbicides and pesticides. Although this regime is highly labour intensive it allows maximum use to be made of available land in the main growing seasons by limiting the time the crop occupies the field and maximising the potential return.

Under these conditions of natural labour intensity mechanisation has been rather limited. Ploughing is usually performed by buffalo although the two wheel tractor or power tiller is becoming a more frequent sight even the labour abundant regions of South Asia. Larger tractors are unsuitable for a number of reasons. Plot sizes are generally too small and access to individual plots would be difficult without disturbing the intricate design and lay out. Moreover, deep ploughing may have an adverse impact on the soil structure where traditional practices of shallow ploughing and puddling or stirring are infinitely better suited to wet rice conditions. The introduction of small and medium scale technology in Japan and Taiwan has meant that many of the technical problems associated with larger scale mechanisation have been overcome with machinery that has been specially designed for use in small scale paddy cultivation. In both Japan and Taiwan the rapid growth in off-farm opportunities has encouraged the process of integrated mechanisation from ploughing to winnowing. This pattern is unlikely to be adopted elsewhere until the demand for off-farm labour increases substantially. At present, the only stages of cultivation that have been mechanised on any scale in most parts of South Asia are ploughing, threshing (using a standard 4 wheel tractor) and winnowing with the aid of a fan attachment mounted on to the motor of the 2 wheel power tiller.

In spite of these innovations, farm equipment is mostly of a traditional non mechanised variety. The most common general purpose implement is the mammoty. Other tools that nearly every farming household will own include the sickle in both a long and short handled version, threshing stick, measure, mats for drying and transporting, woven storage baskets, broadcasting container and hand leveller. Those households that own working buffalo will also own a plough, yoke and a levelling board. Only a small number of households own other equipment such as hand sprayers, rotary weeders or seeders.

Farming skills are usually acquired from an early age. Young children often accompany their parents to the paddy fields and are well exposed to the whole farming process by the age of ten. Between the ages of ten and twelve boys will begin to help their fathers in land preparation by undertaking some of the smaller tasks, while both boys and girls may join in the harvesting process. By the age of fourteen a boy may begin to plough usually starting with the third ploughing which can be less precise, the ground already having been turned over twice. By sixteen some boys can already undertake all ploughing operations but often it is not until the age of eighteen that a boy will be regarded as experienced enough to complete all cultivation tasks including broadcasting. Women work extensively in the paddy fields monopolising most transplanting work and helping equally with manual weeding and cutting and filing. Winnowing is also traditionally a female activity but with the introduction of mechanised winnowing they are now less involved.

In some areas in the past it was common practice for parents to allocate some paddy land from the family 'pool' to an elder son once they feel sufficiently confident in his farming ability. Today with increasing pressure on paddy land, this level of early independence is not always forthcoming and young people often complain that paddy farming can no longer provide them with a reasonable level of economic independence.

Organisation and features of labour use in paddy cultivation

The evolution of the labour pattern in paddy cultivation has, to a large extent, been determined by a complex cultivation schedule spanning the various processes of land preparation, planting and harvesting. For the purposes of this assessment a typical cultivation schedule has been broken down into twenty two separate stages. Some of these stages may not always take place depending on whether or not transplanting has been adopted on a particular holding. The sub-division of the main processes of land preparation, planting and harvesting also facilitates the more accurate collection of farm data, as cultivators tend to estimate factors such as labour type and man hours in easily relatable units. Each of the twenty two stages involves a distinct investment of labour time and the use of particular tools and techniques. Cultivation methods have been handed down verbally through generations forming an extensive body of indigenous knowledge. Villagers often explain, for example, that cultivation should not begin until the arrival of certain migratory birds which traditionally mark the beginning of paddy operations. This kind of practice has an important rational basis when it is understood that such birds (eg the Indian Pitta or Pitta Brachyura) are weak fliers and take advantage of the strong northeast monsoon winds that carry moisture to the fields for the main cultivation season. The first cries of the bird thus indicate the onset of the much needed rains, signalling an appropriate minimum risk period to begin cultivation (see Senanayake 1983).

Today, the majority of paddy farmers seem to prefer to delay cultivation until the monsoon has firmly established itself with consequent water wastage. Farmers with land around the perimeter of the paddy tracts begin farming operations by engaging in land clearance and tree cutting to reduce any shade caused by overhanging branches, shrubs or undergrowth. The clearance of undergrowth also helps to control vermin as the shrubs provide a natural habitat for rats, mice and other insects. Soft leaves and cuttings are then dumped onto the fields as compost. Labour time spent on clearance varies depending on how exposed a plot is to natural vegetation. Farmers report anything from 4–10 man hours per acre with some farmers spending more than 24 hours per acre on field clearance.

The first of three ploughings takes place after preparation. Ploughing by buffalo is still the most common method in South Asia. This is sometimes known as 'earth lifting' since the purpose is to turn over the soil in order to loosen it and facilitate decomposition. Around one inch of water is the accepted level for this ploughing which can take anything from 20–35 man hours per acre depending upon the location of the plot, the moisture content of the soil, the soil type and the efficiency of the farmer. After the first ploughing, it is necessary to begin preparing the terraces/bunds by scraping and clearing the ground of any weed growth. This is a time consuming process and if a cultivator has a number of plots scattered on small terraces, the increased number of surrounding bunds will mean a proportional increase in the labour time spent on this task which usually amounts to at least 15 hours per acre. Some cultivators actually report up to 35 man hours per acre spent on terrace clearance. The second ploughing, often known as mud ploughing, assists the loosening and breaking down of the soil into smaller particles, taking a little less than the labour time spent on the first ploughing. Before the third and final ploughing the bunds that have been previously scraped down and cleared of weed are built up by compacting fresh mud onto the structure. This improves the water holding capacity of the bund and allows the cultivator to repair any damage such as leaks and holes caused by crabs. A similar length of time is spent on this as for terrace scraping but, if the bunds need a lot of attention, the man hour input may well exceed the former task. The final stage of field preparation involves a third ploughing and levelling. This process is often known as puddling and levelling and it consists of turning the soil to eradicate weed whilst improving the texture by creating a muddy consistency prior to a final levelling. These two stages are most commonly undertaken together and seem to take most farmers somewhere between the length of time spent on the first and second ploughing.

After the fields have been prepared farmers are ready to sow or plant. If transplanting is to be adopted a nursery bed will have already been prepared. If weather conditions remain unfavourable at the time of sowing, however, farmers may prefer to broadcast. Transplanting is very labour intensive and can easily take a gang of fifteen labourers two days to complete the process, accounting for up to 240 labour hours. Transplanting is essentially carried out by female labour. After uprooting the young plants from the nursery bed they are transferred to the main plot where they are planted out with even spacings between clusters. Each cluster consists of two to three separate shoots sunk to an optimum depth which the extension service equate to a quarter of a finger's length. Each square foot should contain roughly six clusters whereas farmers tend to overplant to around eleven per square foot at a deeper than optimum depth which ultimately retards growth. This problem is compounded when farmers come to apply fertiliser even at the recommended doses, which will then be inadequate for a higher than optimum per acre plant distribution.

Broadcasting is still more commonly engaged in than transplanting. When broadcasting, farmers rarely achieve maximum potential, because of their tendency to sow at very high levels of density. Random field trials have shown that the number of plants per square foot can be as high as forty four compared to the recommended ten. Farmers sow thickly in the belief that the more paddy that grows, the fewer the weeds that can penetrate. The result is simply a reduction in the number of shoots per plant, reduced access across the field and consequently less chance of detecting weed growth. Weeding by hand or through the application of weedicide often leads to plant damage in this context.

In many parts of the countryside the use of chemical inputs in the form of weedicide, fertiliser and insecticide has increased. The applications of fertiliser and insecticide are relatively short processes totalling not more than around 14 hours of labour time. Weed control, however, is often a mixture of the application of a chemical weedicide and/or intensive manual weeding by hand. Hand weeding is carried out by a mixture of female and male labour often supplemented by additional child labour within the family. Weeding time is extremely variable between households depending on the method of sowing or planting, the application of weedicide, the level of water maintained in the field and natural levels of weed growth. An average of around 40 hours per acre appears to be the norm for weed control. This is supplemented to some extent by a routine task which is rarely taken into account when examining labour use but comprises an important aspect of the overall labour schedule. This consists of the daily maintenance carried out by almost all farmers throughout the growth phase. Water levels are identified, the bunds are inspected for leaks and repaired if necessary, weeds are checked and uprooted and attempts are made to prevent attacks from birds and insects. With farmers spending up to an hour a day almost every day the total number of hours per season for maintenance can exceed 90 hours per acre. This task is very rarely carried out by wage labour.

Once the paddy has ripened, coinciding with a period of dry weather, the harvesting begins. The plants are cut by hand sickle in an intensive operation which, along with filing, requires more than 100 labour hours per acre and lasts for a varying number of days depending on the size of the labour gang.

16

Filing immediately follows cutting and is performed mostly by women as they pile up the harvest into small bundles which are then transported to the threshing floor and stacked to await threshing. Transporting and stacking averages around 45 labour hours per acre and is the second most labour intensive activity of the harvesting process. This is mainly due to the fact that nearly all threshing takes place mechanically by a four wheel tractor. Tractor threshing takes roughly 2 hours compared to 35 hours if threshing is carried out in the traditional manner with buffalo. Even if a tractor is employed for the task it is still necessary for a cultivator to be on hand to fork through the paddy as it is threshed. This exercise can easily take up an additional 40 hours of labour time in order to ensure that all the paddy has been separated from the remaining straw. Winnowing completes the harvesting process and is most often carried out by means of a mechanised fan attachment driven from the motor of a two wheel tractor. This has commonly replaced the old method of hand winnowing which was carried out by female labour. Despite a reduction of winnowing time to 4 hours by fan for an acre of paddy, cultivators remain working on the threshing floor for 20 hours to complete the task. The final stage of transporting paddy to the household store varies in time depending on how near the cultivator's house is situated to the threshing floor. In most cases threshing takes place on land within the settlement area, so that farmers traditionally work on floors near to their houses.

The main feature of the organisation of labour is that the most intensive operations are the stages of preparatory tillage, transplanting and maintenance including weeding and cutting. It will therefore be particularly relevant to focus on these operations when considering any changes and adaptations that have taken place in the labour system as a whole. A survey conducted by Herath (1983) in Sri Lanka shows a lower total labour use for a sample from Anuradhapura and a rather higher labour use from a Kandy sample (1983:30–37) when compared to the figures outlined above. These findings reflect the greater level of mechanisation to be found in dry zone cultivation in Sri Lanka and the extremely labour intensive methods of the fragmented paddy holdings of hill country Sri Lanka, where twice the labour input of that for the dry zone was noted.

Minor irrigation and input use

Minor tank irrigation has a long history in many parts of Asia and as Bray (1986) has shown gave rise to large scale irrigation systems such as those found in Upper Burma, Cambodia, Java and South India and Ceylon. Leach (1959) argues that the great dry zone irrigation kingdom of Prakrama Bahu I (1164–97) in Sri Lanka, in many respects resembled Wittfogel's model of hydraulic civilisation based on a degree of despotic coercion. Leach draws on the historical works of Sir J Tennent (1860) to demonstrate that this famous Sri Lankan king was a warlike expeditionary tyrant as well as a celebrated builder of many thousands of large and small tanks. Gunawardana (1971) accepts that by the end of the C12th there was a vast network of irrigation that had ben developed over a long period and that irrigation was one of the most important public works of the ancient Sinhala State. However, Gunawardana contends that there were also numerous minor village tanks and systems which involved less sophisticated technology and were sponsored by non governmental sources reflected a more decentralised and multi centred society.

The maintenance of an irrigation tradition has been at the centre of many rice economies where water control is synonymous with more intensive production. Undoubtedly, as Gunawardana (1971) argues and Bray (1986) emphasises, despite the large tank and canal network of medieval Sri Lanka, irrigation was technically divisible and survived the breakdown of strong central control. In this context it is likely that the present level of development of the forces of wet rice production in Sri Lanka are inextricably linked to intricate production systems and procedures developed in the past. Here, numerous tank rehabilitation schemes under the various Integrated Rural Development Projects (IRDP) are a case in point. As is to be expected, however, the rehabilitation of an important piece of past technology has rarely been accompanied by a straight reintroduction of past water management practices designed to optimise distribution for intensive cultivation. A number of economic and social developments have meant that various traditional cooperative practices are either no longer favoured or are impossible to administer. The net result is a compromise solution which although not ideal is perhaps more realistic in the contemporary village setting with many conflicting demands and interests. At the same time this compromise solution still allows the majority of farmers to engage in more intensive cultivation methods gaining the benefit of increased labour and biochemical inputs.

In practice, the rehabilitation of any former irrigation system often involves the complete reconstruction of a tank. One such case has been closely by the author in Kurunegala district under the World Bank funded (IRDP) project. Here, the tank was one of 1,298 similar minor tanks in Kurunegala district, which contains the largest number of minor tanks in Sri Lanka, and together with Anuradhapura district accounts for over 75 percent of all the nation's minor tanks (Madduma Bandara 1984). On average the Kurunegala tanks are much smaller in capacity than others in the dry zone and yet the average acreage under their command is much larger in proportion to tank size. This could be due to more favourable climatic conditions and the greater pressure of population on land in Kurunegala which has resulted in an increase in the total aswedumised area in the district (Madduma Bandara 1984). The particular tank in question formed part of a local cascade system which is seen by a number of experts as less wasteful of water and better able to withstand social pressure than the partly modified systems seen on colonisation schemes or the completely modified Mahaweli type development.

A number of topographical features indicated that it was likely that there was a tank on the same site in an earlier period. High ground at either end of the existing bund could well have constituted the original bund axis, while a minor stream that previously flowed through the paddy tract was probably the main spill channel. Over the years the dry tank bed had been developed as private coconut land. Work on the tank started at the end of 1979. A seven hundred foot earthen bund abutting the high ground at either end was constructed on existing paddy land. An impermeable membrane of puddle clay acted as the essential barrage while the dam profile was formed from locally available 'filling' material. A one hundred foot natural spillway with a suitable spill tail channel and definition wall was built on the right bank with the spill tail channel being directed into the existing stream rather than the distributary channel. Since farmers had aswedumised the old stream bed the spill tail channel runs off into a number of centrally located paddy fields. Two sluices were located at either end of the bund opening on to a right and left bank canal system which replaced the old field to field irrigation system. The tank itself covered six acres of former paddy land and over nine acres of former coconut land.

The tank catchment area consisted of a quarter of a square mile of sloping forest reserve and coconut land. According to the Irrigation Department the average annual rainfall and corresponding catchment yield provided adequate water for regular issues during the cultivation season. Farmers, however, pointed out that the catchment area was insufficient and that a feeding channel should be extended to tap the local Dedura Oya river as a plentiful water source. Official resistance to this idea came from the fact that such a scheme would disrupt an adjacent major system which was fed by the Dedura Oya. Irrigation officials pointed out that the more efficient use of water by farmers would serve the same ends.

The irrigation system was completed in December 1980 at a cost of Rs 570,895 (KIRDP 1981). The Irrigation Department constructed distributary canals of 1,400 feet in length down both the right and left bank. The left bank farmers cooperated by substantially extending the canal by up to twice its original distance. The right bank farmers, however, appeared unable to cooperate in a similar way to those on the left bank and the distributary channel thus remained in its original state. The reasons for this were complex and had more to do with poor inter household relations in this particular part of the village than with technical difficulties.

Official estimates showed that water issues of 0.5 feet per acre during the maha season, when tank water was supplemented by rainfall from the northeast monsoon, allowed the tank to irrigate up to two hundred and twenty five acres of cultivable land. The Irrigation Department pointed out that these were optimal figures and that the actual tank command area was probably much smaller at around sixty acres. Farmers did not always cultivate simultaneously nor did they adhere rigidly to a timetable which meant that water wastage was invariably high. There was a general tendency among farmers to try and delay the start of cultivation operations until there had been adequate rainfall and the tank was nearly full, thus ensuring greater water security. This prevented them making efficient use of the early rains and made them much too reliant on the tank for providing all the necessary water for cultivation.

The water management practice that was advocated by both the Irrigation and Agrarian Service Departments was based upon a system devised at the Maha Illupalama Research Station known as the Walagambahuwa model. The method of implementation had been via institutional and participatory instruction through government officers and field training classes. The main thrust of the programme was to advance *maha* (wet season) cultivation and adhere to the timely completion of all cultivation tasks using the correct seed variety. An Assistant Cultivation Officer (ACO) was responsible for water management. He was elected on a three year term and was himself a farmer operating a smallholding of around one and three quarter acres of predominantly tenanted land. Many of the water management objectives were established at a public seasonal meeting (*kana*) prior to cultivation. Theoretically, staff from the Agrarian Services and Agricultural Departments should have attended each *kana*. However, during the dry season of 1984 only two of the six staff were observed to be in attendance. A number of issues such as the type of seed variety, the dates for starting cultivation, channel clearing, land preparation, sowing and harvesting, the provision of fencing and the level of fines to be instituted for failure to comply with some of these measures, were all decided upon at the seasonal meeting.

There appeared to be little cooperation over canal clearance in certain parts of the village particularly down the right bank. There was no complete conformity over the cultivation timetable and it was not uncommon to find that some farmers had already begun land preparation before the *kana* was held. Many cultivators did not fence their land and the resulting encroachments were be quite damaging to the water management system. A number of these farmers complained that they did not have the means to provide adequate fencing in the interests of the community.

Water issues were a constant source of minor dispute and conflict. The lack of a canal extension down the right bank meant that more complaints originated from this source where there was greater opportunity for illegal tapping and draining and correspondingly a greater need for fairer distribution. Farmers in the most northerly paddy tract often resorted to blocking the stream in order to divert water to their fields. This tended to leave the middle fork of the right bank without water and had, in the past, forced the ACO to divert water across from the left bank. Farmers in the northerly tract complained that during the dry season they received many fewer water issues than those on the left bank. One of the more vociferous right bank farmers, who was descended from a notable family in the village, took pains to stress that it was an interesting coincidence that the ACO happened to hold land on the favoured left bank. The ACO, however, was under instruction not to issue water to this northerly tract if it was in short supply since the particular soil conditions of this area resulted in a high level of percolation with a water retention capacity that was five times less than elsewhere. The ACO's task had been made all the more difficult by the failure to introduce an efficient pole system in the new portion of the canal which meant that, in order to gain access to water, farmers either had to use hollowed out tree trunks as pipes or simply cut straight into the canal banks themselves.

Water was issued downstream first to reduce the ease with which farmers upstream could tap water illegally. Water was rarely issued for land preparation and the first issue was normally between seven to fifteen days after planting and again twice per month during the growing season. On the right bank, however, the general lack of cooperation among farmers led the ACO to ignore all but the most serious breaches of practice. One farmer was known to dam up the main canal in order to raise the water to a piece of higher adjacent land that he had recently aswedumised.

In spite of these problems, the village tank functioned reasonably well and those responsible for water management had managed to revitalise a number of traditional cultivation practices and values in order to ensure a reasonable level of operational success. Farmers were encouraged, for example, to be meticulous about the maintenance of bunds, canals and ditches and to ensure a neighbour's water supply was not interfered with. Although the level of cooperation which characterised traditional village agriculture no longer existed, the tank did manage to renew many cultivators' interests in working together for improved water management. This contrasts with many of the larger modified systems that require greater external management, often leading to extensive bureaucratic intervention and the disintegration of traditional paddy farming communities.

In helping to expand the irrigated area of the village the tank also contributed to what Madduma Bandara argues is the single most important historical factor influencing national production in Sri Lanka. He goes on to show how the benefits of irrigation are related to yield increases, increased crop production and greater food security. The first benefit that farmers always mentioned in relation to the new tank was concerned with increased crop production. Since 1980 double cropping had become much more widespread although it rarely extended to cover all paddy land under the tank. Increased land productivity relating to increased yields and farm incomes was only been possible as a result of the introduction of an intricate system of irrigation and water management which, in turn, led to an increase in the intensity of production.

Finally, enhanced security, as a result of greater water availability, which has alleviated the hazards of variable rainfall, encouraged farmers to apply a greater level of biochemical inputs including fertiliser, weedicide and insecticide. In some cases, such as with urea, there was widespread over adoption by farmers. An important issue, here, is whether or not the current concern about the long term health effects associated with the widespread use of artificial fertilisers and pesticides will lead to a revival of traditional organic cultivation methods based on seed varieties that have been engineered to respond to reduced chemical inputs. There are a host of well documented problems concerning crops grown with artificial fertiliser. They tend to be poor in nutritional quality, with a poor storage life and contaminated with chemical residue. The widespread use of nitrogen fertilisers has led to the pollution of surface water and ground water with nitrate thus effecting drinking water supplies and river and stream purity. In addition to this, artificial fertilisers are a major source of nitrous oxide and a possible cause of stratospheric ozone depletion.

In a similar and equally alarming way, pesticides cause extensive environmental pollution. Pesticide poisoning is a growing problem in many developing countries where spraying is uncontrolled and haphazard. Based on a revision of the 1972 WHO figures for pesticide poisoning, it has been estimated that there are around a million cases of poisoning each year, resulting in approximately 20,000 deaths. Although pesticide residues in the environment are generally low, they tend to concentrate in the body fats as they move up the food chain. Many pesticides are either known or suspected carcinogens, mutagens or allergens. Thirty eight pesticides in common use in the UK, for example, are now banned in other countries and the position is much worse in developing countries such as India and Sri Lanka. It is possible that in the future farmers may be encouraged to adopt traditional soil enrichment and pest control techniques without any significant effect on overall yield levels. The intensive adoption of integrated paddy and livestock farming could help to supplement the already fertile soils in a manner that might reduce the dependence on artificial remedies. At the same time alternative pest management practices might usefully rely more on the careful management of natural predators to control target species rather than indiscriminate spraying with broad spectrum poisons which eliminate pest and predator alike. These changes may have little effect on overall yield levels but would have the effect of reducing costs without reducing intensification.

Coconut production

A great deal of non paddy land at village level in monsoon Asia is given over to plantation crops such as coconut. This land is often divided into smallholdings based on monoculture and mixed home gardens where other fruit crops and vegetables are interplanted with coconut. Coconut trees grow well on sandy soil at temperatures of around 27'C. In ideal conditions the trees are also fertilised with coconut ammonia and urea. Irrigation is rarely practised even on the larger holdings but villagers often construct drainage ditches and may irrigate by hand in a drought. The trees are susceptible to insect attack, particularly from white ants but insecticides are rarely applied to combat this menace.

An ARTI (1981a) survey in Kurunegala district in Sri Lanka showed that effective cultivation practices were little adopted. The survey reported only 4 percent of cultivators practising soil conservation; 5 percent using fertilisers; 3 percent underplanting in an intensive manner; 11 percent engaged in regular weeding. Typical yields vary between 900 – 1,200 nuts per acre under village conditions, rising to 7,500 nuts per acre on a typical large estate. The lifespan of an average tree is around sixty years and thus replanting is essential to maintain maximum productivity. Harvesting may begin at around six to ten years with a productivity peak at around thirty years. Increasingly, loans and grants are provided for a variety of activities such as for underplanting and replanting, spacing, tree felling, contour drainage provision etc. In many cases villagers do not make use of this assistance when it is available since some feel that the conditionality attached to the loans and grants is too difficult/expensive to comply with, while others simply fail to understand the grant mechanism and are naturally suspicious of official intentions and procedures. On the whole the extension effort for subsidiary smallholder activity is less effective than for than for staple crops and production is consequently less intensive than it might be.

For many smallholders in monsoon Asia, coconut cultivation is seen as a useful supplementary source of income as well as providing for all their own domestic consumption requirements and for some smallholders, incomes can be quite substantial and form an important part of total income, despite the low level of development of new techniques and innovation. The important factor here, however, is that the degree of existing crop diversification does provide for an additional margin of agricultural intensification that could be further exploited in the future. Another interesting feature associated with coconut cultivation at village level has been the proliferation of local people attempting to engage in coconut trading. The more successful entrepreneurs manage to form solid links with wholesalers who send a regular distribution fleets into coconut growing villages.

Subsidiary crops

Commonly grown home garden crops include chillies, coffee, betel, bananas, limes, papaw, mangoes, oranges and jak fruit yams, manioc, brinjal and various hydro plants. Paddy farmers mostly grow these crops on homestead plots but do occasionally grow subsidiary crops in the paddy fields during the dry season although the work is considered rather cumbersome, requiring a good deal of drainage and the preparation of raised beds. It is also seen as potentially disruptive to the main activity of paddy cultivation which farmers view as a priority, providing a secure income and a staple food on which a family can subsist. Agricultural extension services have been actively encouraging farmers to grow subsidiary crops on dry paddy land for some time. They point out that this would not only optimise land use but might also subdue potential conflict over water distribution in sensitive areas.

A number of subsidiary crop programmes have been introduced in different countries to encourage farmers to diversify and maximise potential output in line with variable weather conditions and irrigation capacity. Most families have traditionally managed to maintain a home garden plot and thus homestead extension programmes are simply an attempt by extension staff to encourage a more systematic approach to garden cultivation.

Other subsidiary crops include dry grains, cowpeas, black grams, green grams, soya and groundnuts. The cultivation of these additional crops is not particularly widespread in rice farming communities in spite of a good deal of local extension effort. Farmers argue that they require considerable attention and yet often do not reap satisfactory rewards as they do not possess adequate storage facilities and are thus forced to sell any surplus directly after the harvest when prices are generally low.

Tobacco

One example of a cash crop that can be found in some rice growing areas is tobacco. On the whole tobacco cultivation depends firstly on the availability of local infrastructure, since it is usually grown on a contract basis, and secondly, on prevailing prices. It tends to be seen as a compromise strategy for marginal land holders in the dry season who farm under contract to one of the large tobacco companies (domestic or multinational) through a registered barn owner in the locality who supplies inputs and purchases the product on behalf of the parent company. In tobacco cultivation the soil is first prepared, weeded and loosened before planting. After about seven days, an initial application of fertiliser is made and this is followed up with a second application after one month. Weeding and planting is fairly labour intensive. Harvesting begins after the end of the second month. The first of six pluckings takes place at intervals of about eight days between each plucking. The leaves are then weighed, purchased and transported to the local tobacco barn owner.

The barn owner is then responsible for tempering and grading the leaves which are first racked in a room where the temperature is steadily increased over a period of one week. Each stage of the heating process has a different function from colouring the leaf, to drying it and expelling all humidity and finally drying the mid rib. The green leaf is divided into two qualities dictating the price paid to farmers. Around ten kilos of green leaf will produce one dry kilo.

There are a number of advantages to tobacco growing as far as small cultivators are concerned. The first is that all plants and necessary inputs are provided by the barn owner. The cost of inputs has to be repaid after the harvest but unlike a loan there is no outstanding interest payment. Farmers realise that the input provisions are simply a means for the parent company to maximise production. If there is a poor harvest farmers must still repay the cost of the inputs to the barn owner with no element of shared risk. Since labour requirements are relatively high farmers argue that if they were to calculate the cost of their own labour they would only be earning marginally more than a casual agricultural labourer. Yet, in a number of places tobacco has been more of a success than other subsidiary crops. Although the labour inputs are high, the opportunity costs of labour, which is almost exclusively family based, are generally lower during this period.

Livestock

In most rice economies there is little extensive livestock production at the household level. Many families maintain a few buffalo for draught purposes in agriculture such as for ploughing and threshing and also for general haulage and transportation work. In a situation where agricultural land is under significant pressure grazing takes place in marginal areas such as along the roadside, on tank bunds and in forest reserves. In the fallow period between the cultivation seasons, buffalo may graze in the paddy fields. Due to the lack of adequate permanent grazing land, buffalo owners supplement fodder intake with cut grass from the paddy terraces. Artificial feedstuffs are rarely used except in cases where cross bred milch cows have been introduced as part of a stall fed cattle programme to generate incremental income for smallholders and marginal householders as, for example, under the Indian IRDP programme. In the evenings, the buffalo are normally brought to the domestic compound for protection. Any manure is then collected and recycled on to the home garden plot. Buffalo are rarely milked since villagers commonly believe that this would drain their energy. The majority of farmers who keep buffalo are those who farm full time with little or no off-farm employment. The tasks are shared between the family and children often watch the herd in the afternoons after school. Many buffalo owners are smallholders or tenants who may hire out their animals during the cultivation seasons.

Overall, paddy farming is by far and away the single most important agricultural activity in most rural monsoon economies and the paddy cycle still dominates almost every aspect of village life in most of rural Asia. This has become all the more marked since the introduction of widespread irrigation linked to newly constructed canal systems and the construction or rehabilitation of village minor tanks. For most households paddy is viewed as a staple crop which provides greater domestic security. Paddy cultivation has simultaneously become more intensive with the increasing use of biochemical inputs and techniques such as transplanting. The extraordinary degree of intensity has served to increase land productivity which has, in turn, either increased real family incomes or stabilise incomes in the face of increasing land fragmentation and diminution. In this way, increased agricultural intensity, has simultaneously help to maintain the smallholder environment which has given rise to a growing off-farm economy, the character of which is determined by a combination of State policy and economic forces. This argument will now be examined in more detail in theoretical, historical and empirical form in the following chapters.

2 Theoretical perspectives on rural transition

Attempts to theorise the process of rural transition in developing countries have consumed much intellectual energy over the years. Despite this, many would now argue that the debate has become rather sterile in approach and has largely failed to capture the complex reality of the world as experienced by ordinary people. This is, perhaps, best exemplified by the preoccupation of the debate with overarching economic and political systems and the precise degree of determination that such systems are seen to exert in the final instance.

Given this, it is not surprising to find that much writing on rural development in recent years has been more concerned with how to alleviate the immediate problems of vulnerability, sustainability and food security than with the question of the contradictions of the production system itself and related social formation. Where structural issues have been addressed, it has increasingly been in an attempt to promote neoclassical thinking on the supremacy of the market as a means of generating and dispersing wealth in the rural economy. However, an inadequate understanding of some of the complexities and subtleties of local production systems may result in such policies not achieving their stated goals. Raising producer prices and eliminating subsidies could be a case in point where, for example, most of the rural population may be small subsistence farmers or landless labourers and nonfarm workers unable to sell to the market and dependent on low cost inputs. Rather than abandon the theoretical analysis of the rural economy altogether, an attempt will be made in this chapter to reexamine certain aspects of the debate in the light of contemporary rural change. This will entail a brief discussion of both the neoclassical and marxist development paradigms alongside recent reformulations of the debate which appear to shed more light on certain aspects of rural transition which have hitherto remained neglected and thus inadequately conceptualised. The problem with an alternative approach that might advocate an almost exclusive concentration on a concrete historicist model is that, although one might avoid a degree of theoretical posturing and arcane semantics, there is a grave danger of ending up simply contemplating the unique or engaging in senseless empiricism, based on numerous accounts of the particular, that fail to provide even the roughest of guides on the direction of future change.

Neoclassical modernisation

Much post war theorising about the direction of change in developing countries was strongly influenced by a number of models designed to explain the nature of economic growth. Drawing heavily on concepts embodied in the 'Harrod Domar' model where, for example, growth is seen to be dependent on the level of savings and the productivity of investment, contemporary theory began to focus on the means of raising the savings capacity as the central issue in economic development.

A number of theories were formulated around this model which assumed that modernisation as represented by the developed capitalist economies, embodying high rates of growth, was the central objective of development. The concept of economic dualism, which was reflected in much of the writing of W.A. Lewis in the 1950s, assumed that rapid development would be brought about by a transformation of a traditional (rural) subsistence sector being gradually replaced by a modern (urban) capitalist sector with a high propensity to save and reinvest. Likewise, Rostow's theory of growth assumed a steady progression through various stages of development from traditional to take off and finally self sustaining growth and maturity with savings capacity as the main propellant.

Economic theories of growth and development were further reinforced by a substantial sociological literature which was in turn rooted in Parsonian structural functionalism. Parsonian theory laid much emphasis on the importance of goal directed behaviour advocating the rational organisation of available means to achieve specific ends. At a societal level, this notion led to the formulation of particular structural determinants based on the reproductive needs or functional requirements of society. It was argued that within this structure there existed a series of pattern variables or choices which could be defined into specific role categories when society was in equilibrium. Any change in equilibrium would require adaptation and reintegration based on greater levels of specialisation leading to greater functional cohesion.

Hence, different pattern variables or choices could be associated with societies at different levels of development. Modern pattern variables were associated with ideal type orientations such as achievement, functional specialisation etc, while traditional pattern variables were associated with self orientation, diffusion, ascription etc. While Parsonian theory regarded these pattern variables as an effect of a given structure, development theorists saw them as determining the structure and thus perceived the task of development as that of promoting behaviourial reorientation towards the systems and values embodied in western capitalism (see for example Hoselitz 1960, Eisenstadt 1961). A further extension of this concept was developed by McClelland (1961) in a psychological interpretation of achievement motivation which was seen as a crucial factor in development and dependent upon particular social and cultural practices such as those of child rearing.

Despite the fact that these theories have been subjected to much criticism over the years (see Taylor 1979), they continue to provide the theoretical justification for many modernisation programmes aimed at economic and political reform, institution building, industrialisation and urbanisation. Indeed with the revival in neoclassical thinking over the last few years, many of the concepts embodied in modernisation theory have re-emerged in the dogmas of the new right. As a means of explaining rural transition in the developing world, however, these theories fail on a number of accounts. Most importantly, they lack any historical perspective viewing each country in isolation from the world economy. At the same time they lack predictive capability since they mainly operate at a descriptive level failing to identify the causal factors in the process of change that might illuminate the whole process of rural transition beyond simply measuring an economy against a scale of modernisation.

Neomarxist dependency and world systems theory

In contrast to the modernisation approach, dependency theory offers an explanation of change in the periphery that draws upon notions of surplus extraction and distorted economic development which are seen as a corollary of advanced capitalist reproduction. This model assumes that within the capitalist system extended reproduction is limited because of an eventual lack of demand which results in the falling rate of profit in the domestic economy necessitating territorial expansion. Frank (1967), in developing this argument from concepts such as those devised by Sweezy (1942) and Baran (1957), has been successful in providing an understanding of the structural character and conditions of particular capitalist forces contributing to underdevelopment. He argues that internal contradictions within the metropolitan economies serve to reproduce capitalism in the periphery which is based upon the appropriation of locally produced surplus leading to the development of the metropolitan core and the underdevelopment of the periphery.

However, the theory has in turn been criticised on account of its rather generalised description which is seen as simply providing a reverse mirror image of the earlier functionalist paradigm (Browett 1982) and its failure to specify the concrete process of surplus extraction whilst at the same time lacking any prescriptive formulae (Taylor 1979). Laclau (1971) has criticised Frank and the dependency school on a number of accounts. He has pointed out that Frank has defined capitalism on the basis of it being a relation of exchange rather than a relation of production. He has also criticised the notion of seeing the early period of Western expansion as capitalist. This is closely associated with a further point which relates to Frank's view that the market is the defining characteristic of capitalism since this implies that feudalism is characterised by the absence of a market. Yet analysis of the feudal mode demonstrates the existence of a fairly well developed market.

World systems theory has attempted to refine global theorising by undertaking an historical analysis and periodisation of the various stages of capitalist expansion throughout the world economy (see Wallerstein 1974). Both Friedman (1976) and Ekholm (1981) have defended the notion of a global system arguing that the analysis must focus on external exchange relations. Friedman views an understanding of the dynamics of global links that determine exchange as the key to understanding exploitation, where the external arena is seen as the crucial place in which relations of production are ultimately formed and reproduced.

Both theories lay undue emphasis on the role of external factors without sufficient regard for autonomous internal forces which, as will be argued below, are of crucial importance in understanding the particular character and complexity of rural transition. In spite of these attempts to conceptualise the nature of change in the periphery, there still appears to be a need, as expressed by Browett who draws on Arrighi (1971) and Bernstein (1976) for 'a more specific, concrete and diagnostic approach (Browett 1982:151). As Gordon (1982) points out, social structure and class struggle are fundamentally ignored in any analysis where social relations are visualised at an international level.

Modes of production and the capitalist economy

The mode of production approach represents an attempt to come to terms with some of the theoretical weaknesses outlined above. A mode of production consists of the totality of the forces of production and the means of production (land, water, labour, machinery etc) linked to the relations of production (how these are owned and controlled). It focuses on the underlying structure of a given social formation which is seen as consisting of a set of relations of production acting upon particular forces of production. A mode of production will thus define a specific set of relations between various classes and the level of development of the associated forces of production. At a broader level, a social formation may change as a new mode of production begins to develop with a new power structure that challenges the former order.

The overall concept derives from Marx's theoretical account of capitalism and the falling rate of profit. In the capitalist mode of production all commodities are produced by wage labour which has been divorced from the means of its own production and generates surplus value (labour time) in the form of profit. Marx demonstrates how the subsumption of the productive forces under capitalist relations of production encourages extended reproduction, and that with an eventual rise in the organic composition of capital brought about by increased surplus, there will be a tendency for the rate of profit to fall. This is checked by a series of counterbalancing forces which serve to increase the rate of exploitation. From this, as Taylor points out, one can see how the long term trend of falling profit rates due to the over production of constant capital will lead to the export of capital. This contrasts with the dependency theorists' view of peripheral domination due to under consumption in the core.

Laclau (1971) has modified this notion in the contemporary context to argue that there are a series of modes of production within any one social formation that articulate with a dominant capitalism. The structural characteristics of capitalism necessitate the reproduction of traditional modes in the periphery to supply the capitalist core with cheap labour. This does not represent a dual economy since the peripheral mode is maintained specifically by capitalism and functions for capitalism.

Attempts to theorise these traditional or non capitalist modes of production have revolved fairly extensively around French marxist anthropological scholarship. Meillassoux (1972) argues that pre capitalist relations are subsumed by dominant capitalist relations, as does Terray (1972) in his study of the Guro in West Africa. Although these notions of articulation give a measure of independent identity to the mode under observation; they simultaneously recognised its dependence upon the metropolitan system. Implicit in this formula is the idea of dissolution and conservation. This appears to be a somewhat contradictory idea, but is necessary in order to maintain the articulationist stance of assuming that pre capitalist modes are both independent from yet formally subsumed to wider capitalist relations. Others, however, have argued that the notion of articulation fails to recognise the essential characteristics of a mode of production at a given time (see for example Banaji 1977a) and consequently fails to provide an adequate understanding of the prevailing economic and social system.

Many of the issues concerned with this approach were raised in a parallel argument with specific reference to Indian agriculture. Harriss (1982) demonstrates that the question of what constituted the necessary conditions of capitalist production in agriculture remained prominent in this debate. For some, a structural transformation in the mode of production was represented by the introduction of generalised commodity production and in particular the existence of wage labour (see Chattopadhyay 1972). Others argued that a pre requisite of capitalist transformation was a marked trend towards expanded reproduction through capital investment (see Patnaik 1971, 1972) mainly on account of the fact that although commoditised labour appeared to exist, it was largely in an embedded form rather than as free wage labour (Harriss 1982:10).

This empirical debate (see the collected works in Patnaik, Banaji et al 1978) resounded between Rudra, who denied that any such transformation was taking place in the Indian countryside and Patnaik who at first argued that the evidence pointed towards a marked capitalist trend but later drawing upon an historical examination of change, relating in particular to the colonial period, qualified her interpretation of contemporary developments, seeing them as only partly transformative. This contrasts with the almost orthodox interpretation of change by Ram and Chattopadhyay in the context of historical materialism and the inevitable development of capitalist production relations. Ram (1972), for example, in a classically Leninist posture attacks Patnaik for attributing too much importance to types of cultivation that are not obviously capitalist. Her major fault, he contends, is in failing to comprehend relations and tendencies as opposed to immediately observable categories.

The colonial mode of production and the post–colonial state

One approach adopted in response to some of the theoretical inadequacies contained within the Indian debate mentioned above, has been developed by Alavi (1975) with the concept of the colonial mode of production. He dismisses the Indian debate as part of an 'empiricist illusion' and argues that the concern over the degree to which various aspects of cultivation in various regions are more or less capitalist, reflects an overall failure to accept the underlying structure which determines development in the last instance. As Harriss has emphasised, Alavi's main point of contention with both Patnaik and Chattopadhyay is their failure to show any underlying conflict between rural capitalist and feudal landlord classes representing the co existence of and articulation between different modes of production (Harriss 1982:12). Having demonstrated that feudal conditions did not pertain to the colonial period in India, Alavi (1975) then develops a theoretical construct designed to show that change is most often neither fully developed in terms of a capitalist transformation nor completely dependent upon capitalism. It is rather a specific form of colonial capitalism expressed in terms of a colonial mode of production. Other commentators such as Otto–Walter (1978) argue that this approach accepts an underlying unity of change while stressing the necessary specificity of changes in particular class formations.

Alavi has since refined this analysis to emphasise the form of colonial capitalist penetration in relation to post independence change (see Alavi 1980). He draws on the historical works of Habib and Mukherjee to refute the notion of Indian pre capitalist society as being an essentially static entity. Alavi traces a gradual breakdown in traditional relations based on increasing forms of hired labour and merchant sponsored out work industries. He argues that land tenure was characterised by a complex system of localised rights, not in land itself but in the rights to surplus. There was also a fusion of economic and political power at the local level which characterised the social formation in terms other than Asiatic. Villages were self sufficient and organised along caste lines with individual rights over land and access to common land and services.

The main impact of colonial rule, according to Alavi, was the dissolution of political and economic force at the place of production and the dispossession of peasant ownership under zamindari authority. Here, the form of surplus extraction based on extra economic coercion was gradually replaced by direct economic coercion or contractual ties. Alongside these changes, the increased burden of land revenue, overseas transfers and the destruction of the indigenous manufacturing industry to create markets for British goods enforced by high tariffs on Indian exports, and the loss of European export markets to the British after the Napoleonic Wars, all served to distort the form of expanding capitalist relations.

In Alavi's theoretical paradigm illustrating the necessary extent of change required to induce capitalism, not only must tied labour, extra economic coercion and the fusion of economic and political power at the local level all become transformed, but particular productive and reproductive change must also be brought about. It is here that the crucial elements of his argument rest. The peasant is forced into commodity production in order to purchase goods that were formerly made at the local level and to make cash payments in the form of land revenues. In order to achieve these objectives the peasant farmer cultivates cash crops. 'We may look upon this process as internal disarticulation and external integration of the rural economy' (Alavi 1980: 393). In this situation the reproduction of capital is not achieved by strictly conventional means since surplus is not accumulated locally, expanding the form of local reproduction, but instead serves these purposes in the metropolitan core. In this way the specific colonial mode becomes characteristic of change in the periphery. Although it is accepted that the form of colonial production differs from place to place, the underlying principle is seen as the same.

A number of analysts have argued this colonial mode of production has been transformed into a neocolonial mode after independence. Gordon (1982) has emphasised this in his interpretation of the Indonesian economy which he sees as suffering a collapse after 1942 and remaining in a series of stagnant phases until the 1965 coup. He contends that the establishment of a post-colonial social formation after 1965 has resulted in the destruction of the former political elites and the growth of an economic system where production and surplus extraction revolves around the importation of capital and technology. The new class alignments are mediated by a bureaucratic oligarchy to ensure behaviourial consistency towards the sources of metropolitan patronage.

Evers (1978) has attempted to refine the post colonial concept by first dividing up the reproductive circuit into various sectors before analysing the forms of ownership and control over the means of production. He argues that the subsistence sector, where production takes place outside the market and reproduction is based upon the cultivation and provision of food and the provision of shelter, can appear to be isolated and self-sufficient. Yet he points out that this sector, in both the rural and urban context, plays a crucial role in sustaining dependent capitalist relations through the reproduction of cheap labour. Although Evers recognises the difficultly in identifying the more powerful groups within the subsistence sector, where production is consumed before entering the market, he claims that analysis of the main beneficiaries should focus on land ownership and access to government bureaucrats.

Ibrahim (1982) has conducted research into the penetration of capitalist relations in Malaysia and the ensuing reconstitution of the peasantry. He discusses the impact of colonial policy on society where plantation enclaves and mineral extracting enclaves coexisted with a commoditised peasantry producing a mix of staple food crops and cash crops. Land alienation policies encouraged a growing differentiation within the peasantry. The ensuing reconstitution of the peasant community evolved into what Ibrahim terms 'hybrid' relations of production. The transition from the production of use values to exchange values and the integration into the circulation circuit of capital had specific class ramifications. He notes that the post colonial State, although no longer directly under the authority of foreign capital, still serves to perpetuate a social formation determined by capital and subsumed under the metropolitan core.

The colonial concept has been attacked by Banaji (1977b) for its lack of specificity in identifying the form of smallholder production and the mechanism of surplus extraction. Based on historical evidence from the Deccan he contends that small producers, although maintaining a measure of independence over the means of production, were simultaneously reliant on

34

comprador capitalists for their reproduction. Roseberry (1978) similarly highlights the plight of Venezuelan smallholder coffee producers, caught up in a debt bondage relation with capital, which is today controlled by the State, to illustrate the subordination of the peasantry. Agricultural modernisation and technical innovation can be seen to complete the process of the subsumption of labour by drawing smallholders into the circuit of capital.

Alavi (1989) stresses that indigenous developments in the post colonial State may now have altered elements of the economic structure but that it has still not been able to shake off its dependence on metropolitan capital which continues to be perpetuated through technical collaboration with foreign multinationals. Gunasinghe (1980) has also argued that in the post independence economy of Sri Lanka, indigenous production relations in the countryside have been reactivated as a means of surplus extraction and are related to a peripheral capital formation dominated by metropolitan capital. On the question of the agrarian structure in India, Byres (1989) emphasises the pattern of emerging class formation and polarisation around an increasingly prosperous group of capitalist farmers, formerly small and medium landlords and rich peasants, and an impoverished group of poor peasants, landless labourers and artisans. He argues that the new biochemical technology in agriculture which has been steered towards the regions where richer farmers have been in the ascendency has hastened the process of differentiation as these richer peasants have secured access to resources and inputs. Undoubtedly, the dominant farmer groups of western Uttar Pradesh, Haryana and parts of the Punjab and Rajasthan have commanded a great deal of political influence which they have turned to economic advantage. The various kisan (farmer) leaders from the 1940s onwards including Sardar Patel in Gujarat, Gobind Ballabh Pant in Uttar Pradesh, Pratap Singh Kairon in the Punjab, and more recently Charan Singh and Devi Lal in Uttar Pradesh and Haryana respectively, have all been successful in gaining advantage for farmers in the region. One of the current kisan lobbies led by Mahendra Singh Tikait, with a membership drawn from the Jat community and richer farmers from among the Yadav, Ahir and Gujjar caste groups has been actively agitating on a number of fronts including farmer exemption from water and electricity charges.

What is interesting in this context is that although the case of India provides Alavi with evidence of dependent capitalism and Byres with evidence of agrarian capitalism, both indicate, either implicitly (Alavi 1989) or explicitly (Byres 1989) that the situation may be less rigid than first appears. Alavi is certainly on less than firm ground in the case of India with its well developed industrial base, plethora of regulations and restrictions relating to foreign investment and its willingness to disregard international patent and copyright conventions. The United States Trade Department, for example, has in the past placed India on its blacklist for disregarding international intellectual property laws. Although foreign capital and technology is now more welcome than in the past and has risen from Rs 100 million in 1980 to Rs 2.4 billion by 1988, this has to be seen in the context of total industrial investment with public sector investment alone standing at around Rs 720 billion (India Today, Jan 1990). Most foreign firms operate in collaboration with Indian business and are by no means free of intervention. IBM, for example, had a subsidiary in India until 1978 when the Indian Government insisted on acquiring a major shareholding. IBM was unable to resist Government pressure and ultimately had to pull out of India altogether. As for the Indian electronics industry, there has been increasing indigensation of production which has grown at a compound rate of 35 percent in the 1985–90 period and 25 percent in 1980–85. Exports in this sector have risen dramatically with a cumulative annual rate of 40 percent in the 1985–90 period compared to 27 percent between 1980–85. In the software segment alone, India has over 400 software organisations of which 150 are software exporters. However, the wider economic picture is somewhat mixed. While the composition of exports has changed dramatically over the years, the rate of growth of total exports has been slow and with an increasing import bill for petroleum products the trade gap has been widening. Yet, the World Bank development report (1986) concluded that India's overall economic performance under the sixth plan 'was a tribute to the quality of its economic management in adjusting to a variety of challenges while keeping external borrowing and inflationary pressure in check' (1986: 101). This position has changed in recent years with increased government expenditure leading to a growing current account deficit and a dramatic rise in foreign borrowings producing a debt of $70 billion, up from $19 billion in 1980. Interest payments on past loans have become one of the fastest growing elements of government expenditure (Economist, Jan 1990). In response to this situation India's high international credit rating has now been downgraded.

It does appear that despite many underlying weaknesses in the economy, which only managed to achieve a growth rate of 3.5 percent in the three decades following independence, there is, as Harriss (1989) points out, sufficient strength to withstand external pressure. Furthermore, some recent economic indicators have shown a marked improvement. India's annual average rate of growth in the 1980s reached 5.5 percent while industrial production has been growing at around 9 percent since the mid 1980s. This has led some commentators to conclude that during the 1980s there has been a maturing of the economy which despite its ups and downs 'continues to display remarkable resilience (India Today, Jan 1990: 37).

As far as rural transition is concerned, Byres (1989) makes a number of important qualifications to the notion that conventional agrarian capitalism can be generalised throughout the country. He points to the circumstances of employment creation in both country and town to indicate that the capitalist transformation has only been a partial process and furthermore draws attention to the fact that in other parts of the country, such as the rice growing south, a different set of inherited characteristics may lead to a different rural structure. This is a crucial point in the argument and will be returned to later.

Towards a synthesis

What has emerged from the debate up to this point is an underlying recognition of the need to understand more fully the logic and character of the domestic economy in general and the rural sector in particular. As we have seen above, to some, the survival of smallholder production merely represents a transitional phenomenon that will disintegrate in the wake of the progressive march of the forces of commercialisation and mechanisation, generating a marked differentiation within the rural population as capitalist production relations become finally established. This argument has been propounded by authors such as Chattopodhyay (1972), Ram (1972) and Banaji (1977a) in the Indian context, with a more recent qualified interpretation by Byres (1989) drawing almost exclusively on the wheat growing belt of north India, as well as authors such as Arrighi and Saul (1973) and Cliffe (1977) in relation to African rural transition. Others have been more concerned to recognise economic and social diversity either in the form of the articulation of different but coexisting modes or as part of the structural development of a particular colonial or post colonial mode.

An important distinction in the debate concerns Marx's concept of formal and real subsumption. Since the peasantry often retain a measure of independence over the direct means of production and capitalists appropriate surplus labour in the form of absolute surplus value, labour is only formally subsumed. Real subsumption, however, with full control over production leads to the increasing organic composition of capital and the appropriation of relative as well as absolute surplus value (Harriss 1982). Bernstein (1979) outlines the process of formal subsumption in his analysis of how smallholders become increasingly dependent upon the market for their reproduction in a situation that does not actually destroy the family farm. The conditions in which smallholders reproduce themselves, according to Bernstein, constitutes a situation which categorises them as 'wage labour equivalents'. Others have seen the position of labour being formally subsumed by capital as one of producing a 'disguised proletariat'.

The central problem that still remains in spite of these more specific attempts to conceptualise the nature and form of rural change in the periphery, is their adequacy to account for the continued existence of commodity production centred on the household as the basic unit of production. Most interpretations, as Long (1984) has pointed out, appear to accept that a smallholder sector is preserved by capitalism which is seen as selectively maintaining non-capitalist elements on account of their useful or functional character for the reproduction of the system as a whole. Here, the provision of cheap labour is seen as one of the main functional incentives. One question that must therefore be raised in relation to this notion, is the lack of an adequate explanation accounting for the willingness of capitalism to limit itself to consequent low rates of capital accumulation, limited technological development and to incur the opportunity cost of reduced surplus appropriation.

Another problem with many of the interpretations that focus on the concept of formal subsumption and notions of a 'disguised proletariat' is that although they accept that household producers are neither fully dependent upon the sale of their labour power, nor fully expropriated from the means of their production, there is an underlying theoretical implication of transition and disintegration (Glavanis 1984) or decomposition (Long 1984) which appears rather over deterministic.

This view of rural transition has also been criticised by Harriss (1982) with specific reference to empirical evidence highlighted in an agrarian study in Tamil Nadu. In addressing the problem of the separation of the direct producer from the means of production, Harriss questions existing interpretations that appear to depend upon concepts of simple determination. This, he argues, has led certain commentators such as Banaji to slide over the issue of total separation which in many local agrarian contexts has not actually taken place, by stating that partial control over production will over time lead to full control over the entire means of peasant production. The plausibility of such an argument is 'derived from an historicist view of a necessary process of capitalist development' (Harriss 1982: 291). Here, we might return to the point raised by Byres (1989) who hints that in parts of India, other than the wheat growing belt, the rural structure may take on different characteristics.

An alternative neopopulist interpretation of agrarian transition is represented by urban bias theory (see Lipton 1977) which reformulates class struggle in terms of a system of surplus extraction and investment which markedly favours the urban population over the rural. In spite of the obvious appeal of this argument there has been a certain amount of criticism based on empirical evidence that does not support the view that agriculture is more heavily taxed than industry. Byres (1979), for example, reinforces the view that agriculture in India operates as a free rider or favoured sector showing that farmers have consistently avoided taxes, lobbied for the maintenance of high prices and generally prospered from inter sectoral terms of trade. In fact close examination of the composition of government revenue in India appears to bear out these findings with 41 percent of central revenue being generated by customs and excise duties and 23 percent from internal borrowings. Moreover, India taxes producers goods such as cement, coal, plastics, rubber etc in addition to manufactured goods. The urban bias argument has been revisited by Harriss and Moore (1984) with a number of interesting reformulations such as Moore's core-periphery model designed to capture the political dimension which cannot necessarily be reduced to urban-rural economic interests. Lipton (1989) appears to recognise the limitation of a strict urban-rural dichotomy in certain parts of the world by referring to the recirculation of money in the form of rural investment in many parts of Asia. In India, for example, the share of agriculture and rural development in the budget has been raised from 44 percent in 1989-90 to 49 percent for 1990-91.

The suggestion to formulate alternative analyses of agrarian change has been made by Kahn (1981) in order to challenge and supplement existing theories which, on account of their level of generality are often an inappropriate means of conceptualising change at the local and regional level. In their comprehensive critique of Marxist anthropology, Kahn and Llobera (1981) reject structuralist attempts to encapsulate a universal interpretation of totality and materialism, characterised by functional determinism. Finding inspiration in the works of Terray and Reay they contend that a solution depends on the restoration of specific historical analyses in which concrete studies using the basic concepts of historical materialism may begin the task of a 'post structuralist' critical evaluation.

A more precise examination of the dynamics of household or petty commodity production appears to require a reassessment of the Chayanovian debate and elements of peasant resistance to capitalist forces. Friedman (1980) illustrates the viability of the family farm in the context of agrarian capitalist developments in the United States, illustrating the type of survival strategies adopted by family members. Although in many cases it is unlikely that a smallholder system will be preserved in its original state on account of its own internal logic, what is required in analysis is a means of understanding the nature of the links between the internal system and the external structure. This may help to avoid the problem noted by Long (1984) of presenting a much too homogeneous impression of the household enterprise and that noted by Kahn (1980) where the phenomenon under observation is seen as part of a complete and definable capitalist system with its own logic and structure.

The development of a more satisfactory understanding of the nature of the rural economy first involves an elucidation of the internal dynamics of household production, as pointed out by Long (1984), which entails looking at the division of labour within and between households and the definitions of cognitive orientation and economic rationality that form part of the process. However, since change is to be explained in terms other than demographic evolution and simple social processes, external factors that relate to production and consumption must also be considered (Long 1984: 6). This emphasis has been applied in a recent study of the Mahaweli irrigation scheme in Sri Lanka which focuses on the interactions of bureaucrats, farmers and traders which are seen to reshape planned intervention in a manner which reinforces peasantisation rather than commoditisation (Siriwardena 1990). The importance of such a study is that it questions assumptions made about the nature of rural change from a dynamic empirical basis which is not simply concerned with the problem of conceptualising the continued existence of traditional social formation in a wider framework.

To sum up so far, there are three strands to the theoretical debate on the changing nature of production systems in the rural economy. It is worth pointing out at this stage, incidentally, that these same arguments are parallelled in a similar debate concerning the nature of contemporary change in advanced western economies. The determinist position is that the modern corporate capitalist system and its weak counterpart in developing countries is an economic form that is destined to dominate in all circumstances resulting in the final convergence of disparate economic systems. Interestingly, this view has now been widely criticised in both the developing country and advanced western context. Weiss, for example, points out in relation to Italy that 'although these determinist and essentialist notions still linger in the literature with surprising tenacity, there is now less need to do critical battle with a set of theories whose defects have been so lucidly exposed elsewhere' (1988: 2).

The second strand contains a strong functionalist logic which views the continued existence of non capitalist or small capital relations as useful and indeed necessary for the functioning of national and international capital. This dualist model remains prominent in the developing country debate and has simultaneously been reformulated in the context of advanced industrial societies by Berger and Piore (1980) and Goldthorpe (1984).

As indicated by a number of commentators above, there is now a growing recognition that neither the highly deterministic convergence model nor the functionalist dualist interpretation, represent an adequate conceptualisation of rural change in developing countries. This same objection has been raised by Weiss in her analysis of the state and small enterprise in Italy where empirical evidence of the small scale flexible economy demonstrates that there is no 'law–like tendency *for capitalism* to produce similar economic and social structures' (1988: 1). In response to this, the third strand in the debate has been variously formulated as an autonomous petty commodity model; an independent regionalised production system; a competitive small producer economy. All of these interpretations possess a strong degree of commonality in their opposition to any notion of a unilineal process of capitalist development and indeed could be seen to represent various stages in a continuum of opposition to centralised corporate capitalism. In many parts of the developing world it appears that the family enterprise has been able to resist large scale organised production either in agriculture or in manufacturing and services by simultaneously consolidating traditional strengths and advantages and adopting new business practices. These largely consist of a combination of strategies ranging from household diversification to economic intensification and inter firm cooperation, all of which will be examined in the final chapter.

40

The modern family enterprise and micro-capitalism

Family enterprise is often theorised in the form of petty commodity production combining traditional family property and labour relations with aspects of commoditisation such as market integration. This form of production is often seen as embodying an intrinsic competitive advantage over conventional capitalist enterprise since there is no structural requirement for profit on account of a flexible consumption pattern. Here, the distribution of net income can be redeployed as necessary. It is on account of this fact that a number of commentators have argued that this mode need not be subsumed under a wider capitalist or neocapitalist system. Kahn has clearly demonstrated from empirical evidence in Indonesia, for example, that far from any universal emergence of a class of rural capitalists, what is being witnessed in many cases is the re-creation of a class of peasants based on viable peasant enterprise (Kahn 1980, 1981). Middleton (1989) has shown in an analysis of petty production in Ecuador that the number of petty enterprises has remained stable while their internal structure has been dynamic.

The family farm

There is no doubt that the family enterprise continues to dominate in many parts of agriculture as the family farm in the smallholder setting. This form of agriculture is a particular feature of Asian wet rice farming characterised by the steady fragmentation and diminution of land holding alongside the injection of new technology leading to increased yields. Bray (1986) in an extremely detailed and well documented account of technology and development in Asian rice economies has argued that the continued existence of the small-scale farming enterprise can be explained by its particular ability to raise productivity within the context of severe land constraints.

At this stage it will not be necessary to dwell on the specific character of the family farm which will be examined in more detail in chapter four but it may be useful to consider briefly the main theoretical issues associated with wet rice production as expressed by Bray and others (see Bray 1986, Francks 1984). Bray's main theoretical argument turns on the perceived inadequacies of orthodox accounts of rural transition in Asia. Neither the concept of a specific Asiatic mode of production characterised by a stagnant peasant economy nor a debilitated variant of western capitalism is seen as capable of explaining the underlying character of the Asian small farm. For Bray, the key to this problem lies in the acceptance of the specificity of local conditions and the relativity of the notion of technological progress. The dominant view of progress has been formed on the basis of western notions of rising productivity being associated with efficient forms of labour substitution where extended cultivation and labour scarcity are significant factors in the production equation. Conditions in Asian rice farming are very different. Land is the scarce factor while labour is abundant. In these conditions it makes more sense for productivity to be associated with increased output per unit of land and increased demand for labour and this is precisely what has happened in many parts of Asia.

Bray explains this outcome by analysing the unique characteristics of the main forces of rice production in the form of the plant itself, land use and water control which respond particularly well to intensification and skill application. This process has been reinforced by the high level of divisibility of capital inputs in the form of biochemical technology which has contributed to significant gains in marginal productivity without any tendency towards large scale accumulation and farm consolidation. Both transplanting and double cropping have generated a rise in labour inputs but this has been off-set by increased yields. This intensive method of increasing land productivity is defined as internal augmentation by Kikuchi and Hayami (1985) as opposed to external augmentation relating to the expansion cultivated area and is observed by them in the agricultural evolution of Japan, Taiwan, Korea and the Philippines.

Francks (1984) has also traced the history of agricultural development in pre war Japan showing how productivity gains were based on labour–using, land–saving techniques and inputs during the late Tokugawa and early Meji periods. Francks explains that these technological changes culminated in the Meji *noho* (Meji agricultural methods) based on high yielding seeds of a shorter stem and fast maturing variety which were responsive to high applications of fertiliser, deep ploughing, intensive water management and which facilitated double cropping. These early green revolution type techniques requiring increased inputs, led to higher yields and increased output with a concomitant increase in labour in the form of days worked per year by the basic farm family. Between 1880–1935 total agricultural output increased at an annual compound rate of 1.6 percent per annum while total input increased at 0.4 percent and total productivity increased at 1.2 percent per annum with three quarters of the growth in output being directly generated by technological development (Hayami and Kikuchi 1985: 92). These technological developments led to a gradual shift in the structure of agriculture which, according to Francks, was not characterised by an increase in the size of holdings with larger farms becoming increasingly dependent on wage labour but rather the opposite happened where large scale holdings could no longer benefit from the extended farm system which broke down as these holdings were split up and parcelled out to dependents and tenants. These 'new smaller units relied mostly on family labour which was better suited to the new kinds of careful cultivation technique, and were able to take advantage, as household units, of the increasing scope for non–agricultural by–employment' (Francks 1984: 65). In Meji Japan, technological change was sufficient to counteract decreasing returns to labour on the limited land base.

Similar technological developments have since been introduced throughout much of South and Southeast Asia with massive increases in irrigation infrastructure and the seed–fertiliser combination.

Francks is quick to point out that this does not imply that there was no differentiation within the agricultural community. Many of the former large holdings retained reasonable amounts of core land and were able to take advantage of better access to knowledge and information on cultivation technique while simultaneously profiting from commercial transactions based on post–harvest storage and strategic sales. This complex socio–economic pattern meant that, over time, the mass of small owners and tenants were able to enjoy certain advantages. These largely consisted of having adequate labour supply and the ability to increase income from nonfarm activity while continuing to benefit from patron–client relations which tended to stabilise rents (Francks 1984). However, as Kikuchi and Hayami emphasise these developments have been insufficient to off set increases in population pressure which has gradually led to the stagnation or decline in the marginal productivity of labour, although without internal augmentation through the introduction of new technology the situation would be considerably worse (1985: 97). In a further study of two Indonesian villages, Hayami and Kikuchi draw on empirical data to demonstrate the hypothesis that modern irrigation, seed–fertiliser (green revolution) technology in Southeast Asia has produced a similar land–saving bias to that of pre war Japan. They conclude that where the technology has been introduced it has increased the yield per unit of land and the area double cropped with a consequent rise in the demand for labour and the real wage rate. Finally, they suggest that technological change based on irrigation, modern seed varieties and fertilisers has helped to counter the effects of increasing population pressure. 'Essentially, the new technology saves the use of land (prevents its factor share from rising), and to the extent the technological change is land saving, income inequality between the landowning and the landless classes does not increase' (1985: 107).

The outcome of this particular form of technical progress in most of monsoon Asia has been neither one of increasing agricultural involution as seen in Indonesia by Geertz (1963), nor one of the gradual evolution towards capitalism as seen by Collier (1981) and White (1981) also drawing on Indonesia, but rather the survival of a smallholder system rooted in the family farm. Bray emphasises that the additional labour requirements in agriculture are spread over the year and that 'for most tasks household labour suffices to run a wet rice smallholding' (1986: 5). This point is substantiated in chapter four on smallholder farming in Sri Lanka where attention is drawn to the growing importance of income diversification in the maintenance of smallholder relations and the family enterprise model. This contention is supported by Bray in a diachronic sense by demonstrating the evolution of rural diversification which is seen as having provided much of the traditional dynamic in Asian rice farming.

Economic diversification and local adaptive strategies thus form a central part of new attempts to conceptualise the nature of change in the countryside. This most often takes the form of inter sectoral diversification as illustrated by the expanding off-farm economies in rural Asia and also noted by Long and Roberts (1978, 1984) in Latin America. In other cases it may be seen in the form of intra sectoral diversification as noted by Archetti and Stolen in Argentina (see Long 1984). In this context it is vital to explain the forms of economic diversification by indicating how the different dimensions intersect. What emerges from any review of alternative approaches to the understanding of rural change is the need to move away from treating the farm as the central determining feature of economic decision making and social organisation and a corresponding need to examine the relative weight of non agricultural activities in the formation of different social strata (Long 1984: 6). This is an area of study that has generally been under emphasised in the literature and, as Herath (1983) points out with specific reference to Sri Lanka, has often merely been seen as an example of a transitional labour system representing a stage in the process of the large scale capitalisation of production. Undoubtedly, as opportunities in the nonfarm sector increase there will be greater incentives for certain households to abandon agriculture altogether, especially those engaged in small manufacturing where, as Japanese experience shows, it became increasingly hard for some households to combine agricultural and industrial enterprises while the prospect of tying up capital in agriculture gradually became less attractive (Francks 1984). However, as the contemporary Italian and Japanese cases demonstrate there may well be a continuing role for small household based enterprise in the countryside which may consolidate a form of flexible micro capitalism distinct from a simple mechanistic notion of the development of large scale capitalist production.

The rural firm

Household diversification, which links family members to the wider society by employment in it, may not undermine household production in the village which often retains governing principles other than those of the capitalist market (see Long 1984). Emerging economic structures may not always destroy smallholder agriculture but rather lead to the development of a satisfactory accommodation with the wider regional system. What emerges at the local level is a complex set of production relations which link different activities together. In many instances the family farm may continue as a viable entity while key family members are simultaneously engaged in the organised nonfarm sector as wage earners or in other family based enterprise. In both cases the family retains important access to elements of their means of production with owners or part owners being directly involved in the production process. At the same time, family labour may continue to predominate in part or all of the production system providing an important competitive edge for its own survival while relations of distribution have broadened out so that production is now for the market rather than specifically to order.

What we see then is a pattern of diversity and flexibility which embodies a mix of family and market in the farm and nonfarm sector. These combine to produce a family enterprise model which may display micro capitalist tendencies if sufficient capital is retained in the business for reinvestment. Where this is the case, the enterprises will display certain characteristics of household production based on the continued use of family labour, possibly alongside wage labour, with the owners continuing to be directly involved in the process of production. The inherent competitive edge of this form of production does not necessarily derive from low wages, poor conditions and low quality/low cost goods and services. These secondary labour market characteristics may predominate at any one time, especially in the initial phase of development resulting in short term gain, but will not be capable of sustaining production in the long term. The strength of the small firm model ultimately lies in its intense specialisation in a particular economic process combined with its close proximity to the market and its flexible response to demand. At the same time it is likely to enjoy, either formally or informally, a host of exemptions from charges, levies and taxes on account of its size, structure and dispersion.

The obvious question that springs to mind at this stage is whether or not the family firm model merely represents a residual economy in transition towards capitalist relations of production which are more commonly associated with full commoditisation. This position assumes the inherent advantages of organised mass production capable of matching single purpose tasks to waged employees for the standard production of mass demand goods. If this is the case, the continued existence of small family enterprise, including those that have taken on a micro capitalist character, is a major dilemma and one which is heightened by the important role that small enterprise continues to play in certain advanced industrial economies such as in Japan and Italy.

The conventional answer to this dilemma has already been touched upon in the preceding section and is predictably formulated in narrow functionalist terms where the small firm is seen as performing an important function for organised capital. The question then becomes not so much whether or not it is functional but whether or not it is optimally functional? If it is not then why does it exist at all? The answer generally lies in circumscribing functionality to the economic periphery. As Weiss (1988) points out, mass production by definition does not enter markets where demand is highly unstable. In this case organised capital engages in a 'risk shifting' exercise leaving subordinate units with highly disposable labour forces to operate in this area since they are capable of connecting consumers to the market at levels of turnover which would be unacceptable to organised capital. In other words the growth and demise of the small firm is seen as contingent on the process of large scale capital accumulation.

Whilst not denying the fact that small firms can and do perform an important function in markets characterised by limited or fluctuating demand, there is also growing evidence to show that they do not only operate in the economic twilight while at the same time organised capital does not always dominate in core markets. At this point it will be useful to return to the European setting to provide some insights into the possible survival and future direction of the small firm economy. In an historical examination of small craft based activity in Europe and the United States Sabel and Zeitlin (1985) convincingly demonstrate that craft production contained its own vitality based upon skilled workers operating flexible technology to meet diverse demand. They show that craft activity was capable of increasing productivity and competing with Fordist organisation but that it lost out to an ideologically inspired vision of a superior model of large scale capital and mass production which succeeded in influencing the state and financial institutions. Weiss (1988) contends that these findings on small craft production are of exceptional importance since they challenge the notion of the inherent superiority of, and hence inevitable drift towards, large scale organised capital. Weiss extends Sabel and Zeitlin's explanation of the demise of craft production in most of Europe and the United States to focus more sharply on the direct role of the state as prime mover in initiating a process of economic concentration and centralisation. She argues that in Italy, however, in direct contrast with the situation in most of Europe and the United States, the role of the state has been no less decisive but very different in its promotion of industrial dispersion through a form of small family based production. In contemplating the wider significance of the Italian model, Weiss contends that its roots are not the monopoly of any one organisational form. Although its origins have been attributed to the retention of specific technical, craft and managerial skills associated with the *mezzadria* (share-cropping) tradition (see Paci 1982), Weiss (1988) argues that the mobility data implies greater birth heterogeneity. Thus, the relationship of the agricultural craft tradition to the contemporary family firm is one of 'elective affinity' rather than being an 'indispensable ingredient' (Weiss 1988: 200). This latter finding has also been confirmed in a recent study of small firm development in the Veneto and Emilia Romagna regions of Italy (Slater and Watson 1990).

Goodman (1989) demonstrates that the significance of industrial growth in Italy in recent years is that it has been led by the small firm with large and medium sized enterprises declining in importance. Other important features of this trend include the fact that the small firms remain highly dependent on the instrumental role of the family and that they are not only engaged in producing traditional sector commodities but have also moved into high technology areas. Weiss confirms that Italian small firms proliferate in a large number of product areas ranging from shoes and textiles to domestic appliances and mechanical engineering.

The Italian case neatly illustrates that small family enterprise is not only capable of surviving but also thriving in an advanced capitalist economy. In fact Goodman (1989) emphasises that the strength of the Italian small firm economy lies in its ability to meet demand rapidly and to gain productivity as well as serving specialised markets. Indeed, the evolving nature of the modern market economy has meant that the mass market is gradually giving way to the differentiated market with greater emphasis on product customisation and quality. This has had an important impact on the organisation of production which is beginning to shift from a capital intensive form of standardised production based on flowline engineering and 'Taylorist' management principles to a more flexible, faster, multi skilled craft oriented system. This tendency has been further underpinned by the availability of modern microcomputer technology which has been effectively deployed by the small enterprise to great advantage. This shift has been characterised by those drawing on the French regulation school as a shift towards flexible accumulation where flexibility manifests itself in production technologies, labour processes, markets and consumption patterns. A feature of the Italian model that needs to be stressed at this point is its unconventional structure in the area of production and exchange. This will be analysed in more detail later but at present it will suffice to say that much of the strength of the system turns on collaboration and linkage rather than the straightforward competition of the modern market economy. Piore and Sabel (1983) refer to this collaboration in terms of special producer/client relations, inter firm cooperation between producers and neighbouring producers and intra firm collaboration between owners and workers.

The crucial point in this argument revolves around the fact that economic concentration is less a result of the inherent logic of the market and more the consequence of both direct and indirect state intervention. Weiss argues that particular crisis circumstances such as the periodic threats to national sovereignty during this century provided an important impetus in the drive towards economic concentration. National politics and relations between markets have consequently been a more decisive factor in the development of modern capitalism than any internal logic of the system itself. Furthermore, as the market becomes more complex and sophisticated the advantages of smaller, flexible, skill intensive units become more apparent. Just as for the small farm in Asia where productivity gains have been expressed in terms of increased output per unit of land based on the increased labour intensity, small firm productivity is based on the increased deployment and intensity of multi skilled and flexible labour.

Rural family enterprise

Neither the family farm nor the family firm represent an antediluvian and stagnant form of production. Both have demonstrated their ability not only to survive but also to gain productivity and absorb labour through a form of highly dispersed economic enterprise. In many developing countries where agriculture has intensified and the pressure on land continues to grow, the family farm may gradually combine with nonfarm activity in such a way that the combination of activities begins to resemble a dynamic small enterprise economy.

In much of Asia and in some parts of Africa, such as Kenya, household diversification has already extended the concept of the family farm into a family firm where household members often complement primary sector work in agriculture and animal husbandry with secondary activity in minor agro-processing, tile and brick making, weaving etc and/or tertiary sector services in repairs, tailoring, carpentry, trading, retailing, transport, contracting, government service etc. Although these enterprises may not possess all the advantages of the modern Italian family firm such as high product concentration, inter firm linkages and networking, features that will be returned to in the concluding chapter, many do possess a strong skill orientation, flexibility, local market intelligence and the ability to customize production and distribution. This form of enterprise allows families amongst other things to: optimise on labour deployment and to adjust to seasonal demand patterns; maintain access to products and services that they might otherwise have little contact with; provide greater economic flexibility in a single activity by adjusting internal production and consumption patterns; stabilise rural population in a position of greater food and income security.

Once this becomes clear it is perhaps no surprise to find that small scale or household enterprise as an economic form continues to be of considerable importance in the rural economy of many developing countries, particularly in Asia where some commentators have identified aspects of it as representing 'monsoon capitalism'. This family enterprise model consists of a number of combinations of activity which can be broadly classified into activity sets depending on the particular livelihood strategy of the household. These sets range from smallholder farming alone to a combination of smallholder farming and nonfarm production or service activity or indeed smallholder farming and wage employment. This complex form of activity is by no means free of differentiation which manifests itself both within the various combinations of activity and between the various sets. The upper end of the economic and social structure consists of a mix of households that have been successful in establishing single or multiple activities, both farm and/or nonfarm, which are characterised by retained income as well as households which have secured access to formal employment. At the lower end of the spectrum are

48

households which depend almost entirely on secondary participation in these activities through casual wage labour. Although for census purposes they often appear as agricultural labour, giving the impression of growing agricultural proletariat, in reality they are more often than not multi occupational with diverse income sources which may even combine wage labour with self–employed earnings and exchange labour.

The level of prosperity and deprivation rarely arises out of the production system alone but from a combination of economic and social access linked to local political manipulation. This observation has been borne out by successive studies on clientilism, politics and patronage at the micro level in developing countries and has been interestingly reinforced in a recent study of planned intervention in the Mahaweli irrigation scheme in Sri Lanka (see Siriwardena 1990). Siriwardena draws attention to the process of the reshaping and the reinterpreting of official policy through a series of individual and collective struggles on the part of the key actors at the local level, namely farmers, officials and traders and shows how producers transform policy in accordance with their own needs and how local officials adapt and modify policies and procedures to ensure local survival. Siriwardena contends that the logic of market alone cannot explain the outcome of these struggles and that commoditisation has reinforced a non market outcome. In a general sense then, it appears legitimate to conclude that neither the pre–existing capital base nor the precise categorisation of traditional production relations as owner, tenant or labourer can serve to explain fully the nature of the contemporary economic and social formation and emerging stratification.

The problem of identifying emerging stratification on the basis of agrarian production relations is especially pronounced in a rice producing environment where the capital base of many households in the form of land is already small and diminishing over time. In these circumstances nonfarm activity is of considerable importance. On the one hand it performs an equalising function at the higher and mid levels of the income spectrum whereby those with little direct access to land can nevertheless raise their earnings quite substantially through primary participation in a nonfarm enterprise or through formal off-farm employment. On the other hand at the lower end of the spectrum it can mitigate the extreme disparities by providing diverse secondary participation in a variety of economic activities throughout the year.

From modes of production to means of living

What is apparent from the foregoing is that it may be necessary to seek more realistic ways of conceptualising local economic systems and related social formation. Since much economic activity has become multi–layered and multifarious it may no longer be particularly useful to characterise relations within an exclusive mode of production framework. The inadequacies of most of the conventional definitions of employment, enterprise and income used by economists and policy makers to identify changes and formulate interventions have been highlighted in the context of women's employment by Grown and Sebstad (1989). They contend that these definitions are often too narrow for policy analysis where, for example, employment categories fail to capture the range of economic activities; earnings data provide only a crude measure of household income without regard for how that income is controlled and allocated; enterprise analysis concentrates almost exclusively on the manufacturing sector rather than the services, retail and wholesale trades. One of the most important features of the present feminist school is the emphasis placed on the role of women's reproduction at the household level. As Beneria (1982) points out, this has led to an extension of analysis into the household and the domestic economy providing a more complete picture of the full extent of enterprise and diversification (also see Mies 1982).

In these circumstances it may be more useful to construct a means of living matrix which will be capable of identifying the individual livelihood strategies of households based upon levels of income, patterns of consumption, financial security and human capacity, taking into account various cost of living profiles tailored to different groups. Grown and Sebstad have also referred to the appropriateness of a livelihoods system approach in examining the issue of women's poverty. They argue that this would represent a more comprehensive means of incorporating the numerous dimensions that reveal the dynamics of women's poverty. The fundamental innovation in this approach would be the linking up of the conventional components of employment, income and enterprise with an understanding of the underlying relationships within and between households (Grown and Sebstad 1989: 941). They go on to demonstrate that this approach would focus on the livelihood strategies of individuals and households examining the way resources, including human and physical assets, and opportunities, in the form of institutional mechanisms and informal networks, are mobilised for survival, security and growth depending on the level of vulnerability of the individual or household. For Grown and Sebstad, examination of the mix of livelihood strategies would include analysis of labour market involvement, savings, accumulation, investment, borrowing, use of technology, consumption patterns, social and networking etc.

From this it should be possible to rank households on a means of living index focusing on the flow of wealth arising out of a particular livelihood mix as a first order effect rather than the stock of wealth. This will involve a calculation based on total net income from labour, the income value of all assets and the value of goods and services in kind (ie those provided by the government). These measures and proxy measures will subsume human capacity factors governing access to employment, bureaucratic intervention, political mediation and group/faction membership but may have to be supplemented by certain consumption costs relating to particular taxes, rates and charges.

Given the complexity of these interlocking factors it is by no means easy to separate out common interests. Levels of income are likely to cut across many of the categories so that it is not easy for households to identify with each other in ways other than along traditional demarcations. Furthermore, politicians often reinforce this pattern of loyalty by bestowing benefits and rewards on the basis of primordial ties. A clear example of this is the institutionalisation of caste in India through a policy of positive discrimination in favour of scheduled caste and tribe reservation and representation. This is currently a highly contentious topic in India with the Government wishing to implement the recommendations of the Mandal Commission report which proposes to extend reservation to other backward caste groups. The current recommendations are for a 27 percent quota for backward caste groups on all vacancies in central government in addition to the existing 22.5 percent quota for scheduled castes and tribes and further quotas in all universities, colleges and private sector undertakings with financial assistance from the government. Manor (1984) has identified the contradictions of caste or subcaste loyalty in the political environment of Karnataka where stratification within the *vokkaliga* and *lingayat* subcaste groups as the main beneficiaries of political patronage has led to the unequal distribution of benefits and rewards. Despite these difficulties it is nevertheless possible to identify the means of living criteria which will subsume most of the factors relating to broad production and consumption patterns which will tend to coalesce at different places on the income spectrum. In this way it may be possible to conceptualise households in a manner that allows for a more comprehensive and, consequently satisfactory, categorisation that will in turn enhance the current understanding of rural transition.

This approach emerges from a similar perspective as that adopted by Long and Roberts (1984) in their study of miners, peasants and entrepreneurs in Peru. It represents a shift away from the notion of structural determination and a move towards a model emphasising actor orientation and specific linkages. For Long and Roberts, the mining enclave of the Peruvian highlands is not seen as simply determined by some monolithic form of State capitalism, extracting surplus as a part of the wider system of urban bias, which may result either in the growth of agrarian differentiation or the formal subsumption of the peasantry. Instead they search for a different mechanism that will result in a different response at the local level. For them it is a better understanding of the 'regionalised production system' that may provide some of the necessary answers. This involves analysing the changing interrelations between sectors of production and the elucidation of the complex linkages between the production centre and its economic hinterland. The implication is that these links are not part of some predetermined system but are themselves dynamic.

These linkages may be remoulded by struggles between individuals and with outside forces but at the same time they produce a certain regional and local individuality and independence. Particular life styles and cultural patterns which influence individual and household expectations consequently influence the overall linkage pattern. The interaction of local patterns of politics, power and patronage may not conform to any predetermined national capitalist system. The result of increasing diversification, brought about through the complex structure of networks and linkages within the locality and between the locality and the regional centre, is a tremendously varied set of household strategies at the local level. This is seen by Long and Roberts as an opportunity that gives families space to pursue their own path while simultaneously creating a dynamic element in local society.

This theoretical and methodological stance which has sprung out of the debate on the nature of agrarian transition and which has been inspired by the provision of unsatisfactory answers to recent empirical material (see Kahn 1980, Long and Roberts 1984) has been adopted in this study as a means of approaching and understanding the problems of transition in contemporary rural Asia. It is becoming more widely recognised that 'what emerges from an examination of the recent debates is the real paucity of theoretically informed but empirically grounded studies which focus on the relevant issues, thereby helping us to understand better the complex relations between capitalism and other forms of production' (Glavanis 1984: 34–35). An attempt to address this inadequacy has been made in the following chapters drawing on case studies from Japan and India in chapter three and detailed empirical analysis at village level based on work undertaken in Sri Lanka in 1984 in chapters four and five.

3 From farm to firm in monsoon Asia: case studies from Japan and India

The previous chapter has discussed how wet rice production, upon which much of the agricultural economy of Asia is based, entails a high level of labour and skill intensity which has generated an increase in the output per unit of land and an increase in the capability of land to support an ever rising population. As land scarcity becomes an increasing problem so the pressures to diversify will be considerable. Although this problem is typical of contemporary Asia it is by no means confined to this region. In Africa, for example, 45 percent of the land base is classified as either desert, arid or semi–arid with a further 22 percent having shallow depth and excess water and 18 percent with low fertility. The combination of rapid population growth and sub–optimal agro–ecological conditions found in many parts of Africa can only increase the pressure on families to seek alternative nonfarm employment.

The off–farm sector is beginning to attract the attention of policy makers and researchers eager to explore new ways of generating employment and income for the rural population. Chapter two has already examined the theoretical implications of rural diversification, where the nature and extent of off–farm activity is seen as beginning to determine the overall place of a household in the contemporary local or regional economy. It has also been pointed out that many households are beginning to combine farm and off–farm activity as part of a single household enterprise strategy which continues to display the characteristics of small scale operation such as restricted investment and family based labour with a fairly high degree of risk compensated for, to some extent, by flexible consumption and flexible work patterns. A further group of households have diversified into regular employment. In some countries, such as in Japan or Taiwan, this group may be involved in a modern (rural) manufacturing sector, in other countries, such as in India or Sri Lanka, they are largely engaged in the tertiary sector with a growing proportion in government service. Many of these households retain a continuing interest in smallholder farming and in the less developed economies almost all of them operate within a market dominated by local political forces and degrees of instability that have a particular impact on those aspiring to improve their socio-economic position.

This chapter will begin by examining off-farm diversification in a comparative context and will then move on to a more detailed investigation of the development of the rural off-farm sector in the form of two quite distinct case studies drawn from Asia. The first case study is based upon an examination of the changing nature of the rural economy in Japan, where consistent investment in the agricultural and industrial sectors has produced a particular form of rural family enterprise linked to a dynamic regional and national economy. The second case study is based on the State of Kerala in Southwest India, where severe pressure on land has forced many households to diversify into a less developed and more precarious off-farm economy. This case illustrates a number of features associated with economies at the lower end of the income spectrum. Many of these features will be addressed in more detail at the micro level in chapter five on off-farm diversification in village Sri Lanka.

Off-farm diversification in a comparative context

Off-farm employment tends to serve a variety of needs in the rural sector. It not only provides an important source of income for many landless households but increasingly it is becoming a main source of activity for numerous smallholders throughout Asia and parts of Africa. This is especially the case where agricultural holdings are declining in size but where families are reluctant to sell productive plots which can be worked primarily with family labour and often without undue interruption to the off-farm schedule. In this situation production and consumption linkages between farm and off-farm activity are crucial (see Haggblade, Hazell and Brown 1989). The growing demand in agriculture for goods and services designed to increase output and productivity has provided the off-farm sector with a growing input market. Increased production has also led to an increase in agricultural processing and distribution activities. Rising family earnings resulting from increased output will, in turn, increase the demand for a wide variety of consumer goods and services. Factor market linkages are also important. Agricultural surpluses are commonly transferred out of agriculture through a plethora of fiscal mechanisms. In the African setting this capital often flows into urban areas but it can also provide between 15 to 40 percent of typical nonfarm investment requirements (Haggblade et al 1989). At the same time, off-farm earnings are a useful source of cash and investment for the farm while off-farm employment can indirectly improve access to farm credit and inputs as a result of greater contact with external suppliers and agents. This latter point is highlighted in some detail in the following chapters on rural diversification at village level in Sri Lanka. There is in fact considerable evidence from East Africa of reverse flows of capital from off-farm to farm (see Kitching 1977, Collier and Lal 1986).

Where agricultural output is in decline such as in the drought prone Sahel and parts of Sub Saharan Africa, off-farm activity becomes a critical survival measure offering cyclical and seasonal employment to supplement meagre farm incomes. It is for this reason that the off-farm sector in most parts of Africa is not as developed as in Asia where production and consumption linkages form part of a dynamic rather than a disabled relationship. This is borne out by the observation that for any given level of agricultural income the off-farm multiplier effects are higher in Asia than in Africa (Haggblade et al 1989).

In spite of these differences, Chuta and Leidhlom (1979) have noted that there is a good deal of empirical evidence demonstrating that off-farm employment and income is increasing in absolute terms throughout the developing world. Furthermore, the rural labour force appears to be growing at a faster rate than the agricultural labour force. The actual percentage increase varies from 0.2 percent in East Africa to 0.8 percent in Southeast Asia (Anderson and Leiserson 1980). Corner (1986) argues that this structural transformation has been overshadowed by the fact that off-farm employment has not ben able to expand sufficiently to absorb the growing number of new entrants to the rural labour force.

The percentage of the rural workforce with primary employment in the off-farm sector for selected countries in Africa and Asia is shown in table 3.1 below. The definition of nonfarm activity that has been adopted by Haggblade et al (1989) appears to include both livestock and forestry. This will have the effect of pushing up the nonfarm percentage figures for all countries particularly those where pastoralism and smallholder livestock production play a more important role in relative terms in the total rural economy. India has a large livestock population based primarily on stall fed milch cows but the percentage of main workers employed in livestock and forestry is only 2.4 percent (1981 census).

Other definitional ambiguities are likely to have had the opposite effect of underestimating the true extent of off-farm activity since the macro data rarely accounts in an adequate manner for the extensive secondary employment in the off-farm sector. Nor does it always include larger rural towns which act as a catalyst for off-farm growth.

Table 3.1   Percentage distribution of primary employment in the rural nonfarm sector in selected African and Asian countries

Country	%
Africa	
Benin (1961)	41
Ghana (1960)	27
Mauritania (1977)	21
Senegal (1970–71)	18
Togo (1970)	16
Sierra Leone (1974)	14
Ivory Coast, Bouake Region (1963)	10
Malawi (1977)	9
Mozambique (1963)	9
Cameroon (1976)	8
Mali (1976)	6
Rwanda (1978)	5
Chad (1964)	3
Asia	
Taiwan (1980)	67
Thailand (1985)	31
South Korea (1980)	19
India (1980)	19

Source from Haggblade, Hazell and Brown (1989: 1176)

Many studies of off–farm activity have noted an inverse relationship between farm size and off–farm income (see Anderson and Leiserson 1980 on Pakistan, Thailand and S.Korea; Shand and Chew 1986 on Malaysia; Ho 1986 on Taiwan). Ho (1986) demonstrates that in rural Taiwan, although off–farm activity has increased for all farm size groups, the share of off–farm employment is considerably higher for smallholdings of less than 0.5 ha than for farms of over 2.0 ha. The percentage share for the two size categories in 1975 stood at 63 percent and 32 percent respectively. A similar study in Malaysia has shown that the off–farm share of total income stood at 70 percent for smallholdings of less than 0.5 acres but was only 21 percent for farms of over 5 acres (Shand and Chew 1986). Data from South Asia (India, Pakistan, Bangladesh and Sri Lanka) on the percentage contribution of off–farm employment for different size categories of holding clearly illustrate this inverse relationship. The percentage share of off–farm employment for landless categories varies from around 95 percent in Pakistan to around 52 percent in India. This share declines with an increase in landholding status so that for smallholdings of up to one acre (excluding Pakistan) the percentage share varies from around 72 percent in Bangladesh to 48 percent in India and declines again for farms of over five acres varying from around 45 percent in Bangladesh to 28 percent in India (Islam 1986).

It should be noted that the data is not strictly comparable since the holding size categories do not entirely correspond. The Sri Lanka figures do not include a pure landless category and terminate at the top end with a holding size category of 4.3 acres and above, while the largest holding size category for Pakistan rises to 25 acres and above. The vast majority of off–farm activity recorded in the survey appears to be wage employment. The highest rates of self employment are recorded for the landless and marginal household categories in India with 26 and 37 percent respectively and the lowest rates in Sri Lanka at 6 and 8 percent respectively. Although the Indian average for self employment is only just ahead of Bangladesh and Pakistan it is certainly higher for the landless and marginal groups. This may reflect the initial impact (up to 1982) of the Indian Integrated Rural Development Programme which was targeted at these categories and specifically designed to generate self–employment. This issue is discussed in more detail in the Indian case study below.

The equity effect of off–farm income in levelling disparities between families of different landholding status has been widely explored in the literature. The growing contribution of off–farm income, particularly for the smallest land holding groups, has been seen in the case of both Japan and Taiwan to have improved the overall distribution of rural family incomes (see Ho 1979 and Chinn 1979). Micro level evidence from Sri Lanka presented in the following chapters substantiates this notion of the equity effect of off–farm income. Detailed analysis of households at village level shows that in some cases tenant farmers had been successful in securing higher family earnings than owner operators through the more effective exploitation of off–farm opportunities. Shand (1986) accepts that off–farm earnings have generally led to a substantial reduction in rural inequality, a fact which may help to explain the surprising lack of social protest in the countryside, but qualifies the over generalisation of this phenomenon by pointing to survey evidence from Thailand reporting that off–farm income has improved the distribution of income in only two of four provincial samples. His own study in Kemubu in Malaysia also showed little improvement in the distribution of income (Shand and Chew 1986).

Recent off–farm experience in Southeast Asia

Off–farm diversification is most advanced in East and Southeast Asia. Japan presents a particularly interesting case of off–farm development and will therefore be examined in more detail in the following section. The present discussion, however, will be confined to a more general comparative analysis of one or two countries which have reached different points in the development of a diversified rural economy within the Southeast Asian region.

Taiwan has probably experienced the most development in this regard, and indeed the speed of rural transition has in many respects been as impressive as in Japan. The share of the labour force in agriculture, for example, has declined dramatically during the last 3 decades. By the beginning of the 1950s around 67 percent of the labour force was in agriculture. This had declined to 56 percent by 1960 and thereafter declined rapidly to 37 percent by 1970 and 20 percent by 1980 (Oshima 1986b). Agriculture's share of GDP has also declined sharply from 35 percent in 1952 to 26 percent in 1965 and 6 percent by 1984 (Williams 1988). Off-farm income meanwhile has risen from being roughly half of on-farm income in the mid 1960s to double the farm income by 1980 (Oshima 1986b).

The pattern of rural development in Taiwan has been similar to that of Japan. Oshima argues that the intensification of agriculture through the introduction of new crop varieties, inputs and the expansion of irrigation and rural infrastructure contributed to the initial rise in farm family incomes. Multiple cropping reached a ratio of 1.9 by the mid 1960s (Oshima 1986b). Once agricultural growth began to decline, full employment was maintained by the diversification of labour into off-farm activity. Chinn (1979) argues that between 1960-62 and 1970-72 off-farm income was largely responsible for rising real income in Taiwan. The combination of industrial export growth, rising domestic demand for non-farm products and the strategic introduction of monsoon type (small scale) mechanisation releasing labour from full-time farming, all served to bring about the current pattern of decentralised development.

Williams states that 'travelling through the lush green countryside of Taiwan, one is impressed by the extraordinary degree of human occupancy. The entire area from the seashore to the lower slopes of the mountains in the centre of the island is minutely parcelled out in tiny fields and irrigation ponds, punctuated by innumerable rural villages and larger cities and towns' (1988: 27). Williams goes on to note the small size of agricultural holdings, with 43 percent of farm households in 1980 of less than 0.5 ha and 73 percent of less than 1 ha, which has led to a substantial rise in the phenomenon of part time farming. Ho (1986) has examined the extent of part time farming in the rural economy, the incidence of which is summarised in table 3.2 below.

The table shows the decline in full time farming since 1960 from just over 47 percent to around 10 percent by 1980. It also illustrates that, of an astonishing 90 percent of part time farming households, a large majority regard off-farm activity as their main occupation. Ho (1986) contends that a substantial share of the demand for off-farm labour has come from modern enterprises that require a near full-time commitment. Initially, this demand was met by female participation in fast growing labour intensive industries such as textiles, apparel and electronics. As off-farm employment opportunities have expanded farming is increasingly being undertaken by the older and less educated members of the household.

Table 3.2   Incidence of part time farming in Taiwan

Year	Full-time	Part-time	
		Farming as main occ	Sideline as main occ
1960	47.6	29.9	22.4
1965	31.9	40.9	27.1
1970	30.4	40.6	29.2
1975	17.7	47.6	34.6
1980	10.2	34.4	55.4

Source   from Ho (1986)

The growth in part time farming and off-farm opportunities has been greatly facilitated by Taiwan's decentralised industrial structure. In an earlier review of industrial dispersal in Taiwan, Ho (1979) demonstrates that between 1956 and 1966 rural manufacturing industry grew at around 7.2 percent per annum outstripping the rate of growth in the urban sector. The 1971 industrial census showed that 50 percent of all manufacturing employment was located outside the main urban centres accounting for 48 percent of manufacturing value added (Ho 1979). Ho has characterised rural industry as generally small scale, employing less than 20 workers (in 1971 the average size was c 15) with a low capital-labour ratio. Although this has had the effect of reducing labour productivity relative to urban units, rural industry appears to enjoy a higher ratio of net value added to the book value of fixed assets implying a more efficient use of capital than its urban counterpart (1979: 88).

The Taiwan experience of rapid rural diversification has hinged upon the development of a highly productive smallholder agricultural system, consolidated by the 1949–53 land reforms and based around investment in appropriate inputs and infrastructure and diversification into commercial crops. Ho (1979) concludes that this created a vigorous market for non food products facilitating the growth of domestic manufacturing and services. In any rural setting, rising demand is likely to lead to a growth in services which tend to be location specific, and the production of certain goods with high income elasticity, such as furniture, furnishing, clothing etc. However, in Taiwan widespread industrial dispersal has been possible on account of the high level of development of rural infrastructure (electrification had reached

70 percent of farm households by 1960) with a well developed rural transport system. As industry has oriented production to the growing domestic and export markets, the demand for low cost labour has led to an expansion in rural employment in small and medium units. This has meant that households have not had to break family farm ties while simultaneously engaging in a local micro capitalist economy.

Elsewhere in Southeast Asia, few countries with the exception of Japan, have experienced the same level of off–farm diversification as in Taiwan. The majority of monsoon economies remain at an earlier stage of rural transition and may well only manage to develop a less dynamic variant of rural micro capitalism based on a less stable form of family enterprise employment. The key determining features of this transition are the level of development of the agricultural economy and the degree of unemployment and underemployment in the rural sector generally.

In the Philippines, as in many rice producing economies in Asia, agriculture has greatly benefited from the development of irrigation and new high yielding varieties of seed and associated inputs. As rice cultivation has become more intensive with the introduction of divisible technology, so the labour absorbtion rate in agriculture has increased, reflecting higher inputs of labour per hectare as land productivity has steadily risen. Kikuchi (1986) estimates that this trend continued from the introduction of improved irrigation in the late 1950s up until the mid 1970s. Fabella (1986) indicates that around this time, off–farm employment varied between 24–25 percent depending on the period of the agricultural cycle against a general backdrop of expanding agricultural employment while employment in this sector grew by 22 percent between 1967–74 (Fabella 1986). He goes on to examine the nature and composition of off–farm activity at a macro level demonstrating that a good deal of this activity complements rather than competes with agriculture. It is interesting to note in this context that the major off–farm growth area was seen to be in wages and salaries rather than in self–employment. The largest single source of off–farm employment was in manufacturing which had a 7.4 percent share of total employment, closely followed by commerce at 6.1 percent and government service and transport at 3.6 percent and 2.4 percent respectively (Fabella 1986). Overall, service based activity was more than double that of manufacturing.

Since the mid 1970s, although the labour force in agriculture as a main occupation has been increasing, there has been a reduction in the number of workdays per working member and a shift towards part time farming. This is well illustrated by Kikuchi (1986) in a study of a Philippine rice village. Here, the bulk of off–farm opportunities have been in hired employment outside the village and by 1980–81 this form of employment accounted for 28 percent of total employment. This structural shift was accompanied by rises in real wages and growing wage differentials between farm and off–farm employment attracting more labour into off–farm work. Kikuchi observed that as real family incomes rose new off-farm enterprises began to spring up in the village itself. Such activities included bicycle operations, store keeping, small trading and even a mobile soft drinks and snack business run by landless labourers.

Empirical evidence from other Southeast Asian countries shows that off-farm employment and income is rapidly growing in importance. In Thailand, for example, the annual compound real growth rate of regional GDP from 1971–72 to 1978–79 was 7.8 percent, just ahead of agriculture at 7.2 percent, while the growth rate of off-farm income was an impressive 12.3 percent. Furthermore the growth rates of off-farm income for all regions exceeded 10 percent, well ahead of agriculture (Onchang and Chalamwong 1986).

For many countries, however, the push factor still dominates this process of transition as farm sizes decrease and productive smallholder employment is converted into unproductive labour. Off-farm activity may expand in response to this process but without complementary pull factors as experienced in the case of Japan and Taiwan, the off-farm sector is unlikely to become substantially more dynamic.

The evolution of rural diversification in Japan

Japan provides one of the best documented cases of the evolution of farm and off-farm employment in a rapidly changing agricultural and industrial economy. Indeed, the early experience of Japan is highly relevant to many contemporary developing countries which are moving into a phase of rising agricultural productivity coupled to a growth in domestic demand for manufactured goods and services and steady opportunities for manufactured exports. The importance of off-farm employment in Japan is all the more relevant when one considers the rate of increase in the rural population of most developing countries and the persistence of widespread under employment and unemployment resulting in continuing deprivation and poverty for a large proportion of the rural population. Some of the more significant changes in Japanese agriculture date back to the post restoration Meji period after 1868. This period is taken to represent the beginning of modern Japan. In order to examine the growth of off-farm employment it will be useful to consider the place of agriculture and non agriculture in the earlier Tokugawa period where the preconditions for accelerated growth became firmly established.

By-employment in the Tokugawa period

In Tokugawa Japan (1600–1868) land ownership was nominally vested in a feudal overlord who had the right to levy taxes on the peasantry often amounting to around 40 percent of agricultural product in kind and services.

The village headman was responsible for the prompt payment of taxes which were paid on the basis of family groups as tax units (Hirschmeier 1964). As with all feudal societies there were strong patron–client ties which encouraged the poor to provide labour for the rich in return for access to marginal plots for cultivation. In Tokugawa Japan the emphasis was on social and economic stability, cohesion and control. Despite this preference for continuity, Hirschmeier argues that from the second half of the eighteenth century onwards many changes took place in the rural economy leading to a substantial rise in production as a result of an increase in the cultivated area and the introduction of new techniques. Far from being a sector that was reproducing itself at a little above subsistence level by the end of the Tokugawa period, output had in fact doubled since the beginning of the period and although this was not a spectacular increase given the time span involved, agriculture was well above the subsistence level (1964: 73–74).

One of the major factors that contributed to the rise in output in agriculture, and which would continue to lead to higher yields per hectare and increasing intensity of labour per unit of land in the Meji period, was the well developed irrigation infrastructure. Booth (1989) emphasises that these irrigation systems not only absorbed a great deal of labour in their construction, maintenance and management but also enabled a more intensive system of cultivation to be introduced which had the effect of placing a technical limit on the operated holding size of any one household. The average holding size was already under one hectare in many parts of the country by the late Tokugawa era (Booth 1989).

With the increasing commoditisation of agriculture came a rise in the demand for consumption goods and services. In response to this demand many rural entrepreneurs began to invest in off–farm enterprises providing a ready alternative to the restrictive practices of the traditional urban based guilds. Hirschmeier shows that off–farm opportunities were wide and varied depending on local conditions and the availability of capital. Larger entrepreneurs with landed or trading interests were able to invest in activities such as sake brewing often combined with miso and soy sauce making while those with less capital might engage in cotton and silk spinning on a putting out basis. Smith (1969) has undertaken a detailed study of off–farm or by–employment using primary survey data from the 1843 Kaminoseki survey in southwestern Japan. Although 82 percent of all families were classified as farmers, 55 percent of the income of all households was generated from non agricultural sources. This figure was seen to rise to as much as 70 percent in some districts despite the fact that the occupational returns implied an overwhelming dominance of agriculture. This discrepancy has been noted in chapter one as a serious problem in the measurement of off–farm employment.

Smith estimates that off–farm income was between 2 to 7 times larger than one would have expected from the proportion of nonfarm families in the population and he goes on to consider a number of possible explanations. Firstly, he examines the possibility that farm income might have been grossly under estimated but admits that there is no evidence to support such an inference, arguing that if anything returns were more complete for farm earnings than for off–farm income. Next, he considers that the higher level of productivity of off–farm work might explain the difference but feels that the discrepancy is too large to be accounted for by differential rates of productivity. Finally, he concludes that it is the widespread incidence of by–employment which explains the surprisingly high level of off–farm earnings. The proportion of total income of farm families generated from by–employment ranged between 15 to 30 percent in the most heavily agricultural districts to over 50 percent in other districts. Furthermore, in almost all districts the majority of off–farm income was generated by farm households and in 5 of the districts they accounted for as much as 70 percent of all non agricultural income (Smith 1969: 696–697).

By–employment was obviously an important feature of Japanese rural life in the late Tokugawa period and the particular characteristics of Asian wet rice cultivation, which supported a growing population in agriculture based on the survival of the small family farm, provided an appropriate environment for increased levels of rural diversification. Family members would spend all their available time engaged in by–employment when they were not actually farming and Smith estimates that on average could expect to earn as much in a day off–farm as they would working on the farm. A good deal of by–employment was carried out at home but work was also undertaken away from the farm on salt fields, for example, often on a group basis. Smith identifies a number of features associated with by–employment apart from its linkages to the family farm such as its dependence on the rapid expansion of trade mediated through market towns which provided villages with a constant flow of goods and services and an outlet for domestically manufactured products. There was also a marked division of labour among different districts with some generating the bulk of off–farm earnings from industry while others relied on trade, transport or remittances.

By–employment provided one of the most effective ways of increasing household income for farm families in Japan in the pre industrial period. At the same time agricultural output continued to rise and would show a marked increase in the post Meji period. Although the pressure on land brought about by population growth resulted in a surplus of agricultural labour, Smith shows that the number of working days available to the farm population doubled as did the total output from this population as a direct result of the growth in off–farm activity.

It was during the Meji period after 1868 that Japan experienced a substantial rise in agricultural growth expressed in terms of rising output per capita and output per worker against a background of land scarcity and a relatively constant agricultural labour force. As already mentioned in chapter one, Francks (1984) has shown how the introduction of land–saving technology in the form of new higher yieldin/fast maturing seeds and greater applications of fertiliser combined with techniques such as deep ploughing and double cropping to result in increased output and higher productivity. Francks emphasises that the particular nature of land saving technology encouraged increased inputs of labour whilst not preventing households from engaging in off–farm employment. Analysis of the long term trends in the rural sector during this period reveals that from 1880 to 1935 there was slow but steady growth in agricultural output at an annual average compound rate of 1.6 percent while total productivity increased at around 1.2 percent (Hayami and Kikuchi 1985). What is also clear is that there was no massive increase in the capital–output ratio during this period. In fact there was a slight decline up to 1919 and it then remained fairly steady through to 1938 when it ended at the 1919 level. Ohkawa (1969) concludes that this demonstrates the 'capital–saving' nature of agricultural development during this period. Francks (1984) has stressed the high divisibility of agricultural innovation which reinforced the consolidation of landholding in the small to medium sized category as larger owners released land they could no longer afford to cultivate. Francks argues, however, that the new agricultural technology and off–farm opportunities were incompatible. From 1900 to 1917 industry grew at an impressive 6 percent per annum while the population growth rate rose from around 1 percent in the 1880s to 1.5 percent by the late 1930s. The increasing off–farm employment opportunities open to the farm population did begin to place some strain on the 'capital–saving' technology mix that had been introduced into agriculture.

Francks examines the effects of this strain on farmers in the Saga plain in southwestern Japan, demonstrating that after 1920 the problems arising from the outflow of labour, which were compounded by a fall in rice prices, were rectified by further technical changes which reduced the labour requirement at certain critical points and over certain critical processes. The two main developments in this direction related to improvements in the irrigation infrastructure and crop rotation. One of the main labour bottlenecks had revolved around the provision of water for irrigation by means of the traditional foot operated water wheel which was a basic mechanical task absorbing a great deal of labour and remained a common feature in Japanese rice farming until after the second world war when rural electrification became more widespread. In the Saga plain area this problem was overcome by the

64

implementation of small scale static electric pumps which offered the cheapest means of providing the necessary horse power. The final product was a 2 hp electric motor attached to a centrifugal pump by a belt. The pump was static but the motor was portable. These pumps were capable of serving units of 10 to 15 hectares (Francks 1984: 224–225). The mechanisation of irrigation was also important in another sense in that it facilitated a shift to the new cultivation practice of unified late planting. The main advantage of this was to help eliminate the destructive rice borer pest which thrived under the traditional phased rotation system of cultivation moving from one plot to the next. Farmers were at first resistant to change since the phased rotation system allowed for exchanges of labour during transplanting between different families. Francks points out that eventually these developments led to new labour peaks during transplanting and harvesting where hired labour became more common but at the same time family members were now able to engage more easily in off–farm work free of the former demands associated with irrigation which had been a constant burden throughout much of the year (1984: 232–245).

Improved agricultural techniques and general commercial expansion thus enhanced the opportunities facing the rural population but did not result in any substantial increase in the unit price of labour on account of the continued growth in the labour supply. Tussing (1969) argues that increased agricultural output had the effect of stabilising food prices and land rents in the context of low rural wage rates. Despite this, however, total household earnings increased dramatically due to the rise in off–farm employment, both in aggregate and per worker terms. We have already seen that by the beginning of this period a large number of households were registered as cultivators although in many cases they were already earning the majority of their total income from by–employment. This trend continued as opportunities in the rural industrial sector continued to expand particularly in areas such as metal working, silk reeling and weaving, ceramics and building materials. The growth in the export market for raw silk necessitated the mechanisation of hand reeling which had been widely practised under the former putting out system. Mechanisation relied on imported machinery but did not alter the size or location of the operation which continued to be small scale and rural. 'The silk–export boom brought prosperity to the villagers, and rich farmers, merchants, and other moneyed men took up silk reeling on a putting–out basis or in small factory–like establishments' (Hirschmeier 1964: 94). Hirschmeier has examined biographical sketches of a large number of those involved in the silk industry in Gumma. He specifically draws attention to the fact that the vast majority did not consider moving to the city and that the new village enterprise was a direct and simple continuation of what they had done in the past with the addition of modern machinery. He goes on to emphasise that in spite of inefficiencies, assured profits meant that raw silk production continued as a village industry.

Farm households and small rural workshops continued as the main source of rural manufacturing. Table 3.3 reflects data drawn from 43 prefectures in 1884 on the location of manufacturing units in selected product areas. The

Table 3.3   Distribution of manufacturing establishments by location (1884)

	metal working	ceramics building materials	spinning weaving	all
number	159	238	1206	1981
% rural	81.8	76.5	71.4	62.4
% urban	10.1	8.8	19.1	19.2

Source   Francks (1984: 53) from Yamaguchi 1963.

table clearly illustrates the importance of rural industry in a number of key product areas. In other areas such as chemicals, machinery and foods the percentage of manufacturing establishments in the rural sector was significantly less at 26.4, 15.8 and 10.3 respectively. The vast majority of these establishments had less than 20 employees. At first, industry was closely related to agriculture and agricultural labour demand governed much of the process. This situation gradually changed as heavy industry began to locatein urban areas with access to surplus labour. Yet, off–farm activity continued to be an important source of income and employment to farm households, a trend that has continued up to the present day.

One of the more detailed accounts of the size and extent of off–farm employment during this period is provided by Tussing (1969) who has undertaken a quantitative analysis of the labour of the labour force of Meji Japan based on data drawn from Yamanashi Prefecture. As we have seen, a number of non agricultural activities had already become well established throughout the country by this time. These included activities that had to be conducted at the point of consumption such as retail and construction, and those based on easily obtainable raw materials and widespread demand, such as sake brewing and home–based miso making. Elsewhere there was a degree of specialisation with particular activities concentrated in particular areas. Yamanashi Prefecture was noted for sericulture, paper and crystalware. Tussing contends that the period saw a significant rise in the demand for locally manufactured items with agricultural labour being deployed during the slack season for the manufacture of indigenous products. What is interesting about the Yamanashi data is that it reveals that there was a significant transition in the composition of the rural labour force from the beginning of the period, when off–farm work was an important source of secondary

66

employment, to the Taisho era (1912–26) when off–farm work was largely undertaken on a primary basis while agriculture had become a major source of secondary employment. This is reflected in table 3.4 below. The heading

Table 3.4 Sectoral distribution of labour force by primary P and secondary S occupation and S as % of total (Yamanashi Prefecture 1879 and 1920).

	1879			1920		
	P	S	%	P	S	%
agriculture	194,164	29,238	13.1	196,259	127,511	39.4
industry	26,418	21,375	44.7	64,059	14,245	18.2
services	14,498	15,035	50.9	46,991	11,786	20.1

Source   Tussing (1969: 207).

agriculture in table 3.4 includes forestry and fishery while industry is taken to include mining. The number given under 'secondary occupation' in each sector includes persons whose primary occupation is also in that sector, thus the sectoral totals in the table are greater than the actual number engaged in each sector.   Although the labour input in the non agricultural area increased in both relative and absolute terms, the proportional change in the different sectors was fairly mild. The number of people engaged in agriculture remained steady steady throughout the period with the census returns showing 193,872 in 1879 whereas by 1920 this figure had hardly changed at 193,714 (Tussing 1969). A breakdown of the changes in the sectoral distribution of the labour force in Yamanashi, as a percentage of the full time equivalent labour input, is provided by Tussing in table 3.5 below.

Table 3.5   Distribution of labour force as a percentage of total labour input

Years	Agriculture	Industry	Services
1879–82	78.6	13.5	7.9
1883–87	78.7	12.9	8.4
1888–92	75.5	14.8	9.7
1893–97	74.1	15.4	10.5
1898–02	73.5	15.6	10.8
1903–07	74.7	14.5	10.8
1908–11	71.8	16.5	11.7

Source Tussing (1964: 204)

Tussing has divided opportunities in the off-farm sector in the prefecture along conventional dualist lines to emphasise the different growth characteristics of the modern and traditional activities. He claims that over a period of 41 years, between 1879 and 1920, the modern sector grew in terms of persons employed by around 21 times from 445 to 9,260. This excludes the case of silk reeling which, as discussed above, remained a mixed activity combining modern machinery run on traditional small scale lines. The modern sector largely comprised commerce, transport and finance with manufacturing employing around 3,068 persons. The traditional sector, meanwhile, continued to prosper and those engaged in it increased from just over 22,000 to 65,000 over the same period, which was 7 times the size of the modern sector. 'To the extent that this pattern was that of all Japan, it testifies to the enormous vitality of the indigenous sector of the Japanese economy, particularly to the remarkable elasticity of both supply and demand with respect to income of the traditional Japanese manufactures and of traditional productive organisation' (Tussing 1969: 208).

As off-farm opportunities increased in both sectors, especially in the area of traditional or semi-traditional activity, total household earnings rose considerably. Tussing shows that in silk reeling, for example, the average number of days worked per year doubled between 1883–1911 with a concomitant rise in the annual earnings per worker despite the low overall wage rates. The significance of these findings lies in the impact of low wage rates on total household earnings. The debate on the ethics of employment in rural manufacturing enterprise has long seen the driving down of wages in the face of excess labour supply as an inevitable feature of extortion and exploitation in the countryside, with the implication appearing to be that this sort of activity should be discouraged at all cost. The important point in this regard, as illustrated by the case of off-farm activity in Yamanashi, is that for many earners the opportunity costs of nonfarm work were low and for some, as Tussing again argues, productivity around the home was close to zero. Furthermore, these earnings represented a regular and substantial income that did not disrupt the family's pattern of work or other traditional forms of livelihood.

Part-time farming and the off-farm sector in the contemporary period

The particular pattern of Japanese agricultural development has in many ways been well suited to local conditions. Rises in output have largely been obtained through increases in the productivity of land as the scarce resource via the more intensive use of labour resulting from the introduction of new divisible technologies and intricate cultivation practices. In this way monsoon paddy agriculture, which was characterised by high levels of labour intensity and marked seasonality, was able to sustain a dense farm population within the context of the gradual diminution of holding size. As average yields

68

increased and double cropping became more widespread, farm incomes began to rise, helping to stimulate growth in the non agricultural sector which had long provided additional employment and income during the slack season. Oshima (1986 a & b) has emphasised the importance of achieving year round full employment where the annual real return per farm family is growing faster than the growth in the total labour supply, as a necessary pre-condition of development. The experience of Japanese development in the prewar period shows that the growth in rural technology and infrastructure provided the basic foundation for the subsequent transition to a modern East Asian economy. Improved irrigation, rural electrification and communications all served to promote a pattern of rural development which depended on rising farm output and income producing a steady growth in off-farm opportunities which, in turn, boosted total household income. This pattern of diversification was facilitated by the introduction of simple labour saving rather than labour replacing technologies such as the mechanisation of irrigation, which then released labour for further off-farm activity without creating widespread unemployment.

This pattern of development accelerated in the postwar period once the initial impact of postwar devastation began to subside and allied policy changed in response to the outbreak of war in Korea and the perceived threat of communism in China. The rapid growth in industrial exports during this period provided increased opportunities in the non agricultural sector leading to a decline in the agricultural labour force and a rise in the marginal productivity of labour and agricultural wages. Two points are significant here in relation to the changing composition of the labour force. Firstly, this shift was accompanied by institutional change in the countryside brought about through land reforms which were introduced between 1945-50 and resulted in the transfer of ownership of roughly one third of all farm land with a decline in tenancy from 45 percent to about 10 percent. This resulted in a drastic reduction of rents in the countryside and the creation of a larger number of small independent operators who were less tied to traditional village activity. Secondly, an increase in the availability of appropriate labour substituting technology in the form of two wheel mechanical tillers, rotary seeders, weeders and mechanical threshers, encouraged widespread diversification.

Structural changes in the labour force brought about first by a war economy and later by postwar export led growth, saw the decline in agriculture as a primary source of employment and income for the majority of workers. Although agriculture provided the main source of labour for industry, it acted less as a pool of disguised unemployment which could be returned to during periods of economic downturn and rather more as a source of part time employment for an increasing number of rural commuters and off-farm workers. Inheritance laws had traditionally encouraged all but the eldest son to secure employment outside agriculture while those engaged in agriculture also sought to supplement farm incomes in non agricultural activity. These laws were subsequently revised and the practice in recent years has been to divide property on an equal basis thus increasing the pressure on land. The tendency for agriculture to evolve into a side occupation is not a recent phenomenon as demonstrated by Tussing with reference to the Yamanashi data outlined above.

Interestingly, the main source of surplus labour absorbtion during periods of economic downturn has been the tertiary sector with its lower entry barriers and high labour turnover. Shinohara (1970) has shown that 84 percent of the total increase in the labour force during the long depression of 1920-30 was in the service sector. The rate of increase in the male employed labour force during 1920-1930 among a variety of service activities ranged from: over 200 percent in bakery and confectionary; between 80-90 percent in meat dealing and leather production; between 40-70 percent in fish selling, green grocery, tea dealing and china and glass selling. The rate of increase in agriculture over the same period, meanwhile, was only 0.1 percent (Shinohara 1970). After the depression and during the build up to the war, manufacturing industry once again absorbed the vast majority of the increase in the labour force and this trend has continued, with the occasional interruption, to the present day. The rapid growth in manufacturing industry and related off-farm activity in the postwar period can be linked to the extraordinarily high personal savings ratio in Japan at around the 16-17 percent level. This compares to a typical savings ratio over the same period in the USA of around 8-11 percent and in the UK of 1 percent (Shinohara 1970).

Shinohara confirms that between 1952-61 agricultural income increased very little while off-farm income began to increase rapidly. He examines the percentage of off-farm income to farm income in 1961 across five classes of agricultural holding to demonstrate that off-farm earnings were becoming particularly significant for the smaller farm households. This is shown in the table below.

Table 3.6 Proportion of off-farm income to farm income by farm size (1961)

Size (acres)	%
< 1.2	79.6
1.2 - 2.4	46.9
2.4 - 3.6	17.4
3.6 - 4.9	12.4
> 5	9.0

Source Shinohara (1970)

He argues that once the proportion of off-farm to farm income developed a steadily rising trend it began to have a marked impact on the savings ratio, despite fluctuations in agricultural income. Between 1960-67, the savings ratio of farm households kept increasing while the rate of increase in farm income changed very little . He concludes that it was the rising share of off-farm income to total household income that contributed to this high marginal propensity to save displayed by rural households but recognises that off-farm income was nevertheless still complementary to agricultural income and thus likely to have a higher marginal propensity to save attached to it.

As the Japanese economy began to grow at unprecedented levels in the late 1950s and 1960s there were important knock on effects for rural households. The increase in employment opportunities as a result of industrial expansion fuelled an enormous migration of workers from country to town. This eased the pressure on land and allowed rural households to remain in a position of full employment, especially since this was accompanied by a marked rise in off-farm income and an absolute decline in the agricultural labour force leading to an increase in rural productivity. As the economy moved from being in labour surplus to labour shortage small and medium industries proliferated in rural areas to overcome labour supply constraints. These structural changes were facilitated by the high level of development of rural infrastructure particularly in the field of electrification and transportation. The extent and efficiency of the railway network not only enabled factories to obtain raw materials and distribute finished or semi-finished goods but also enabled the rural workforce to secure easy access to off-farm employment. The steadily rising output from the car manufacturing industry was almost exclusively destined for the domestic market resulting in a sharp rise in private car ownership and the increasing use of private vehicles in rural areas.

These changes are reflected in the growing incidence of part time farming since the early 1950s. As already noted the Japanese definition of part time farming is extremely inclusive and, when coupled to the quite impressive historical levels of agricultural growth and rural diversification, the percentage of part time farming households to total farm households was already high by the end of the prewar period in 1938 at around 55 percent. By 1965 Misawa (1970) shows that the percentage of part time farming had risen to 78.5 percent. Up to this point, however, off-farm income although important, especially at the bottom end of the farm size spectrum, did not exceed total farm income despite the fact that per capita earnings were often considerably higher for off-farm earners. The percentage of part time farm households with a larger off-farm income remained fairly constant between 1938 and 1950 but rose steadily thereafter as shown in table 3.7 below.

Table 3.7 shows that the vast majority of farm households are now engaged in some form of off-farm work and the percentage of those with off-farm incomes that exceed farm income has risen steeply from 21.6 percent in 1950 to just over 65 percent by 1980. According to the various Farm Household

Surveys of the Ministry of Agriculture, the percentage of off–own–farm income for all farm households rose from 12.2 percent to 19.6 percent between 1921 and 1941. By 1950 this had risen to just over 27 percent but it was from 1955 onwards that the rise in off–own–farm income really began to accelerate reaching 45 percent by 1960, 63.5 percent by 1970 and just

Table 3.7   Incidence of part–time farming

Year	Total	Type 1	Type 2
1950	50.0	28.4	21.6
1960	65.7	33.6	32.1
1970	84.4	33.7	50.7
1980	86.6	21.5	65.1

Source   Ministry of Agriculture, Census of agriculture in Kada (1986)
Note   For Type 1 households net farm income exceeds off–farm earnings and for Type 2 households total off–farm earnings exceed net farm income.

under 80 percent by 1980 (see Oshima 1986b and Kada 1986). The wages and salaries component represented by far and away the largest portion of off–own–farm income and this share increased at an annual average rate of 4.6 percent (Oshima 1986b). It is important to note that some agricultural labour is included in the wages and salaries component when undertaken off an individual's own farm in a physical sense.

Table 3.8   Percentage of off–farm income per farm household

Year	Share of off–farm income %
1950	27.0
1955	28.6
1960	45.0
1965	52.0
1970	63.5
1975	66.4
1980	78.9

Source   Farm Household Economic Survey

Once again, table 3.8 demonstrates the rapid rise in off-farm earnings since 1955 although these figures also include off-own-farm agricultural work. The increasing importance of part time farming and related non agricultural incomes has had the effect of equalising overall income distribution between rural semi-farm and urban nonfarm households. At the same time, off-farm income has provided smaller farms with an opportunity to equalise income with larger units of 1.5 hectares and above. The equalising effect will obviously depend on the number of family members engaged in off-farm activity. All this has meant that the per capita consumption expenditure of rural households has risen significantly, closing the prewar expenditure gap between the farm and nonfarm sectors.

During this period, a number of important changes took place in the agricultural sector. Between 1950-1975 the agricultural population halved from around 16 million to 8 million and changed its composition so that it became dominated by a female and elderly workforce (Kada 1986). Labour bottlenecks were overcome by the introduction of small scale mechanisation in the form of the two wheel tractor, the modern equivalent of which is represented by the ubiquitous Kubota. This eased the pressure on tilling, and with certain adaptation, on harvesting especially for winnowing operations. The number of farms remained stable, according to Kada, since non agricultural workers did not have to leave the rural environment in search of work. The effect on agriculture was that rice remained the most popular crop with an accompanying decline in paddy land planted to winter crops from 34 percent in 1960 to just under 9 percent by 1975 (Kada 1986). Kada goes on to show that those part time farm households which were more reliant on off-farm income were generally half the size of other part time households with a lower labour intensity as expressed by the multiple cropping index. These farms relied on labour inputs from family and friends, often at weekends, after work and during the holidays. Indeed many employers continue to operate a degree of flexibility with work schedules to allow critical farm operations to be undertaken at certain periods of the year.

Misawa (1970) sees one of the main factors contributing to the growth of part time farming as the increasing consumption pattern of rural households based on the growth of real family incomes leading to increased demand for goods and services. This, in turn, is related to the growth of off-farm employment opportunities which further stimulates consumption and the accessibility of off-farm employment arising from a decentralised industrial structure seeking to overcome labour shortages.

The divisibility of industry and off-farm employment

A glance at the evolution of the industrial structure in Japan provides a clue to the growth of opportunities in the rural nonfarm sector. We have already refered to the development of rural industries in the prewar period. Merchants and wholesale traders were instrumental in the putting out system distributing materials and inputs and marketing products often on a national basis. This system grew alongside the factory sector and at the same time modernised and diversified into new product areas. Many of these small enterprises supplied the growing factory sector but as prices were squeezed quality deteriorated it became necessary for larger industries to attempt to rationalise the subcontracting web. Watanabe (1978) has examined how this took place in the form of vertical grouping whereby the most efficient petty producers were integrated into the factory structure by being given regular work orders and technical assistance and equipment to encourage greater specialisation.

Subcontracting became one of the defining features of the Japanese industrial structure in the postwar period. With the inherent advantage of utilising cheap labour and reducing fixed capital requirements, subcontracting offered a crucial means of lowering production costs and passing on price advantages which became essential to the process of industrial expansion. As larger firms concentrated their efforts on production processes requiring high levels of capital and technology, basic parts and component production was taken up by subcontractors. As production became more sophisticated vertical ties deepened with parent companies providing more support to accommodate greater demands. A useful review of the growth of subcontracting is contained in Annavjhula (1989) who shows that parent companies began to provide subcontractors with financial management systems, improved quality control and enhanced engineering techniques to reduce costs and increase product standardisation. In many cases this meant changing machine configurations from the batch process to a flow system. Annavjhula goes on to provide quantitative evidence of the importance of the subcontracting chain, demonstrating that by the mid 1960s, 54 percent of all manufacturers were subcontractors and by the late sixties the share of subcontractors in some product areas was as high as 79 percent. Areas of particular growth included precision machinery, transport and electrical machinery and for some of the larger companies in these areas, subcontracted labour accounted for more than 50 percent of total labour input (Annavjhula 1989).

This type of industrial structure has led to a wide dispersal of industrial units throughout the country. In many cases rural workers commute to off-farm employment in nearby towns and cities. Vertical integration has meant that employees in all sizes of enterprise are linked into a manufacturing chain which enjoys a certain amount of security through its ability to access both domestic and export markets at the industrial apex. At the same time intense horizontal competition at home coupled to pressures in the international market have generated an innovative momentum which ensures that enterprises at all levels in the chain are associated with various degrees of technological progress. Community based industries also form an important element of the off-farm sector and the rural industrial structure in almost every prefecture. Many of these industries employ less than 20 people and are to be found in high concentrations of specialised production. Annavjhula (1989) claims that there are about 350 clusters or production regions in Japan manufacturing a range of consumer, capital and craft goods largely for the domestic market. Some of these industries operate an integrated factory system of production selling under the brand names of wholesalers and retailers which can greatly facilitate the marketing process. Others operate through a complex subcontracting and re-subcontracting chain with a wholesaler and/or producer as the mother unit determining the design and production schedules of subcontractors who, in turn, may draw on homeworkers on a piecework basis (Annavjhula 1989).

Community industries tend to be prevalent in product areas dominated by traditional labour intensive processes and those which rely heavily on manual skills. Yet, as Weiss (1986) has demonstrated in the case of small enterprise districts in Italy, there are many market niches which require flexible production processes capable of specialising in the adaptation or modification of products at different stages of the production chain. Just as in the case of agricultural development in Japan, where the divisibility of technology enhanced agricultural productivity and labour intensity, industrial development has also been characterised by a high level of divisibility with low entry barriers and reduced capital requirements which have increased labour intensity and maintained high levels of productivity. Consequently, the small farm economy has a parallel small firm structure which has increased the number of off-farm opportunities open to rural households and facilitated the growth of the part time farm phenomenon.

The case of Japan has demonstrated an almost natural progression from family farm to rural firm in a monsoon economy. The enormous emphasis in the early years of the modern period on agricultural intensification was consistent with prevailing conditions of land scarcity and labour abundance. Increased output arising from greater labour inputs helped maintain reasonably high levels of employment which could be supplemented by the steady growth of off-farm activity. With greater access to diverse sources of employment, many of which are integrated into the national economy but maintain a measure of local independence, the rural population has been able to achieve near full employment leading to the growth of rural family incomes and the further stimulation of the rural economy. At the same time the farm lobby accuses the government of fixing rice prices at an unrealistic level via the Committee of Rice Price Consultation which is made up of a mix of consumer interests, farmer interests and experts. Others argue that this simply reflects decreasing costs against a strong Yen.

The Japanese case, while offering an illuminating model of a highly developed rural enterprise economy consisting of farm and off-farm and in many cases non rural activity, is by no means typical of contemporary monsoon Asia. A number of distinguishing features about the Japanese setting include: the early rise of an imperial tradition leading to the planned

75

development of an impressive industrial arsenal; an inheritance system which eased the pressure on land and provided core industries with a permanent workforce; major postwar support in the reconstruction phase after the outbreak of war in Korea; and perhaps most significantly, Japanese culture itself. A final point worth mentioning is that while agriculture has become less attractive to rural households, high land prices and the desire to retain land as future security have resulted in the maintenance of a smallholder system operated by residual labour, often at less than optimal levels of productivity and relying heavily on farm subsidies. This problem will have to be addressed in future years and could lead to a policy of land consolidation which might have the effect of reversing the trend towards rural off-farm activity.

Induced diversification in Southwest India

One or two countries, or regions within countries, now appear to display a number of the characteristics associated with rural Japan, while a host more only display a few of the characteristics, such as the growth of part time farming, but without the advantage of a solid nonfarm productive base. As one moves from East Asia to Southeast and South Asia the latter conditions appear to prevail. The State of Kerala in Southwest India provides one such example of rural diversification within the context of a contemporary wet rice economy at the lower end of the income spectrum. The stark reality of this setting in somewhat tempered by the fact that the State has a well educated labour force which has traditionally enjoyed an impressive welfare system and one of the highest physical quality (PQLI) indexes in the country.

The population of the State was 25.5 million (1981 census) with an increase of 19 percent during 1971–81, down from 26 percent during the period 1961–71. The per capita income at 1986–87 prices is estimated at Rs 2,371 (c.Rs 34 to £1) slightly lower than the all India average of Rs 2,559 and below that of Tamil Nadu at Rs 2,732 and West Bengal at Rs 2,988 (both major rice growing States). Despite the low levels of income, the literacy rate in the rural areas in 1981 was 74 percent for males and 64 percent for females. Infant mortality rates were low at less than 39 per thousand with a birth rate well below the national average at 24 per thousand. Out of the major States in the country, excluding Himachal Pradesh and Jammu and Kashmir, Kerala ranks second in terms of per capita expenditure on education at Rs 189 behind Punjab at Rs 194 and third on health at Rs 80 behind Punjab at Rs 95 and Rajasthan at Rs 87.

Kerala, like many wet rice environments, has an extraordinarily high population density at 655 persons per sq km (1981 census) which is over three times the national average at 216 persons per sq km. Much of the State, especially the coastal region, is characterised by a continuous settlement

76

pattern forming a rural–urban continuum dotted with paddy fields interspersed with plantation crops. This has resulted in a high proportion of the population at around 80 percent being classified as rural.

Traditional society was heavily stratified along caste lines and included the widespread practice of agrestic slavery. Although the State has one of the oldest Christian communities in the country in the form of the Syrian Church, the mushrooming of Latin Catholicism after 1504 was largely the result of the widespread conversion of low caste groups such as the Mukkavans from among the fishing community. It is not surprising, given this traditional social structure, to find that political loyalties are still largely expressed in caste and communal terms despite the long history of democratic Marxism which saw the first communist government between 1957–59. Various Marxist led regimes have left their mark on the State but policy has often been the outcome of considerable compromise between partners within a left alliance. Nossiter (1988) points out that the CPI(M)'s share of the vote over a 20 year period from 1967–87 changed very little from 24 percent to 22 percent while the Left Democratic Front's share of the vote in 1987 was 45 percent. It is also interesting to note that the nature of the alliances changed over time. In the 1980 Assembly elections the CPI(M) led a Left Democratic Front comprising 'two components of the planters' party, Kerala Congress, and one of the Muslim league, as well as a chastened CPI and a progressive wing of Congress' (Nossiter 1988: 179) while in the 1987 elections they avoided the communal parties of the Kerala Congress and the Muslim league and won office from the United Democratic Front.

The agricultural economy and smallholder production

This political structure has had an important impact on the character of the rural economy. Kerala pioneered the introduction of land reforms in 1957 and followed this up with a series of agrarian relations and land reform acts in 1961, 1964 and 1969. Although these reforms had the intention of granting full ownership rights to all operators and establishing a land ceiling of 15 acres, loopholes and slow implementation meant that many landed interests were able to make 'alternative' arrangements. Basic needs programmes in the form of education, health and welfare have met with more success and have helped create an educated workforce with an incentive to diversify, although high levels of political consciousness have led to rather turbulent employee relations and have been a disincentive to private industrial investment.

One of the distinguishing features of a rural monsoon economy, as noted above, is the marked tendency towards the scarcity of land and abundance of labour. Kerala is no exception in this case and the high growth of population in the early post independence period and the limited area of land suitable for cultivation has led to a land–man ratio of 0.14 ha per capita. The land concentration ratio is extremely high despite land reform legislation. George

(1986) argues that the concentration ratio has increased since the mid seventies since the gradual increase in the number of agricultural holdings has ceased to be off-set by an increase in the area operated by smallholders on account of a decline in the number of holdings in the larger size category. This has led to the increased fragmentation and diminution of agricultural holdings. Table 3.9 below illustrates that the average size of holdings under each category is extremely low. Of a total of 4,1772 farms falling in the categories below, over 37,000 are in the marginal category with an average operational holding size of 0.2 ha. This category accounts for 89 percent of all operated holdings. The average size of all holdings declined from 0.5 ha in 1970–71 to 0.4 by 1980–81 and is much lower than the all-India average of 1.8 ha. The percentage of holdings under 0.5 ha increased from 72 percent in 1970–71 to 79 percent by 1980–81.

Table 3.9 Average size of operational holdings by major size classes, marginal to medium (1981)

Class and Size (ha)	Kerala	All-India
marginal (<1)	0.20	0.39
small (1–2)	1.37	1.42
semi-medium (2–4)	2.68	2.76
medium (4–10)	5.45	5.98

Source Farm Guide, Govt of Kerala (1987)

In spite of the mounting pressure on land, Kerala has not experienced the same level of agricultural intensification as seen in the case of Japan. The average yield for rice increased from around 1,164 kg/ha in 1955–56 to 1,720 kg/ha by 1984–85. At the same time growth in productivity through different periods has been rather variable. Pillai (1982) argues that the highest annual compound rate of growth for food crops was in the period 1952–53 to 1960–61 (2.8 percent) before the introduction of recent green revolution technology. Productivity continued to rise in the sixties but the growth rate in productivity has declined in the post 1975 period (Pillai 1982). Despite a marginal increase in productivity in 1985–86, total production in this period fell by 6.6 percent. Being a largely rainfed based economy with two annual monsoons and an average rainfall of over 3,000 mm per annum, irrigation has been less well developed than in high productivity areas. The percentage of irrigated area under crop to net area sown is about 12 percent compared to 28 percent for India as a whole (Farm Guide 1987). The percentage of irrigated area under paddy stands at around 39 percent. Investment in major and medium irrigation is nearly six times higher than for minor irrigation. Consequently, paddy farming is less intensive than in other wet rice environments and many farmers continue to cultivate traditional rather than high yielding varieties. Although farms are small and family operated, agricultural wages have forced up cultivation costs during the critical labour bottlenecks of planting and harvesting. At the same time rice prices have been kept in check by inflows of rice from high producing areas in other States. Kerala currently buys nearly half the rice that it consumes. All this has led to paddy cultivation becoming less popular and, in many cases, being relegated to a secondary activity although this situation is likely to have improved with good monsoons in the three consecutive years up to and including 1990. In fact the 1990 kharif season saw rice production in the country as a whole rise to a record 68 million tonnes.

One of the most significant factors in the agricultural sector relates to the nature of the cropping pattern. There has been a marked decline in the share of land under food grains in general and paddy in particular and a rise in land under cash crops. The area under food crops as a percentage of the total cropped area was 40 percent in 1983-84 as compared to 78 percent for all-India. The area under rice declined by over 52,000 ha in 1985-86 while arecanut decreased by 2,311 ha, tapioca by 1,776 ha and groundnut by 1,723 ha. In the same year, the area under rubber increased by nearly 10,000 ha. Alongside the steady structural shift from food grains into cash crops there has also been a general decrease in the area under crops and an increase in land being used for non-agricultural purposes. This has been particularly marked in areas which have seen large-scale migration to the Gulf where the heavy demand for land for the construction of new houses has led to land being taken out of agriculture.

Much of the land taken out of rice production has been converted into coconut groves. Coconut production is the second most important agricultural activity in the State. It accounts for around one third of the State's agricultural income and occupies a large area under cultivation on a smallholder basis with 75 percent of total production on plots of less than 2 ha. Since much of the expansion of coconut cultivation has been on to unfavourable land without adequate drainage or the implementation of proper spacing and cultivation techniques, output has not been expanding as might be expected. This change in cropping pattern is problematic as far as the smallholder is concerned. Throughout the world coconut production tends to suffer from low yields, fluctuating prices and competition from other oil palms. Smallholders often rely on over-aged palms and minimum soil and water management systems. Research has shown that more intensive use can be made of coconut land by careful attention to inter-cropping with a complementary crop such as cocoa and annual crops beneath.

Smallholder farming in Kerala has developed a semi-intense rather than intense form of production. Pressure on land leading to the fragmentation and reduction in size of operated holdings has forced family members to seek off-farm opportunities as a means of avoiding severe underemployment. The shift in the cropping pattern from food grains to cash crops has also reduced the labour input in agriculture and encouraged off-farm diversification.

Changes in the composition of the labour force

The off-farm economy has become an important source of employment and income for a large number of marginal farmers and landless labourers in the rural sector. This situation has been facilitated by a well developed physical and social infrastructure. The State enjoys a good transportation system based upon a network of roads, waterways and railways. Health care has been extended to all areas and the State has one of the best population to bed ratios in the country. Rural literacy levels are impressive and the educational infrastructure is above average. There are, for example, over 187 arts and science colleges in the State. The State also operates a widespread food distribution system with over 11,000 fair price shops selling basic commodities such as rice, kerosene, vegetable oil and sugar at subsidised prices. These developments have served to meet basic minimum needs and increase access to the wider economy.

Under these conditions it may not be surprising to find that there has been a significant structural shift in the composition of the labour force. A clue to this situation can be seen in the declining share of agriculture as a percentage of State domestic product from just over 55 percent in 1961 to 49 percent by 1971 and down to 39 percent by 1981. Kerala has one of the lowest proportions of population in agriculture in India and the figure still appears to be falling.

The breakdown of the distribution of main workers by primary occupation based on census data for 1981 is listed in table 3.10 overleaf. The table demonstrates the significance of off-farm employment both in the State as a whole and for the rural population where just over 52 percent of all main workers are engaged in work other than agriculture. Non-agricultural work in this context includes other primary sector activities such as animal husbandry, forestry and fishery. A surprisingly high 54 percent of male workers are involved in non-agricultural work with almost all of these outside household industry. The highest participation in household industry is from among rural female workers at just over 8 percent of all rural workers and exceeds the participation rate in household industry among female urban workers which stands at 5 percent of all urban workers.

The census breakdown of the percentage distribution of total workers by occupational group is given in table 3.11 and provides a more detailed picture with some minor differences in the data when compared to table 3.10. Table 3.11 shows that secondary and tertiary sector activities provide the main source of employment for just under 48 percent of the workforce. It is

80

Table 3.10 Percentage distribution of main workers by broad category, Kerala (1981)

Occupation	Total			Rural		
	Persons	Male	Female	Persons	Male	Female
cultivators	13.06	15.66	4.95	15.31	18.62	5.53
agricultural labourers	28.24	23.32	43.55	32.46	27.08	48.38
household industry	3.69	2.42	7.65	3.86	2.45	8.02
others workers	55.01	58.60	43.85	48.37	51.85	38.07

Table 3.11 Percentage distribution of total workers by occupational category, Kerala (1981)

Occupation	Persons	Male	Female
cultivators	13.83	16.04	8.02
agricultural labourers	29.35	24.34	42.47
livestock, forestry fishery etc	8.98	10.31	5.49
mining & quarrying	0.74	0.93	0.25
manufacturing, processing servicing & repairs			
a) household	4.05	2.41	8.34
b) other	12.79	12.00	14.87
construction	2.93	3.79	0.69
trade & commerce	10.34	13.16	2.96
transport	4.75	5.99	1.49
other services	12.24	11.03	15.42

Source Statistics for planning, Dept of Economics and Planning, Trivandrum

obvious from the table that tertiary sector activities account for the single largest group of workers after the primary sector with 27 percent of workers employed in trade, transport and other services excluding servicing and repairs. This figure rises to 30 percent for the male workforce. Between 1971 and 1981 the primary sector declined from 55 percent of male main workers to 50 percent while the secondary sector grew from 16 percent to 18 percent and the tertiary sector from just under 29 percent to 31 percent. Department of employment statistics for the period 1975 to 1984 show that while the percentage of those employed in agriculture has declined so has the percentage of those employed in some services balanced against increases in transport and commercial services. One of the major problems with much of the data is that it does not disaggregate the rural population nor does it account for the growth in part-time farming where agricultural work has nevertheless been identified as the main source of income.

Reflections on the all-India setting

It may be useful at this stage to reflect on the data in relation to the country as a whole as a means of providing some form of broader comparison. Certain parts of India, such as the Punjab, display many of the characteristics associated with rapid agricultural growth based on an impressive expansion of the irrigated area and increased agricultural intensity. Chadha (1986) has examined the Punjab case showing that increased agricultural employment has led to a rise in real family income which has had the effect of stimulating demand in the off-farm sector and creating new opportunities for the diversification of employment. These opportunities are often seasonal and located in nearby semi-urban areas. Although the Punjab only covers 1.7 percent of the total area of the country and by 1981 only accounted for around 2.4 percent of the population, it could boast 11.6 percent of the total irrigated crop area and consumed 40 percent of total fertilisers and 20 percent of total electricity (Chadha 1986). This has led to a massive rise in rice and wheat output and the complementary growth of off-farm activity. Chadha estimates that off-farm income contributes from 18 to 29 percent of total household income and rises to 60 or 70 percent for marginal households. However, it should be noted that these figures are particularly high since dairying has been included in the off-farm category.

At the all-India level the extent of employment and income in the off-farm sector is less marked although the macro data mainly focuses on primary activities. The number of main workers in India in 1981 was estimated at 222 million with an additional 22 million marginal workers constituting around 36 percent of the total population. The growth rate of the workforce between 1961 and 1981 was 1.3 percent compared to the growth rate of the population of 2.1 percent. Roughly 78 million workers were engaged in the non-farm sector accounting for nearly 32 percent of the total workforce. This category absorbed around 37 percent of the additions to the workforce between 1961–81. Taking the rural workforce alone, the position of the off-farm element is significantly reduced. Table 3.12 below shows that just under 17 percent of the rural workforce in India were engaged in off-farm work in the secondary and tertiary sectors. The table also shows that this figure almost doubles when considering the total rural and urban workforce and rises again to over 34 percent for the total male workforce. The increase in secondary and tertiary activities for the rural workforce as a whole has been rather slow and has not kept pace with the overall rise in the rural workforce.

Table 3.12 Percentage distribution of main workers by occupational category (all-India 1981)

Occupation	Total	Male	Female	Rural
cultivators	41.6	43.7	33.2	51.1
agricultural labourers	24.9	19.6	46.2	29.9
livestock, forestry	2.2	2.3	1.8	2.4
mining & quarrying	0.6	0.6	0.4	0.4
household industry	3.5	3.2	4.6	3.1
other industry	7.8	8.9	3.6	3.4
construction	1.6	1.8	0.8	1.0
trade & commerce	6.3	7.3	2.0	2.8
transport	2.7	3.3	0.4	1.1
other services	8.8	9.2	7.0	4.8

Source 1981 Census

A significant point which often escapes attention is the fact that about 40 percent of the rural population are engaged in non-farm employment as a secondary source of income (Sudhakar Rao 1985).

One factor that has had an important impact on the incidence of rural off-farm employment is the stagnation of household and village industry in spite of the emphasis given to this sector in the various plans and policy statements of the government. Industrial policy has long been associated with the protection of small and village industries through capacity ceilings, reservation of product items and preferential purchase schemes. The initial emphasis in the early plan periods on pilot programmes for village industries gave way to various industrial dispersal measures in the 1960s and 1970s tending towards small-scale industry in the urban and semi-urban areas. The emphasis changed once again in the Draft 6th Five Year Plan (1978–83) under the Janata Government of 1977–80. In an effort to revive the intent to promote village and small industries as expressed in previous policy declarations, the number of items reserved for small-scale and village industries increased from 180 to over 500 and District Industry Centres were established to act as a single window agency for the promotion of such industries.

Subsequent policy statements in 1980 and 1990 reiterate support for this sector with the latest statement announcing a rise in the ceiling limit on investment, liberalising import assistance for technology upgradation and streamlining credit procedures. These initiatives, alongside existing support through a village industries commission with a network of boards in each State, have not been sufficient to reorientate the basic industrial structure of the country in spite of public support through the procurement and distribution of raw materials, marketing of finished goods, provision of grants and subsidies etc. The quantum of investment in the total and village and small industry sector fluctuated from Rs 1,870 million in the Second Plan period (1956–61) to Rs 5,930 million in the Fifth Plan (1974–79) and then rose to Rs 19,450 million in the Sixth Plan (1980–85) and to Rs 27,530 million in the Seventh Plan (1985–86 estimates). This has to be compared to investment in the large industry sector over the same period of Rs 9,380 million (Second Plan) to Rs 89,890 million (Fifth Plan) and Rs 150,020 million (Sixth Plan) and Rs 197,080 million (Seventh Plan 1985–86) (Sandesera 1988).

Specific programmes embracing the khadi and handloom sector, for example, have included the establishment of workers cooperatives, provision of subsidy for workshed construction (Rs 1,500 subsidy and Rs 6,000 loan), supply of yarn at reasonable rates, modernisation of looms, common quality and testing facilities and a rebate on sales of khadi and handloom varying from 10 to 35 percent. In the handicraft sector raw materials are supplied at subsidised rates of 20 to 25 percent below market rates and support is extended through training and production centres and buyback arrangements with State handicraft board (Vijaykumar 1990).

The net result of intervention in the khadi and village industries sector appears to be an increase in the number of units established and aggregate output but due to low labour productivity at the unit level the sector does not possess a strong internal dynamic. The highest growth rates in output, value added and employment, have been recorded by the cottage match industry, lime manufacturing, carpentry and blacksmithy and non–edible oil and soap, although much of the increase in output and value added is likely to be the effect of inflationary pressure and not real growth (Sudhakar Rao 1985). Rural industries have been largely characterised by low performance resulting from the low level of technology development and dissemination coupled to an investment bias towards the less the less productive khadi sector as opposed to other village industries. The Khadi and Village Industries Commission (KVIC) has tended to under capitalise most activity while simultaneously failing to invest in ways of increasing productivity, product diversification and product quality. The technology problem in relation to this sector has been examined in detail by Leurs (1988).

While the village industry sector has been unable to make much of a contribution towards the expansion of off–farm employment, the centrally sponsored poverty alleviation programmes are likely to have had a more significant effect, although this will not yet be apparent from the macro data. The Sixth Plan adopted a strong anti–poverty focus embodied within a cluster of major programmes which were implemented on a national scale. The Integrated Rural Development Programme (IRDP) has probably had the greatest impact on off–farm activity. The programme was launched in 1978–79 and extended to cover all areas in 1980–81. The programme is designed to provide subsidised credit to families below the poverty line (currently Rs 6,400 but with a programme cut–off of Rs 4,800) for the procurement of productive assets for self–employment. The pattern of subsidy varies from 25 percent to small farmers to 50 percent for tribal groups. The programme is implemented through District Rural Development Agencies and Block offices. Around 16.5 million families received support during the Sixth Plan with a total investment (grant and loan) equal to $ 3,374 million. During the first four years of the Seventh Plan 13.4 million families received assistance under the programme. An important aspect, here, is that many families have received a top–up or "second dose" of assistance and thus the actual number of separate families assisted is somewhat lower. Kurian estimates that by March 1988 around 23 million distinct families had been assisted or around half of the 44 million rural families below the poverty line (Kurian 1989). The performance of the programme has by no means been uniform but concurrent evaluations show that performance has improved. In about 70 percent of cases the assets remained intact with 51 percent of beneficiaries generating incremental income over Rs 1,000 and a further 17 percent generating incremental income over Rs 500. In the Sixth Plan the largest share of assistance flowed towards animal husbandry activities, particularly the promotion of stall–fed milch cattle. However, this trend has been reversed in the majority of cases with central recommendations that at least 60 percent of assistance should be for the promotion of self–employment industry, services and business, with the latter two categories much the most popular on account of lower entry barriers.

The other programmes which will have had some impact on off–farm diversification are the two former wage employment programmes – the National Rural Employment Programme (NREP) and the Rural Landless Employment Guarantee Programme (RLEGP) now merged into one. These programmes were designed to provide employment for the creation of durable productive assets of a community nature. By 1988 the employment programmes had succeeded in creating around 700 million persondays of employment per annum. Although this is an impressive figure in absolute terms, if one assumes that the objective should be to provide at least one member of every family beneath the poverty line with 100 days of employment per annum, 700 million persondays only represents around 16 percent of the total requirement (Kurian 1989).

Off-farm opportunities and the growth of the tertiary sector in Kerala

The poverty alleviation programmes will undoubtedly have had an important impact on the employment strategy of many rural households at the lower end of the income scale. Although neither IRDP nor the employment programmes have been particularly successful at raising families permanently above the poverty line, which is notoriously slippery, the programmes have increased the employment options open to poorer households and in the last few years IRDP has been increasingly oriented towards the tertiary sector.   As already pointed out, the composition of the labour force in Kerala is quite distinct from other States in India. The sizeable proportion of the rural population outside agriculture demonstrates that off-farm activities have been a crucial part of the livelihood strategies of rural households for some time. However, the particular pattern of development in Kerala has meant that rural diversification has not been associated with the growth of a dynamic industrial sector capable of sustaining long term growth and development outside agriculture. The industrial sector does, however, employ a larger proportion of the total workforce than the all-India average. A number of factors, including large-scale migration to the Gulf, have resulted in a rise in consumption but this has largely not been complemented by vigorous growth in domestic production although there has been a rise in local service provision.

Analysis of the industrial sector highlights the backward character of most industry. The State is generally regarded as one of the most industrially backward, with few large and medium-scale industries and 30,000 small-scale industries, only ahead of Orissa, Jammu and Kashmir and Himachal Pradesh from among the larger States. Capital investment per worker in the industrial sector in 1975 was only Rs 3,737 compared to the all-India average of Rs 5,830. Industries such as cashew production, coir, textiles and brick and tile manufacture have traditionally accounted for around three fifths of factory employment. The highest investment levels of productive capital in 1983 were found to be in fertiliser production, cotton textiles, chemicals and tyres and rubber (Dept of Economics and Statistics 1986). Indices of industrial production for different product areas from 1970 to 1983–84 indicate that the largest rises have been in the manufacture of metal products (excluding machinery) especially since 1978–79, followed by chemicals, electricity, non-metallic minerals and rubber and plastics. The poorest performance has been in areas such as machinery and machine tools, electrical machinery and appliances and a range of miscellaneous industries (Dept of Economics and Statistics 1986).

Kerala has what many regard as a lopsided industrial pattern without sufficient industrial diversification. One of the major obstacles in the path of increased industrialisation has been the lack of willingness on the part of the central government and private capital to invest due to high "psychic costs" based on region specific factors relating to restrictive labour practices, strong unionisation etc (see Subrahmanian and Pillai 1986). There are over 10,000 registered unions in Kerala which act as important vote banks for political parties. Their existence and demands have severely dampened potential enthusiasm for industrial investment. For example, of the 65 units approved by the Cochin Export Processing Zone in 1983, 13 had been established by March 1990 of which only 3 were exporting. Large segments of the cashew, coir and beedi (local cigarettes) industries have moved to neighbouring Tamil Nadu where wages are lower and workers more docile. Central investment has also been low in recent years. In 1970 Central investment for industry in Kerala was about Rs 1.16 billion not far below Maharashtra at Rs 1.2 billion. By 1988 this had changed dramatically with Central investment in Kerala amounting to Rs 13 billion while investment in Maharashtra had grown to Rs 139 billion (India Today 1990).

In response to this deteriorating situation the State Government is now anxious to attract inward invest in much the same way as the CPI(M) Government in West Bengal. In order to achieve this objective, the Government has announced a number of incentives which include: a capital subsidy of 5 percent subject to a ceiling of Rs 300,000 in certain target areas such as electronics, light engineering etc; sales tax exemption for large and medium units set up after April 1989; exemption from power cuts for all new industrial units; investment subsidy of 5 percent; exemption of purchase tax on rubber bought within the State. Since the present Government assumed office in 1987 it has helped to set up over 23,000 industrial units and has recently established an industrial promotion and coordination bureau to assist entrepreneurs in business start–up. The Kerala State Industrial Development Corporation is currently in the process of implementing 46 projects compared to a total of 146 implemented over the previous 29 years. The Nayanar Government has also rehabilitated over 1,220 small–scale units in the three years it has been in office (India Today 1990). In order to capitalise on its highly educated labour force, the Government is in the process of expanding the electronics sector through the establishment of three technology parks in Trivandrum, Cochin and Calicut, the first of which involves an investment of Rs 60 million and is due to be operational in the near future.

While these initiatives are highly commendable they are, at the same time, long overdue. The consequence of slow growth in the smallholder agricultural sector coupled to long term industrial retardation has been an economy characterised by high levels of off–farm employment but without sufficient productive capacity capable of matching demand and sustaining a growth momentum. This has been partly obscured in the recent past by the inflow of sizeable remittances from migrant labour in the Gulf. Kerala has traditionally accounted for over 50 percent of total Indian migration to the Middle-East. Nair (1986) estimated that were around 800,000 Keralites working in the Gulf, mainly in the UAE, Saudi Arabia and Kuwait. An indication of the volume of this activity, up until recently, can be seen from the fact that in March 1988 Air India increased the number of direct flights from Trivandrum to the Gulf from 11 to 15 per week on a route which the airline termed its "golden run". The largest group of migrants have been involved in construction activity but Kerala has also supplied a sizeable number of doctors and nurses. The majority of migrants, however, are typically below 35 years of age, from rural backgrounds, having passed matriculation and employed in a variety of low skilled and semi-skilled occupations (Nair 1986).

Analysis of the utilisation pattern of Gulf remittances shows that the bulk of expenditure has been in the area of construction which has manifested itself in the mercurial rise of the "Gulf house". Nearly 30 percent of total remittance income between 1982-86 was used to finance the construction of domestic houses, shops hotels etc. The second largest investment has been on the acquisition of land for construction. A good deal of remittance income has simply been deposited in rural banks while a similar amount has been spent on the purchase of gold ornaments. The major impact on families in terms of percentage change in the value of assets has been most marked for certain consumer durables such as washing machines, TVs, radio cassettes etc as well as vehicles (see Slater, Watson Tripathy 1989).

Although Gulf remittances have contributed to a rise in State domestic product and foreign earnings accompanied by a reduction in regional disparity on account of the fact that districts with a lower per capita SDP (eg Trichur) have benefitted disproportionately, they have not succeeded in bringing about a structural change in the rural economy. There has been a certain amount of investment in service activities, especially those related to construction and transport but little growth of employment other productive activities. In fact returning migrants are now calling on the State to provide rehabilitation assistance to help their re-entry into the job market.

A case study of off-farm employment in Trivandrum district

The following case study is based upon a rapid village survey undertaken by the author in Trivandrum district in March-April 1988 and follows on from a field research project in Trichur district in 1987 (see Slater, Watson and Tripathy eds 1989). The objective of this investigation was to identify a rough pattern of rural diversification at the micro level within the context of a densely populated district with reasonable access to different forms of employment. The survey was conducted with the help of two research assistants and involved various forms of rapid rural appraisal data collection techniques ranging from key informant interviews, household interviews with 30 families on a variety of random walks, and analysis of official statistics at block and village level.

The population of the district in 1981 was just under 2.6 million and the density of population was 1,184 persons per sq km. This is well above the State average at 655 persons per sq km and is the second highest density after Alleppy at 1,486 persons per sq km. The percentage share of off–farm activities in the district is roughly the same as for the State as a whole. The district has 84 panchayats (local councils), 12 blocks (lowest tier administrative unit), 4 municipalities and 1 corporation. The major crops in the district include paddy, coconut, tapioca and arecanut. The literacy rate in the various blocks ranges from around 68 percent to 76 percent. A household survey was undertaken in a village in Nemom block which links the coastal area to the western ghats within reasonable proximity to Trivandrum city. The block is spread over 134 sq km with a population of 211,607 (1981).

Table 3.13 below shows the percentage of working population engaged in farm and off–farm activities for the 12 blocks in the district. The table demonstrates that there is a wide variation in the percentage share of off–farm employment between the various blocks in the district. The average share of off–farm employment stands at just over 50 percent but this masks the fact that 4 of the 12 blocks record an off–farm share of more than 60 percent with the figure rising to almost 80 percent as the proximity to Trivandrum increases (code i in the table below = Trivandrum block).

Table 3.13 Percentage distribution of working population by main activity for 12 blocks in Trivandrum district

Block code	Farm	Off–farm
a	30.2	63.8
b	28.6	71.4
c	30.8	69.2
d	65.6	34.4
e	60.1	39.9
f	49.2	50.8
g	55.1	44.9
h	72.6	27.4
i	20.2	79.8
j	68.7	31.3
k	45.9	54.1
l	66.4	33.6

At the same time 5 blocks record a less than 40 percent share in off-farm activities but only 1 block has a share of less than 30 percent, which is itself not a small proportion in national terms. Obviously, the further the distance from urban centres the lower the percentage share of off-farm activity. Although the off-farm pull effect from Trivandrum corporation will be apparent in the district it should be pointed out that Trivandrum is not the largest corporation in the State. The largest urban centre is Cochin with a population of just over half a million in 1981 compared to 483,000 for Trivandrum. Nemom block is represented by code f in the table with an off-farm population that is about average and, in turn, not so dissimilar to the State average. For this reason it was felt that a more detailed breakdown of the employment pattern at village and household level would be of considerable interest.

Key informant interviews and rapid household surveys were conducted in 4 hamlets within a village area with a population of around 2,000. The hamlets are located a few kms from a small roadside town with a bank, primary cooperative society, health centre and around 15 or so retail outlets. The landholding pattern is highly fragmented. Average plot size is between 1/4 – 1/2 acre with only a few families owning more than 1 ha. The main crop is coconut followed by paddy and tapioca. The dominant off-farm activity in the area is brick making. Key informants estimated that there were around 35 brick production units within the panchayat with some employing as many as 50 people. Wages in these units are paid on a piece work basis and the units provide casual employment for up to 8 months per year. The average wage for a productive worker is around Rs 40 per day. Informants claimed that this activity had grown rapidly over the last five years in response to the huge increase in construction activities in general and housing in particular. They pointed out that in the past most building materials production was located near to the larger urban centres but that this activity had now spread throughout the countryside. Most of the bricks are sold to agents who, in turn, sell on to builders etc.

The wealthiest family in the locality own 10 acres of land in total of which 4 are cultivated for paddy and the remainder for coconuts. The family also own a retail shop and operates a moneylending and pawn broking business. Other reasonably affluent families own brick production units and a variety of small businesses. There are 3 retail shops in the village selling various food items, general provisions and stationary, a bicycle repair shops, a furniture retailing business, a printing press and a private dispensary. Key informants felt that the village had undergone considerable change over the last ten years. They claimed that in the past the village economy was dominated by agriculture whereas today the majority of families have access to other forms of employment with a growing number of individuals commuting to jobs outside the village. Many of the women who work in the village assist with the cultivation and brick making.

Table 3.14 Household employment profile

Primary Occ	Income Rs	Secondary Occ	Family Size	Landholding Cents
Off-farm				
timber merchant	1,000	furniture making	5	50
army personnel	1,500	match factory	6	20
school teacher	3,500	clerk	5	300
electricity eng	2,500	police constable	5	50
petty shop	600	candle making	5	75
typist	1,000	–	3	10
forest guard	1,200	typist	5	30
copra worker	450	brick work	4	15
carpenter	900	–	4	5
security guard	700	hospital aux	3	60
lathe operator	950	–	4	10
school teacher	1,500	school teacher	4	12
printing press	1,500	–	5	50
cycle repair	1,800	cycle repair	6	30
clerk	1,200	–	5	50
brick business	1,250	–	5	30
auto rickshaw	750	–	4	75
customs officer	2,000	–	4	75
police constable	1,000	building work	7	50
contractor	*	–	4	180
army retired	500	nurse retired	3	50
petty restaurant	800	building work	5	40
Farm				
agricultural lab	500	tailoring	7	–
cultivator	900	–	5	100
agricultural lab	350	brick work	8	10
agricultural lab	400	–	2	–
cultivator	800	building work	5	75
cultivator	500	army retired	6	50
agricultural lab	450		7	20
agricultural lab	350	stone work	4	30

* no income declared but admitted to paying Rs 14,000 income tax

Table 3.14 lists the primary occupation, income, family size and landholding status of each of the 30 households interviewed during a rapid village survey.

The table illustrates the importance of off-farm activity as a primary source of employment for over 73 percent of the sample households. Off-farm employment also provides a secondary source of income for 60 percent of all households. Moreover, almost every household has access to some form of non-agricultural employment even if only on a casual basis between the two major cultivation seasons. Wherever possible households appeared to maintain some form of cultivation activity although the average plot size is extremely small. Most of the landholding units under 25 cents (1/4 acre) are only planted with coconut and little labour time is involved in this process. A further feature that is noticeable from the table is that almost all the off-farm employment is in the tertiary sector on both a self-employed and employed basis. Only 3 of the 22 off-farm workers are engaged in the secondary sector as a primary source of employment.

Much of the work in the off-farm sector is of a precarious nature. Access to employment does not necessarily depend on market forces but on personal contacts and networks. These, in turn, depend on local political links and perceived loyalties based on a web of familial and reciprocal ties rather than any straightforward contractual relationship. Dependence on a variety of mutual reciprocal obligations and personalised networks results in greater emphasis being placed on loyalty than on performance and this may result in reducing the levels of productivity and growth in the off-farm sector and the generation of further employment opportunities of a productive nature.

In this situation households are often unwilling to break their ties with agriculture and prefer to balance farm and off-farm work in such a way that enables them to continue to cultivate as insurance against the uncertainties of off-farm employment. In the case of Kerala, the density of population coupled to the declining productivity of agriculture has tended to force the process of off-farm diversification and this has, in turn, led to a substantial dependence on tertiary employment which has not succeeded in generating long-term growth in the economy. Off-farm opportunities have enabled real family incomes to have been maintained against a background of declining agricultural activity but without a concomitant rise in farm productivity and income and the growth of a more vibrant secondary sector it is unlikely that this will lead to a dynamic monsoon economy of the East Asian variety.

This chapter has examined the importance of off-farm employment and income in a number of Asian rural economies. The evidence points to a growing trend towards rural diversification under monsoon farming conditions. Within this general context, two forms of diversification appear to have become established. Where high levels of investment in agriculture and rural infrastructure have led to increased agricultural intensity, rising output and increased demand coupled to a dynamic industrial response, the result has been a steady transition from family farm based to small firm based employment. Where these conditions have been slower to develop, increasing pressure on land leading to the diminution of holding size has forced households to diversify into service related activities where entry barriers are low and conditions often unstable. Here, the family farm has become part of a wider family undertaking which seeks to secure employment through whatever means and often in a more political rural economy. This latter situation is more typical of the lower income rice economies and will be explored in greater depth at the micro level in the following chapters.

4 The farm economy in rural Sri Lanka

The gradual transition from farm to firm in rural Asia may not necessarily alter the underlying nature of agrarian production relations which may remain smallholder based and family oriented. Indeed the continuing relationship between farm and off-farm employment is likely to reinforce many aspects of smallholder agriculture militating against any general transition to large scale capitalist agriculture. This feature is examined below in relation to a particular rice growing community in Sri Lanka which, by 1984, had experienced considerable development in both the farm and nonfarm sectors. This chapter will aim to examine the main components of the agricultural production system in the form of land, labour and capital in order to identify the nature of production relations and the main agrarian characteristics associated with rural diversification.

The form of ownership and control of the main constituents of the production process will decisively affect the nature of the social relations of production in any rural community, distinguishing the degree of separation from, or access to, these same constituents. Land and water are the principal resources governing agricultural production in Karagahapitiya village. Both have a long and complex tradition of rights and obligations over their occupancy and use in the agrarian structure of Sri Lanka. However, a permanent water resource was only recently established in the village, and although there was significant geological evidence pointing to the existence of a former reservoir or tank, the water distribution system was largely dictated by the general pattern of landownership. The main focus of the first part of

94

the discussion, therefore, will revolve around land ownership, tenure and land alienation prior to a detailed analysis of the agricultural labour system. Here, attention will first be paid to the organisation of farming in relation to the labour pattern for each of the main cultivation practices. This will not only clarify the detailed pattern of labour demand but will also highlight the underlying intensity of paddy cultivation in relation to labour absorbtion. Particular interest will be paid to the extent of hired labour in the village production process as opposed to family or exchange labour and any changes in the operation of these more traditional labour arrangements. The final part of this chapter will consider the role of capital in contemporary agriculture as expressed in the investment pattern, factor markets and institutional development. This micro analysis of production relations in agriculture will link into a broader analysis of off-farm employment in the following chapter as a means of establishing the place of agriculture in the formation of contemporary rural production relations at village level and draws on a case study undertaken in 1983–84 of smallholder rice farming in a precarious South Asian setting.

Karagahapitiya village

The village of Karagahapitiya lies in the Kurunegala district of the Northwestern Province of Sri Lanka. Kurunegala is the third largest of the twenty four districts in the country with a total land area of 1,842 sq miles and a population of 1.2 million (Perera 1979). A World Bank survey of 1979 revealed that the district contained 7 percent of the country's total land area and 8 percent of the total population with a higher than average rural population of 96 percent compared to the national average of 78 percent (World Bank 1979).

The three major agro-climatic zones, namely the wet zone, dry zone and intermediate zone are all represented in the district. These can be subdivided into categories of dry, semi-dry, semi-wet and wet. The village falls within the intermediate category which in its broadest sense covers both the semi-dry and semi-wet areas constituting 70 percent of the total district land area with an annual rainfall ranging from 60 to 70 inches per annum (Perera 1979). The climate is tropical with little annual variation in temperature contrasting with a marked annual variation in rainfall. This is mainly caused by the dual effect of the northeast and southwest monsoon. The reduced effect of the southwest monsoon means that in the drier parts of the district cultivation can only take place on irrigated land during the dry (*yala*) season.

The district's topography is one of sloping hills from south to north and west at elevations of 2,000 to 50 feet. The soils vary in texture and drainage efficiency from the fine and well drained reddish brown earth to the fine but poorly drained low humic gley and course rogosols. All soils have a shallow profile of between 2 and 3 feet and are low in nutrient value. In 1984, almost half of the total land area of 1.2 million acres was under permanent cultivation. Coconut and paddy were the two main agricultural crops with coconut extending over 380,000 acres and paddy over 180,000 acres. The district has the highest extent of land under coconut and paddy in the country at 35 percent and 13 percent respectively of the country's total (World Bank 1979). The four main rivers in the district feed the major tanks (reservoirs) and diversion schemes. Favourable rainfall and run off conditions facilitate the storage of surplus water. The average paddy holding size in the intermediate zone stood at 1.56 acres and in the wet zone at 0.69 acres according to an ARTI survey of 1981. This survey also demonstrated that poor irrigation facilities resulted in low levels of cropping intensity during the *yala* season even under conditions of major irrigation.

The village of Karagahapitiya lies under the Polgama tank, the first minor tanks to have been rehabilitated under the World Bank funded Kurunegala Integrated Rural Development Project (KIRDP). The village is situated under ten miles from Kurunegala town and within a few miles of the smaller town of Madagamuwa. The physical setting of the village in the wider geographical context is dominated by the agro–ecological conditions of the low country intermediate zone which stretches in a corridor towards the town of Matale and then opens into a larger area bounded by the Kandyan plateau to the west, Bibile to the east and Moneregala to the south. The surrounding terrain is a mixture of rolling, undulating and flat lands interspersed with dramatic outcrops of interbanded quartz and granite. The geomorphology of the area is characterised by its setting on the plains that surround the Central Highlands, the northern extension of which is known as the Matale Hills (1,500 ft – 2,500 ft) lying to the east of the village. The land around Karagahapitiya is flat with an elevation ranging between 400–500 feet above sea level and a general slope to the west. A small hill range at 700 feet marks the eastern divide of the village and the tank is situated at the foot of this range in the eastern most corner of the paddy tract. The countryside is hilly towards the west where there is a large extent of forest in which the ancient monastery of Arankele is situated.

Being in the low country intermediate climatic zone, the village has a 75 percent expectancy rate for rainfall in excess of 40 inches per annum. The monthly rainfall variation is high, with peaks of 10 inches and 7 inches in October and April respectively. Local soils form part of the red yellow podzolic or reddish brown earth group and vary in texture within the village. Soils on the higher ground, including one of the main paddy tracts, are of a thinner sandy texture. Being porous this soil allows for a high level of percolation and consequently has a low water retention capacity. Drainage is dependent upon the Dedura Oya river which flows from its source in the Matale Hills to the south of the village. A natural stream runs through the village into an adjacent tank forming a minor cascade system. This has been enhanced by the recent rehabilitation of Polgama tank under the KIRDP scheme.

The rate of literacy in the village was high for both sexes. This was not unexpected in a country which has one of the highest literacy rates in South Asia. By the mid 1970s the level of literacy in the country had risen to 78 percent and school enrolments to over 86 percent which contrasts with an expected literacy level based on per capita income of 36 percent (Uphoff and Wanigaratne 1982). In the village, the rate of literacy stood at 85 percent with an average educational attainment for all household heads at just under grade eight on a scale from zero to twelve. An Agrarian Research and Training Institute (ARTI) survey in Kurunegala district found high rates of literacy in line with all other districts. The rate for males stood at 94 percent compared to 84 percent for females in all zones, with only a marginal interzonal variation (ARTI 1981a).

Villagers have good accessibility to a wide range of services which will later be seen to be an important factor in helping to explain the nature of the contemporary agrarian economy and village production relations. As Uphoff and Wanigaratne (1982) have shown on a national basis, these services have led to an impressive welfare and rural development record especially in the realm of life expectancy, health, education and literacy. A study of the physical quality of life indices (PQLI) for the population of Kurunegala in 1981 showed a PQLI of 88.6 for males and 87.9 for females which compares with 43 for India and 94 for the USA (ARTI 1981a).

For agricultural administration purposes the village is located within the Kurunegala/Hiriyala Agrarian Service Centre (ASC) segment and the Madagamuwa ASC division. In 1984 the ASC command area contained 3,929 farming families on 2,466 acres of paddy land of which 920 acres were under major irrigation, 511 acres under minor irrigation and 1,035 acres were rainfed. A further 5,220 acres were classified as coconut land.

The estimated population of the village in 1983–84 was 833 divided into 153 separate households with an average 5.4 persons per household. The average size of household for the district was 5.3 and for the country was 5.6 (ARTI 1981a). In 1931 the population of the village stood at 352 divided among 88 families. Life expectancy in the village, as elsewhere in the country, is high in relation to the level of per capita income.

In the village there was definite spatial segregation along caste and ethnic lines. There were fifteen low caste households, seven Muslim households and two Tamil households. The remaining one hundred and twenty nine households were Sinhalese of the *goyigama* (cultivator) caste. The low caste households could be divided into four separate castes. The majority were *hena* (washers to higher castes) of which there were at least twice as many households as any other caste group. The second largest group of low caste households belonged to the *hunu* (lime burner) caste. There were two *padu* (king's palanquin bearers) households and one *karava* (fisher) caste family.

97

Although the vast majority of villagers are high caste Sinhalese there were distinct subdivisions among them. Those families that originated from the village or surrounding areas regarded themselves as being of up country Kandyan as opposed to low country descent. This categorisation reflects the different historical evolution of the two communities. It was the Kandyan Kingdom that held out against the early colonial influences of the Portuguese and Dutch and consequently retained a greater link with traditional customs, behaviour and culture. With increasing national awareness after independence, the Kandyan distinction was adopted as a mark of status. Villagers continue to draw attention to such differences and regard low country descent as being inferior to Kandyan.

The land system of Karagahapitiya

The paddy land extends across a number of separate tracts which are divided by highland or non *aswedumised* (ridged in preparation for paddy) land and located below a tank bund. In practice, all the tracts form a single entity in the sense that they are connected both artificially and naturally to the same irrigation source, with the exception of the most southerly tract which, on account of its distance from the irrigation tank, periodically experiences water scarcity. The total paddy acreage is roughly one hundred and seventy acres. A village survey (Final Report) of 1942 placed the total extent of paddy at one hundred and thirty nine acres. This figure has subsequently altered as a result of boundary changes and a minor amount of paddy land extension. The paddy land is divided into roughly two hundred separate plots.

Of central concern in unravelling existing production relations, is the extent to which complex traditional land rights governing property holding and transmission still prevail. The traditional purana system has been well documented in its ideal form by Pieris (1956), Leach (1961) and Obeyesekere (1967). The central characteristics of this system were generally associated with a single 'old field' radiating from a tank (reservoir) bund at an elevated point and without necessarily uniform proportions downstream. Ownership of rights within the field was based upon a complex division of equal shares of land with attendant service obligations related to water collection and distribution. Usually the field was divided into two or three tracts each of which would be subdivided into two or three portions known as *bagas* which would themselves be further divided according to their overall location in the tract. These internal subdivisions would correspond to the elevation of the terrain upon which the paddy field had been *aswedumised*. Each of the *baga* subdivisions would then be further divided into an equal number of strips (*issaraval*) each of which would be of equal dimensions. A share of the land rights in the field would normally be over a number of *issaraval* in the respective elevated divisions of the different baga and tracts. The number of shares (*panguva*)

98

in each field would be a fixed number whereas the number of shareholders would vary and thus the rights and duties associated with a particular share might become apportioned amongst a number of inheritors. In this way, the *issaraval* contained within a *panguva* would themselves become divided either lengthwise or cross wise depending on the number of potential shareholders, who would subsequently divide up their service obligations towards irrigation and fencing accordingly.

During the southwest monsoon cultivation season, a system known as the *betma* was adopted. Here, as long as the village tank had insufficient capacity to irrigate the whole field, an upper portion near the tank would be selected and then divided into cultivable plots either in direct relation to the shareholding of each farmer in the total field, or worked in common with the produce being divided accordingly. This system demonstrates the equitable nature of traditional land rights and duties with the exception of the rule governing village and irrigation headmen, who enjoyed the rights over *issaraval* at either end of the tract exclusive of any service obligations. The theoretical model worked in such a way as to ensure that the effect of the differential status of any piece of land in relation to fertility and irrigation on any shareholding would be minimised by the requirement that shares be held simultaneously within the dividing categories of the original field. However, this system could not be viewed as synonymous with communal land tenure consisting of inalienable and non inheritable paddy land. As the pressure for land increased over the years, shares were divided and even changed hands altogether. This theoretical model, however, forms the basis of a popular understanding of traditional land rights in paddy farming (see Pieris 1956: 236-240; Leach 1961: 146-177).

According to Leach, this theoretical model of land distribution corresponded fairly closely to the actual situation in 1954. The main difference in the system being a change in the form of land share transmissions from a fictional *paraveni* (inheritable only) restriction, to the actual situation where 42 percent of the plots in the 'old field' had exchanged hands by sale over a period of sixty four years. Despite this fact, the continuity of the system had been preserved through kinship regulations, so that land was exchanged between the members of a *variga* (endogamous kin group), thus retaining the essence of traditional custom (Leach 1961: 173). The continuity of such an 'old field' system was dependent upon the operation of a kinship system, that, despite lacking any notion of corporate descent, was flexible enough to incorporate affinal relations into an endogamous group provided that a property claim in the share system could be made. Yet kinship relations themselves did not determine the structure of landownership but rather reflected the fixed nature of the pattern of aswedumised landholding (Leach 1961: 302-304).

Despite the fact that Leach's analysis is not entirely subject to stasis, with the growth of differentiation being alluded to in relation to various non traditional forms of land tenure, it is the implicit technical determinism that we will take issue with. An alternative appreciation of the nature of corporate grouping might well focus more clearly upon changing production relations and their consequent social implications. The influence of growing commercialism and the cash economy on the traditional pattern of landholding has been extensively studied by Obeyesekere (1967). He shows that the Partition Ordinance of 1863 had a decisive impact on the peasantry, precipitating subsequent property sales and supporting co-owners of shares in cases of partitioning, thus establishing final and 'safe' title to lands. This was later superseded by the 1951 Partition Act which further served the ends of speculators who had gradually built up cash reserves as a result of commercial participation in the regional economy (Obeyesekere 1967). Crucially, this trend to partitioning was taking place on a foundation of severe fragmentation intensified as a result of previous legislation concerning Crown land encroachment, grain taxes and Roman-Dutch inheritance law emphasising bilateralism. Having undermined the 'structural prerequisite' of the indigenous system, namely land availability, share fractioning became widespread as ownership multiplied (Obeyesekere 1967). In this way we can see a more dynamic assessment of the development of land rights and ownership from the traditional 'ideal' model.

An analysis of the land ownership pattern in Karagahapitiya village clearly highlights the extent to which any traditional or 'ideal' system has evolved. In the first instance, there was little correspondence between the distribution of holdings within the village's seven main paddy fields and an 'ideal' single 'old field', where a shareholder would have had rights in a number of *issaraval* in the various parts of the paddy field. On the whole, the landholding pattern was characterised by a small number of different plots which were fairly randomly scattered. This appears to indicate that the former equitable distribution of shares in land has little influence on present ownership and distribution patterns. The corresponding ownership link between land shares and endogamous kin groups was no longer perceived by farmers to be an important factor. However, most farmers did express reluctance to sell land in the main centrally placed tract (the 'old field' equivalent) to people considered not to be *'honda minissu'* (good people). This was usually understood in ethnic, caste and social terms to exclude any non up-country *goyigama* (farmer caste) Sinhalese. The conditions defining an acceptable outsider who was not incorporated through marriage and thus terminologically defined into a kin group, were otherwise fairly flexible.

Due to certain historical circumstances associated with the rapid rise in population and the growth of the market economy, landholdings had recently become extensively subdivided and fragmented. Not only did this mean that the reality of Karagahapitiya land rights bore little resemblance to any ideal model, it also differed considerably from the picture described by Leach and, as we shall see below, by Obeyesekere.

The vast majority of land titles were owned by households living within the village. By 1984 land titles had been divided up among seventy six households. Table 4.1 illustrates the distribution of paddy ownership amongst all the households of the village. Table 4.2 is concerned in more detail with the relative size differences within the paddy owning community of the village, comprising just under half the total number of households at 49.7 percent. Table 4.2 is given in half acre categories from 0 to 8 acres. In each category both the number of owners and the percentage of total owners is examined alongside the number of acres and the percentage of total acreage held by the seventy six landowning households.

Table 4.1 Household distribution of paddy landownership by size

Size in Acres	No. of Households	% of Households
none	77	50.3
<1	39	25.5
1.0 – 1.9	17	11.1
2.0 – 2.9	11	7.2
3.0 – 3.9	2	1.3
4.0 – 4.9	3	2.0
5.0 – 5.9	1	0.6
6.0 – 6.9	–	–
7.0 – 7.9	1	0.6
8.0 – 8.9	2	1.3
total	153	100.0

Table 4.1 shows that in terms of paddy land ownership there is a good deal of differentiation, with over half of the total households surveyed owning no land whatsoever and a further 25.5 percent owning less than one acre. Table 4.2 shows the proportional division of owned land in relation to the sum total within each landholding category. Land is owned in small units and under considerable pressure with one landowning household to every 1.46 acres. Table 4.2 also clearly demonstrates that the top 3 percent of landowners have control over 20 percent of the total paddy land. Two of the three landowners in this category were descended from a traditional feudal (*walawaa*) family and had thus retained their relative position in the landowning stakes. However, 36 percent of those households claiming feudal descent had been relegated into the less than half acre category landowning category. This factor probably accounts for the rather unusual multi–modal distribution characterised in a

decaying wave form, brought about by a progressive redistribution of land over time. This could indicate that historically there were at least two larger landowning families of differing status, a supposition that was verified by descriptive accounts of the former elite structure within the village. Table 4.2 confirms Farmer's (1957) findings that land was predominantly owned in the form of smallholdings and Robinson's (1975) observations in relation to Morapitiya village that there were no very large landlords in the community. In Karagahapitiya, the data shows the upper ceiling at around 8.5 acres.

Table 4.2   Household distribution of paddy land by size and proportion of acreage amongst landowners

size in acres	no of households	% of households	acreage	% of total
<0.4	10	13.2	2.5	2.3
0.5 – 0.9	29	38.2	15.0	13.5
1.0 – 1.4	13	17.1	14.0	12.6
1.5 – 1.9	4	5.3	6.0	5.4
2.0 – 2.4	5	6.6	10.0	9.0
2.4 – 2.9	6	7.9	16.0	14.4
3.0 – 3.4	1	1.3	3.0	2.7
3.5 – 3.9	1	1.3	3.5	3.2
4.0 – 4.4	2	2.6	8.0	7.2
4.5 – 4.9	1	1.3	4.5	4.0
5.0 – 5.4				
5.5 – 5.9	1	1.3	5.5	5.0
6.0 – 6.4				
6.5 – 6.9				
7.0 – 7.4	1	1.3	7.0	6.3
7.5 – 7.9				
8.0 – 8.4	2	2.6	16.0	14.4
Total	76	100	111	100

Having noted the detailed distribution of paddy land ownership, it is important to focus on the total picture for all households within the village in order to explore the question of the separation from and access to the means of production. Particular attention will be paid to the seventy seven households with no paddy land. In order to refine the concept of landlessness, it may be important to turn to one additional source of agricultural income,

102

namely coconut highland. Although this land was not intensively farmed on account of the ease with which it can be brought under cultivation, a larger number of households had access to large plots from which they could derive a reasonable income. Coconut highland also provided a considerable amount of waged employment to labourers on a casual basis.

Table 4.3 Household distribution of coconut (highland) ownership by size

Size	No	%
None	29	19.0
<1	70	45.8
1 – 1.9	24	15.7
2 – 4.9	19	12.4
5 – 9.9	8	5.2
10 – 14.9	2	1.3
15 – 19.9	1	0.6
20 – 24.9		
Total	153	100

Table 4.4 Household distribution of paddy land and highland by size

Size	No	%
None	29	19.0
<1	52	34.0
1 – 1.9	31	20.3
2 – 4.9	24	15.7
5 – 9.9	10	6.5
10 – 14.9	4	2.6
15 – 19.9	2	1.3
20 – 24.9	1	0.7
Total	153	100

When aggregating coconut highland with paddy land, the number of landless households falls from 50 percent to under 20 percent of total households. Coconut highland is typically held in larger units, is more widely distributed and at the very least forms the compound that surrounds a family's dwelling place. Despite the higher percentages of total land ownership, the number of landless households still amounts to nearly 19 percent of all households. As already seen in table 4.1, this increases to over 50 percent when coconut highland is excluded. An examination of land tenure may shed more light on the overall land distribution pattern and the attendant social relations of production.

Land tenure

A full appreciation of the differential access to the means of production existing between households cannot be gained until the nature of the separation, that appears to deny over 50 percent of the households control over paddy land, is further explored. A more adequate indicator of total separation from the means of production might revolve around an analysis of land operations within the framework of existing tenurial conditions. Although over a quarter of the total paddy land was held in household units of over five acres, none of it was actually operated in enterprises of such size. All operational holdings fell below four and three quarter acres. The tenurial system worked in such a way as to scale down the units of ownership and redistribute land amongst a larger number of operations. Ninety six households actually operated paddy land and a further six gained income from their land which was entirely rented out. Over 30 percent of all landowning households in the village constituted a semi-landlord group renting out at least some of their paddy land. This group had an average landowning size of three acres per household which was twice the average for all landowners.

Those households with more than five acres of paddy land had all chosen to reduce their direct farming commitment rather than operate on a large scale commercial basis. Indeed, nineteen other landowning households with less than five acres had also chosen this strategy. Simultaneously, the number of landless households had decreased by 34 percent from seventy seven to fifty one. Table 4.5 illustrates the household distribution of operational holdings compared to landownership. Table 4.6 illustrates the distribution of operational holdings highlighting the equalising effect of the land tenure system. Table 4.6 demonstrates that there has been a downward shift in the size of paddy holdings since the late sixties when, with a slightly lower percentage than the national average, 14 percent of holdings in Kurunegala district fell between two and a half and five acres and 9 percent were over five acres (Schickele, 1969). In Karagahapitiya, these percentages had fallen to 9.3 percent and 0 percent respectively whilst the one to two and a half acre category had

104

Table 4.5 Household distribution of landownership and operational holdings by size

Size in Acres	Land Owned		Land Operated	
	No	%	No	%
None	77	50.3	53	33.3
<1	39	25.5	48	31.4
1.0 – 1.9	17	11.1	33	21.6
2.0 – 2.9	11	7.2	12	7.8
3.0 – 3.9	2			
4.0 – 4.9	3	2.0	7	4.6
5.0 – 5.9	1	0.7		
6.0 – 6.9				
7.0 – 7.9	1	0.7		
8.0 – 8.9	2	1.3		
Total	153	100.0	153	100.0

Table 4.6 Distribution of operational holdings by size and proportion of acreage

Size	No	%	acreage	%
<0.5	4	4.2	1.0	0.9
0.5 – 0.9	41	42.7	20.5	18.5
1.0 – 1.4	21	21.9	21.0	18.9
1.5 – 1.9	12	12.5	18.0	16.2
2.0 – 2.4	9	9.4	18.0	16.2
2.5 – 2.9	2	2.1	5.0	4.5
3.0 – 3.4	1	1.0	3.0	2.7
3.5 – 3.9	1	1.0	3.5	3.1
4.0 – 4.4	3	3.1	12.0	10.8
4.5 – 4.9	2	2.1	9.0	8.1
Total	96	100.0	111.0	100.0

remained almost the same while the less than one acre group had increased by 8 percent.

The system by which larger landowners reduced their direct involvement in farming whilst landless or small owners increased their farming activity, was based on a form of sharecropping known as *ande*. The 1962 census of agriculture stated that 55 percent of holdings were owner cultivated whereas 34 percent were sharecropped (Bansil, 1971: 129). Over twenty years later, data from Karagahapitiya village showed that sharecropping was practised by 53 percent of operated holdings, broken down into 27 percent as full sharecroppers, rising to 39.5 percent when accounting for those holdings where sharecropping is predominantly practised. The village appeared to have a lower percentage of full owner operators at 46 percent than the estimated 66.6 percent for the country as a whole. When the percentage of the total acreage under *ande* is aggregated to include *ande* land operated by landowners as well as tenants, it exceeds 40 percent, a figure normally seen for central highland and coastal regions (Pieris 1976: 24).

Some landowners chose to rent out land on *ande* because they were primarily engaged in off-farm employment and did not have the time to cultivate all their lands directly or to supervise wage labour. Others rented out land due to a lack of domestic manpower or ill health. One advantage that landlords clearly perceived as an important aspect of *ande* relations was the fact that any land retained for the landlord's direct cultivation could be partially worked through a tenant's modified service obligations. Landowners claimed that wage labourers work less enthusiastically and intensively than a good tenant although it was widely recognised that some tenants commonly deceived landlords about the true extent of the harvest. A number of landlords pointed out, for example, that they often suspected tenants of not declaring the full extent of their harvest and that when they came to inspect the crop at the threshing floor the tenants would hide a portion of their harvest among the stacks of other farmers. It was later revealed that of those tenants who admitted to this, the relationship between themselves and their landlord was fairly distant often involving an absentee owner.

Under existing *ande* terms, most landowners seemed to feel that there was sufficient incentive in the system for them to rent out land rather than farm commercially employing wage labour. The terms governing share tenancy became legally established after the Paddy Lands Act of 1958 (see Gold, 1977). An earlier and less effective piece of legislation was the Paddy Lands Act of 1953. The 1958 Act provided tenants with security of tenure confirming permanent and inheritable rights to cultivate with protection against most forms of eviction. In addition, it limited the per acre rent payable to a landlord at 25 percent of the total yield or ten bushels, revised to fifteen bushels in 1967 (one bushel is c.28–30 kg) and the landlord had to acknowledge his share by the issuing of a receipt. The interest charge on loans to tenants was also restricted to 10 percent for loans in kind and 6 percent for cash (Hameed 1977). Subsequent legislation contained in the Agricultural Lands Law of 1973 and the Agrarian Services Act of 1979 has reinforced the legal status of the

106

tenant in relation to rent, eviction and service duties to a landlord (see Perera, 1984).

In practice, most of the clauses were often ignored. For example, the local government officers of the Department of Agrarian Services openly acknowledged that the paddy lands register, which serves to entitle tenants to security of tenure, was incomplete. The village survey revealed that nearly 18 percent of the 102 owners and operators were not registered. In this way, nearly 35 percent of those who hired-in land as share tenants were not officially entitled to the protection of the Act. In such cases the landlord continued to pay the acre tax to the Agrarian Service Centre, thus formally establishing himself as the operator of the land.

A further infringement of the law commonly occurred over the amount of rent that was actually paid to the landlord. The ratio of tenancies operated along traditional *ande* lines, where the rent is calculated at half the harvest, compared to those where a strict legal quarter was charged, was roughly 4:1. The half share rent predominated on 75 percent of reported tenancies and was still, therefore, by far and away the most common sharecropping arrangement in the village. However, there appeared to be no significant correlation between the type and size of tenant paying a quarter share rent or the landlords receiving it. For example, in both rental groups there was a mix of caste, ethnic background and social and economic status, whilst the landlords of both groups varied between kin, neighbours and outsiders. The continuing survival of the traditional *ande* system, in spite of the 1958 Paddy Lands Act, has been widely confirmed elsewhere in districts such as Kegalle, Kalutara and the Dry Zone at Minipe (see Amerasinghe 1977; Panditharatna and Gunasekera 1977; Selvadurai 1977). It appears that for most tenants, access to paddy land was the single most important factor governing tenancy relations and that they were not willing to put this at risk by disputing the terms and conditions with their landlord. Many tenants explained that off-farm employment was more important to the family in terms of income and that they were thus prepared to accept the traditional terms and conditions associated with *ande* tenure. For those at the bottom end of the income spectrum, however, the fear of eviction coupled to a level of dependency on the landlord for assistance with the purchase of inputs, the provision of draught animals and credit, along with customary behaviourial norms, combined to conserve the *ande* system.

Another traditional form of tenancy that was occasionally practised was *karu ande*, which literally means a quarter *ande*. Under this system the tenant would plough, level and thresh and in return receive a quarter of the harvest after bearing a quarter of the expenses. The *karu ande* landlord was often a small farmer who did not own buffalo and consequently would have to hire-in draught power. *Karu ande* was seen as a traditional risk sharing means of overcoming a problem that would otherwise entail a capital outlay on wage labour. The distribution of this form of tenancy was low with only 8 percent of tenants reporting being involved in this arrangement. The *karu ande* tenants and their families frequently stated that their quarter share of the harvest was preferable to having received a wage equivalent since it was regarded as 'safe income', where the rewards for the work would arrive at the home in a tangible form.

In some parts of the country farming relations have included the system of *tattumaru* which is a rotation system where co-owners rotate the right to cultivate a plot of land rather than working in a cooperative form. The right of use is rotated annually or seasonally. It is a form of voluntary consolidation and is practised when the pressure on land from population growth becomes extreme. Paradoxically, the districts of Kandy and Badulla, which possess some of the most serious subdivisional problems, actually contain less than one percent of *tattumaru* lands (see Gold 1977) while this form of operation was also negligible in Karagahapitiya village. The low incidence in areas of high population density suggests that these arrangements were no longer perceived to be attractive since the opportunity cost of cultivating ancestral land on a rotating part time basis was higher than effectively relinquishing rights to that land and securing off-farm employment instead. The low incidence of *tattumaru* implies that the cultural value of working ancestral land has declined and siblings are now only prepared to take calculated economic decisions when adopting alternative cultivation practices. What appears to be a crucial component in the decision making process is the ability of the land to contribute effectively to the process of household reproduction rather than any arrangement merely designed to maintain a symbolic land operating status.

Land transmission and inheritance

The characteristics of the social formation within the village will largely depend upon the nature of production relations. Access to land as the key constituent of the means of production in the form of ownership and operational control has been examined above. Land is both owned and controlled in relatively small units and is subject to increasing fragmentation. With the development of the productive forces in agriculture and the commoditisation of land, consolidation could take place through the land market. Analysis of the distribution of operational holdings however, indicates that this tendency may only be slight. What is now important, therefore, is to examine the dominant mechanism of transmission that has brought about this particular distribution of land and the implication for future land distribution.

Analysis of the land market in Karagahapitiya shows that it has been fairly buoyant in the past. The incidence of land purchases or sales were fairly randomly distributed throughout all farm size groups. However, more than 60 percent of these transactions took place prior to the early 1960s. This indicates that as the productive forces in agriculture developed in line with technological advances in developing hybrid seeds and related chemical inputs, outright sales of land appear to have decreased. Since the rehabilitation of the village tank, which increased yields dramatically, very few land transactions had taken place. Indeed a common complaint expressed by many farmers with disposable income was that it had become impossible to buy land under the tank in Karagahapitiya.

One method by which land can be transmitted from a landowner to a cultivator and a cash income generated for the landowner out of the transaction, is through a *badu* (leasehold) arrangement. Since this implies the existence of commodity exchange and monetary circulation where land is subject to commoditisation, many authors see this as representing a transitional phase in the development of capitalist relations on the land. Gunasinghe (1975), for example, argues that in many places a structural shift has taken place from a system of sharecropping or produce rent to money rent. The implication here being that a gradual change could be taking place in many rural areas where traditional forms of tenancy are being gradually replaced by more commercial and profitable leasehold tenure. Landlords would then have the ability to realise the commodity value of land by regularly adjusting the price of short term leases. Leasehold arrangements would replace tenancy as the mechanism by which landlords would gain access to other labour power and the landless gain partial access to land.

The acreage held on lease in the village amounted to no more than 2 percent of total paddy land with only three landlords actively engaged in leasing. There was little evidence to demonstrate that traditional *ande* tenancy was being replaced by new leasehold agreements. Usufructuary mortgages accounted for a larger acreage at 5.6 percent of the total paddy land but were only prevalent amongst 8.6 percent of the landlords. Paddy land was rarely mortgaged for emergency cash raising purposes. Cultivators tended to view both mortgages and leases as temporary arrangements lacking even the security of a tenancy agreement. A mortgage (*ukas*) was often regarded by cultivators as more beneficial than a lease since the cultivator was entitled to the harvest during the season of cultivation and when the arrangement was to be terminated his original lump sum would be recovered, whereas a lease involved permanent and irretrievable cash payment. Most cases of mortgaging out land in the village were found to be for particular non commercial purposes. One landowner had planned to leave the village but had not decided whether or not this would be on a permanent basis and consequently mortgaged his land. Another was reputed to have lost interest in cultivating his land and seemed to prefer the prospect of working off-farm, despite his retirement from a long term service commission in the army. It was widely rumoured that he wanted the cash to pay his liquor bills.

Access to the control and ownership of land was still largely determined by the traditional system of inheritance which governed the transmission of rights in material property and was a function of kinship and conjugality. This system itself has been subject to a degree of change with important implications for the development of the productive forces and relations both in and out of agriculture. Terminologically, the kinship system conforms to a 'Dravidian type' classification, where certain lineal terms are extended to collateral relatives and in turn this determines whether or not their offspring are classificatory siblings or cross cousins. The main distinction in the terminology being related to this parallel/cross or kin/affine division (Stirrat 1977). The symmetrical features of this system have been fully treated elsewhere (see Pieris 1956; Yalman 1962, 1967; Obeyesekere 1967; Leach 1961). This terminological structure, in a cognitive sense, is seen by Yalman as capable of prescribing social relations, characterised by cross cousin marriage, within bilateral and endogamous kin groups. This point is disputed by Obeyesekere (1967) who admits to being more concerned with analysis at the level of 'action systems' rather than 'logical structures'. In sympathy with Obeyesekere, it could be said that empirically, in Karagahapitiya, no such prescriptive rule appeared to be enforced. The dominant marriage strategy did not appear to be aimed simply at preserving some sort of terminological symmetry. Despite the fact that all marriages result in being incorporated into this system of classification, the system itself does not serve to regulate all marriages.

A prescriptive bilateral and endogamous marriage system effects land distribution by protecting and consolidating units while maintaining their economic viability and status. Leach, for example, argues that this is a necessary corollary of the material conditions of irrigated rice agriculture, where 'it is much simpler for the human beings to adapt themselves to the layout of the territory than to adapt the territory to the private whims of individual human beings'. In this regard it is 'locality and not descent' which determines the basis of corporate grouping (Leach 1961: 301). Local group endogamy was enforced through the principle of *variga* or subcaste endogamy which treated any breach as a case of ritual pollution. Sociologically, these rules could be interpreted as maintaining a convenient system of ownership and control over land and property rights, which consequently emphasised territorial endogamy (Leach 1961). Whilst agreeing with Leach's premise that the social structure can be seen empirically to have a material basis, this may not necessarily be fixed in the physical layout of the land system but rather in the nature of a dominant mode of production in a dynamic context.

In Karagahapitiya, the absence of any widespread commercial alienation of land, meant that the marriage and inheritance systems played a crucial role in land transmission. Evidence from the village indicated that these systems had been subjected to degrees of change that had altered the character of the social formation. These changes can be accounted for when one considers the fact that marriage is seen as a conscious strategy and that certain deviations from the preferred form have quite different implications for the mechanism of asset building. Obeyesekere, for example, has demonstrated these differences in relation to the concept of *avassa*, meaning essential or close. A preferred marriage is seen as one between *avassa nayo* or closely related kin as opposed to those simply between *nayo* (related families). The *avassa* marriages are between true cross cousins and intensify already close consanguineal ties, strengthening existing alliances. Classificatory cross cousin marriage has an altogether different effect of creating new kinsmen, often involving large dowry payments. (See Obeyesekere 1967). The formal ideology of marriage is that between kinsmen and the practical limitations are endogamously within one's *variga* or between isogamous subcastes. Many people in Karagahapitiya would talk of a desire to marry outside the kin group as a means of extending family ties and creating new brokerage networks. This would include individuals who had themselves married kin members but who claimed that their relationship was distant and had only been discovered after having chosen their partner. Detailed information on marriage strategy was not gathered in the initial survey, but in a number of cases where the author established a good rapport with a family it was possible to develop the subject. By this means, information was gathered on marriages from thirty two household heads, twenty of whom reported marrying outside their kin group while, of the remaining twelve, eight had married a distant kin member and only four had married an *avassa nayo*. These figures were not drawn from a random sample and cannot be more widely generalised for fear of distortion.

It may be useful to look at aspects of the ideology associated with features of the marriage system. In the past, local group endogamy might have been enforced by notions of ritual pollution at breaches of the subcaste delineation. The villagers of Karagahapitiya, however, rarely expressed any observance of a subcaste limitation. The concept seemed to be little used and little understood. When people did make reference to a subcaste it was seen as a theoretical group of kinsmen who might meet on certain important occasions, such as that of a girl becoming pregnant out of wedlock requiring the sanctioning of a closely related group.

The contemporary emphasis on the nuclear family unit means that the preference for close kin marriage is much less prominent. The manifestation of this fact can be seen in the attitude of many villagers to intra village relations. Villagers often claimed that 'today people mind their own business and worry about their own welfare and if required, help only comes from a small group of people'. In addition, the old tradition of arranged marriage through the services of a broker was less dominant as an increasing number of people found their own partner. Of those spouses who married outside the extended kin group, 35 percent reported meeting their own partner and only obtained parental consent afterwards.

Terminological changes have also crept into local discourse in a similar form to the 'slippage' noted by Stirrat (1977), where affinal terms are replaced by consanguineal terms having the dual effect of formalising relations and reducing the category of marriageable partners from within the kin network. This represents a change in the moral basis of the traditional system which

111

emphasised close kin marriage (Stirrat 1977). Affinal terms were very rarely used in the village in any encounter between relations but they were still used in a descriptive sense when classifying relationships. Although this is not complete 'slippage', it does mark a change in daily perceptions.

All these changes represent a shift away from traditional morality associated with the kinship system. Their significance lies not only in this fact but also in the fact that it is the dependence on land as a tangible resource that can be inherited without capital and the usefulness of cooperative work practices, that has been assumed to underlie traditional morality (see Stirrat 1977). In Karagahapitiya, although the kinship system remains crucial to the process of land transmission, it is no longer dominated by an ideology of protection, consolidation and continuity. The nuclear household strategy that governs marriage choice has a similar effect to the 'classificatory' as opposed to 'true' cross cousin marriage strategy (see Obeyesekere 1967).

The contemporary preference for searching out new 'relatives' to become incorporated in the kin unit was explained by households as a preferred strategy of extending the family unit. This in turn was viewed as increasing potential economic mobility and reducing possible internal tension within the family, albeit a high risk strategy. Rather than consolidating land units and promoting traditional forms of cooperation in agriculture, in the absence of commercial consolidation and consequent differentiation, land has become fragmented and subject to individualised tendencies within nuclear household units. This promotes alliances that need not be based on the ideal of land consolidation in the face of alternative forms of economic mobility within a wider system of choice. The rationale behind these changes underwrites a change in the character of the mode of production and the place of agricultural activity in the overall rural economy. The opening up of employment in the off–farm economy has meant that land protection and consolidation is now less important than access to wider sources of income.

In summary, it is suggested that the land ownership pattern and the distribution of control over land in the form of operational holdings have not been subject to commercial consolidation nor remained equally distributed in the traditional share owning pattern. Land is still predominantly transmitted through the mechanism of marriage and inheritance. Yet changes that have taken place within this social system have undermined traditional forms of protection and consolidation, emphasising in a practical and ideological sense an individual household strategy in which land fragmentation and reduced agricultural cooperation has meant that farming is gradually becoming just one element of a household's overall economic strategy. At the same time the dominance of traditional rather than commercial forms of land transmission result in the maintenance of agricultural smallholdings within this broader economic strategy, where paddy holdings are generally under five acres in size.

The agricultural labour system

The impact of modern techniques associated with HYV farming has been widely recorded throughout South Asia. Research into highly productive crop strains has led to the introduction and widespread use of new dwarf plant varieties accompanied by a package of complimentary inputs in many rice farming areas. Critics have viewed this development with a certain degree of scepticism when assessing the social as opposed to the productive impact of the technology. Pearse (1981) has comprehensively examined these implications in relation to the rural community. He argues that in cases where adoption levels have been high, the increased viability of farming has led to a breakdown of communal tenure structures and their replacement with commercial forms of labour organisation. Similarly, Rudra (1971) has pointed to changes in the organisation of labour in India resulting in a structural shift from semi-feudal to capitalist production relations, characterised by a resumption of land from tenants for the owner's direct cultivation. This process depends on the re-employment of former tenants under conditions of wage labour as a manifestation of a new form of inequality. Rudra has also assessed the impact on overall employment in agriculture concluding that modern farming methods involve a more intensive form of operation and higher levels of labour demand.

In Sri Lanka as a whole there has been a high level of adoption of HYV farming practices (see Farmer 1977). This trend is examined in more detail in relation to Karagahapitiya in the following pages. Despite high levels of adoption in the village, this had not led to any serious impact on the level of tenancy, as was seen in the previous section. This feature obviously has important implications with regard to the level of wage labour as noted above. Intensive farming and increases in the demand for labour are not always interrelated. A labour use survey undertaken in Sri Lanka in 1983 has shown the total number of man days per acre for new crop varieties to have increased by just over 5, from 47.8 man days for traditional varieties to 52.9 for new varieties. The impact on overall labour demand has consequently been rather limited (Herath 1983). Undoubtedly, levels of mechanisation will offset labour demand but, despite this, in the context of the Punjab, Rudra (1971) has noted a 40 percent increase in agricultural employment, compared to a rather lower 10.6 percent found above for Sri Lanka. In Indonesia, Collier (1981) argues that farmers seem to be using less labour during pre harvest cultivation practices when compared to the labour input in work days for former local varieties. In addition to this he notes that changes in the method of harvesting, where cultivators now sell their crop to middlemen before the harvest, have further reduced agricultural employment (Collier 1981:156).

Despite the assumed development of organised wage labour stemming from recent agricultural improvements in production technology, the actual incidence of wage labour may vary greatly under different conditions. Perera and Gunawardena point to high levels of wage labour in peasant agriculture in an Agrarian Research and Training Institute (ARTI) nine village sample in Sri Lanka (ARTI 1980b). Drawing upon earlier ARTI rural studies which showed the proportion of cash outlay for hired labour to total outlay as being 44 percent in Kandy and 47 percent in Anuradhapura, the authors demonstrate that full time wage labour, with the exception of two sample villages, accounts for more than 35 percent of total labour and can reach 76 percent. When this is aggregated with part time labour the figures increase to over 55 percent and 87 percent respectively (ARTI 1980b).

In a labour resource use survey (1974) on the Minipe colonisation scheme, Amerasinghe (1984) found that after the introduction of HYVs, the use of hired labour rose by 100 percent to a point where it constituted 51 percent of the total labour force. However, he concluded that each additional unit of hired labour contributed an amount in productivity terms which was less than the cost of hiring that same labour resulting in a somewhat irrational use of hired labour. When compared to these findings the situation in Karagahapitiya examined appears to be quite different. Interestingly, in the ARTI nine village study, a sample from the wet zone of Kurunegala district showed that only 14 percent of the total labour force constituted a category of full time labourers and a further 14 percent were part time labourers, whereas 72 percent were either owner cultivators or tenants (ARTI 1980b).

A detailed labour survey was conducted in Karagahapitiya village in order to examine the structure of labour use in general and the level of wage labour in particular. Having broken down the main labour components of the farming operation for paddy cultivation into twenty two separate stages, data was gathered on the level of family labour, exchange labour and wage labour for each stage, expressed as equivalent man hours per household. This data was then supplemented by the number of man hours hired out per household for both farming and non farming activities. The results of these findings are expressed in table 4.7 in terms of the various tenurial categories. The total amount of wage labour employed on paddy cultivation is expressed as a percentage of total labour employed. The same percentage relation is also given independently for family and exchange labour.

Table 4.7 demonstrates that both tenant categories operate in a similar way with regard to wage labour in relation to the more traditional family and exchange labour forms. The wage labour component for tenants was higher than for owner cultivators, reflecting a greater tendency for tenants to hire out their labour power than owners. This was most likely due to the fact that tenants required supplementary income since they only received a share of their total harvest. Landlord operators maintained the highest wage labour component at 36.6 percent of total labour employed. Family labour dominated in all of the tenurial categories. Part tenants appeared to use more exchange labour and less family labour than full tenants. This could be explained by the slightly larger holding size of part tenants over full tenants. Over eighty percent of owner cultivators labour was supplied by the family and exchange labour, representing the highest proportion of family labour among all categories while landlord operators used less of both at 63.4 percent, preferring to substitute family and exchange inputs for wage labour. However, in no farm category did a combination of the traditional labour arrangements, in the form of family and exchange labour, account for less than 63 percent of the total labour use and the average for all categories stood at just under 80 percent against an average of 25 percent for wage labour. Table 4.8 below expresses the same data in terms of farm size rather than tenurial category.

Table 4.7 Household labour use by tenurial category as a percentage of total farm labour

Tenurial Category	Family %	Exchange %	Hired %	Family & Exchange %
Full–Tenants	63.9	13.5	22.6	77.4
Part–Tenants	57.8	19.9	22.3	77.7
Owner Cultivators	62.6	18.8	18.6	81.4
Landlord Operators	50.5	12.9	36.6	63.4

Table 4.8 Household labour use by farm size as a percentage of total farm labour

Farm Size in Acres	Family %	Exchange %	Hired %	Family & Exchange %
< 1	56.9	19.2	22.9	76.1
1 – 1.9	53.4	17.2	29.4	70.6
> 2	67.2	4.8	28.0	72.0

Most farm land, as previously shown, was held in units of under two acres and the majority of holdings fell in the less than one acre category. Table 4.8 demonstrates that small farmers used less wage labour and more family and exchange labour than larger farmers. The intermediate category, farming between one and two acres seemed to use less family and exchange labour and more wage labour. Interestingly, the few larger farmers with land over two acres, engaged family labour more fully than any other category but seemed to use little exchange labour. This could be due to the fact that most larger farmers were full time farmers and at the same time remained more isolated from the majority of their neighbours and other villagers. Unable to draw on regular exchange labour, these farmers employed wage labour to make up 28 percent of their total requirement. Once again the average wage labour component was much smaller than the traditional components at around 27 percent compared to 73 percent respectively. The proportional use of wage labour per household as seen above, could also be examined in relation to those cultivating households predominantly engaged in off-farm employment and in relation to the remaining full time cultivating households.

Table 4.9 Household labour use by principal economic activity

Economic Activity	Family %	Exchange %	Hired %	Family & Exchange %
Off-farm	52.9	16.6	30.5	69.5
Farm	62.1	16.0	21.9	78.1

Table 4.9 demonstrates that there is little fundamental difference in labour use between those farming households that were fully engaged in cultivation and those who maintained off-farm employment as their main source of income but nevertheless still operated smallholdings. This latter category used less family labour and more wage labour than full time farming households reflecting their reduced availability for some farming operations. Both categories used roughly the same amount of exchange labour. With a high level of family labour supplemented by exchange labour, totalling just under 70 percent. Part time farmers preferred, whenever possible, to work their own smallholdings with their own labour power in the method of the traditional family farm. Once again this is not a surprising result when it is considered that the majority of these part time cultivators were found to be clustered at the bottom end of a landholding distribution scale at under one acre per household.

All these results indicate that wage labour in paddy farming is an accepted and adopted component of total farm labour but rarely accounts for more than one third of total labour use in farm households. Before examining in the nature of wage labour compared to family and exchange labour in more detail, account must be taken of a remaining category of households so far unexamined. This group comprised the non landowning or non land operating households, although as previously shown nearly all village households had access to at least some coconut highland. This group numbered fifty one

116

households in total and accounted for exactly one third of all village households. Over 70 percent of these non farming families were engaged in regular off-farm employment and their activities will be examined in the following chapter. The remaining 29 percent are of particular interest at present since they come close to constituting a landless wage labour category. Table 4.10 highlights the distribution of all households by number and percentage for each tenurial group of farm and part time farm households, compared to non farming households and landless labourers.

Table 4.10 Distribution of total households by employment category

Nonfarm Operators	No	%
landless labourer	15	9.8
regular waged	36	23.5
total	51	33.3
Farm Operators		
full tenants	26	17.0
part tenants	25	16.3
owner cultivators	28	18.3
landlord operators	17	11.1
landlords	6	3.9
total	102	66.6

The landless wage labour group which totalled fifteen households was the smallest single category, assuming that the two landlord subcategories are combined. This group could be distinguished from the majority of nonfarm operators by the fact that their livelihood depended upon securing casual labouring opportunities, predominantly within the village, as opposed to the more regular employees of the external regional economy. There were a number of interesting features that related to this small labouring group. Very few of the households were of up country or Kandyan *goyigama* (cultivator caste) descent and could consequently be differentiated from the vast majority of villagers and especially those families claiming a long standing hereditary link with the village. Of the total fifteen labouring families, The majority were low caste. None of these labouring households depended solely on income from paddy farming work. They were engaged in a number of diverse labouring activities predominantly centred on work commonly referred to as 'highland labour'. This encompassed manual labouring on coconut land, such as the digging of irrigation ditches and occasional planting and fertilising, working in home gardens and house construction, extension and repairs. This highland income was in most cases supplemented by small amounts of other off-farm income. Here, members of the household undertook *cadjun* (coconut fronds) weaving, coconut husking for local traders, carpentry, wood carving, cooking snacks for local roadside stalls and even the selling of *kasipu*, an illicit liquor distilled from local fruits. A number of the older family members of the washer caste households continued to undertake caste duties at ceremonies and life cycle rituals for a cash income.

Wage labouring in paddy was in many cases less important to these households than other labouring activities on coconut estates, on home compounds and around the village. Given that the most intensive wage labouring activity in rice cultivation is transplanting, which is almost exclusively undertaken by female labour, male householders were forced to seek labouring work from wherever possible. A final point concerning this group of landless labourers is related to how they came to be in their current position. The general limitation of the physical expansion of farm land alongside a gradual increase in the availability of off-farm employment has meant that landlords have tended not to view paddy farming as an attractive commercial proposition. Consequently, there has been little incentive for landowners to develop a fully commercial production system, unlike other parts of the dry zone where conditions might be more favourable. Traditional forms of tenancy were still widely operated in the village and tenant farmers had not been evicted from their former landholdings to find themselves as disenfranchised labourers. The social characteristics of the landless group indicated that they did not originate from the village but came to settle from neighbouring areas a number of generations ago. Their main problem was not one of eviction but their failure to have found land to operate in the first place. In the past their caste status would have been a barrier to securing a satisfactory landholding and this is still the case for prime paddy land. Having encroached onto marginal highland where they were able to meet the most pressing need of securing land on which to build a rudimentary house, they were then forced to make a living from whatever means possible. This has meant engaging their labour power in a number of activities of which wage labour in rice cultivation is simply one component in their overall economic strategy.

The changing systems of labour

Although wage labour accounted for less than family labour, its use had undoubtedly increased over the years to a position where by 1984 it appeared to exceed that of exchange labour. Taking the average use of hired labour per household for each tenurial group compared to the average use of exchange labour, hired labour exceeded exchange labour by 54 percent. The nature of modern farming depending upon the timely execution and completion of various cultivation tasks has assisted this change of labour use even if there is some debate as to whether or not these new practices actually increase the total demand for labour. Chinnappa and Silva (1977) argue, contrary to Herath (1983), that total labour use has increased significantly as a result of HYV farming and they refer to Amerasinghe's findings in 1972 of a 31 percent increase in labour use on the Minipe colonisation scheme. The labour survey findings in Karagahapitiya indicated that there was a relatively high overall demand for labour but as Chinnappa and Silva (1977) found in Hambantota district, there were few operations, with the exception of transplanting, that were exclusively carried out by hired labour. Other operations that often involved an element of hired labour included field preparation, weeding and the application of chemical inputs but none of these were by any means exclusive to hired labour.

Although there has been an attempt by extension staff to popularise transplanting by drawing attention to related output increases, farmers in the village had not widely adopted this technique for two critical reasons. The first was the greater need for water when transplanting which, in spite of the provision of the new tank, was not always available. This was demonstrated by prevailing conditions prior to sowing during the 1983–84 cultivation season, when the lack of water forced nearly all farmers to broadcast rather than transplant. The second reason was the cost of hired labour for transplanting. At 1983–84 wage rates of Rs 15 per female labourer per day, the cost to an employer amounted to around Rs 450 per acre, rising to Rs 600 per acre by 1984, as female daily wage rates rose to Rs 20 per day. Male wage rates throughout this same period rose from Rs 20 to Rs 25 per day. Hired labour for transplanting was obtained through one of the two or three female labour gangs known by the participants as a *kandayama*. Each group was headed up by a gang leader whose task was to coordinate all labour activity for transplanting, acting as an intermediary between farmer and labourer. The gang leaders occupied a higher status within the group than the ordinary members and as a result of their position were able to manipulate contracts and negotiations in their favour. In terms of general prestige and status in the village as a whole, however, wage labouring in paddy was not well regarded and the majority of female householders were keen to emphasise that they did not labour in the fields for daily wages. Since virtually all transplanting labour was obtained through the gang process, the groups become semi–institutionalised. The gang leaders argued that their labourers were professional transplanters and thus more efficient than exchange labour, allowing timely completion and the chance for farmers to begin the numerous post transplanting operations. The final profit to a gang leader after collecting her own wage roughly amounted to the equivalent of two days wages.

In spite of irrigation water from the rehabilitated tank, transplanting was not as widespread as might be expected. Dias (1977) notes that transplanting has been the least adopted component of the new HYV farming method in Sri Lanka despite the fact that it prevents early lodging and therefore raises yields. He notes an adoption level for transplanting of 18 percent which compares to 17 percent noted by the ARTI's five village investigation of 1974 (Dias 1977). Hired labour appeared to be used by farmers who could not draw upon an adequate supply of family and exchange labour for peak cultivation operations. The cause of demand was based upon demographic and circumstantial factors rather than the structure of the agricultural production hierarchy. Some households did not possess the requisite number of family hands to undertake specific operations while other households were headed by the elderly or infirm. Of two households who exclusively employed wage labour for all operations, one was that of an outsider with off–farm employment and insufficient contacts in the village to engage exchange labour while the other was that of an elderly former government servant in the who could no longer undertake intensive labouring work. Many part time cultivators with regular off–farm employment hired labour for land preparation since they were unable to maintain domestic buffaloes of their own for ploughing. With the exception of transplanting work, hired labour tended to be randomly recruited from within the village. Some employers had regular links with particular labourers while others switched according to their preferences and needs.

No farmer liked to depend exclusively on wage labour employment and there was a marked status attached to operating one's own land, even if this was held under tenancy. Farmers claimed that wage labourers 'do not do good work' yet they also admitted that the transplanters, for example, were far quicker and more skilled than themselves. Meanwhile, the practice of engaging labourers on a contract basis for a fixed task rather than paying daily wages was seen as a means of checking labour inefficiency. By no means were all labourers inefficient. On one occasion a labourer was observed to be told to slow down by his employer since he was working too hard. When questioned as to why he exerted himself in this manner he argued that 'it was preferable to do one's best in the field than to be reborn a buffalo'. Consequently, the situation in the village was similar to that found by Robinson (1975) in Morapitiya nearly ten years earlier, where farmers claimed that hired labour should not be used for paddy cultivation as it was considered 'not good for the paddy'. Robinson argues that very few Morapitiyans work as hired labour, with female transplanters being the only exception to this rule (1975). Despite the fact that villagers in Karagahapitiya did not seem to engage in the large scale institutional hiring of labour, they did argue that it was the only way to overcome peak labour shortages. Farmers tended to stop short of making the type of claims that Morapitiyans made when they argued that hiring labour for important work would only produce inequality within the village and that those villages that did not practice exchange labour could never improve their economic position (Robinson 1975). Cultural norms concerned with paddy cultivation did not prevent the hiring of labour in Karagahapitiya but there did appear to be an optimum level for wage labour beyond which full time labourers had to seek employment elsewhere. The outcome of all this was the development of a situation broadly similar to that described by Chinnappa and Silva (1977) where the proportion of people deriving their main source of income from agricultural labour remained low and the new demand for labour was met essentially by part time agricultural workers comprising other cultivators and non cultivators whose major source of income was from diverse casual labouring activities.

The combination of family and exchange labour made up the majority of total labour input into agriculture. Family labour would often involve everyone in the household over twelve years of age. Adult females would transplant and winnow and would be assisted by young girls for weeding and filing. Boys engaged themselves in many of the male tasks and started to plough at around fifteen years of age. Family labour also included close relations living independently in the same house or in adjacent buildings on or near to the family compound. The small size of landholdings meant that a large proportion of total labour needs could be met from the cultivator's own household. This corresponds to the labour use characteristics of Welivita found by Silva 91973) in the Kandyan region.

Two other forms of non contractual labour also existed. The first was a family based voluntary system revolving around close kin. Some householders saw this as an extension of parental respect or duty, depending upon who was performing the voluntary labour. This labour form encompassed all non household labour provided by an extended family group who might live quite separately in the village. It was not part of any formal system of exchange labour but had been classified above in the exchange labour category. In many respects, with the breakdown of a certain level of cooperation in the modern village setting, it was this informal voluntary labour that constituted the majority of non family household labour. With the changing pattern of marriage and kinship seen in the previous section, most voluntary labour outside one's immediate family came from a father's brother's sons, rather than from the more traditional cross cousin link of a mother's brother's male offspring, with whom one had a more informal joking relationship. The second source of intermediate labour came from those non family members who reported working on a *nikan enavaa* (just coming) basis. In its broadest sense this category could include all the voluntary labour of extended family members, as it does for Robinson (1975) who states that its members comprise the 'effective *pavula*' or family of 'first degree relations'. However, it may be useful to distinguish this semi-voluntary labour of effective kin from that of neighbours and friends. *Nikan* labour from the latter two groups was mainly reported from older teenagers or unemployed youths who had not yet secured any land of their own to operate. Again this source of labour has been classified as exchange labour.

The traditional exchange labour system was known as *attam* and was most often used during harvesting operations. Pieris (1956) mentions that the whole village would help each other by performing *attam* on a task specific reciprocal basis such as reaping, until every man's harvest had been cut. Robinson cites the former observations of Robert Knox to demonstrate the long historical roots of a system where all villagers cooperated in the reaping of each others' fields, moving from one to the next until the task was complete. Morapitiyan village ideology represented in statements to Robinson such as 'we are all kinsmen in this village and everyone helps everyone else' and 'if ten come to help you then you will help at those ten households', demonstrate the continuing importance of a system of directly reciprocal cooperative labour (Robinson 1975: 62). Where *attam* still existed it tended to operate within a more restricted network than on a village wide basis, in the form of an action set (Robinson 1975). In Karagahapitiya, recent changes meant that few villagers expressed the sentiments noted in Morapitiya. Rather than extolling the virtues of large scale labour cooperation, cultivators were more inclined to outline the problems associated with *attam*. For example, the need to adhere to a strict timetable in farming meant that cultivators felt that a system of direct reciprocation would result in the creation of a serious time lag in their operational schedule. Also with a large number of part time cultivators attending regular employment outside the village, direct labour reciprocation was difficult if not impossible to administer.

The system of exchange labour that operated in the village was more closely associated with the former *kaiya* arrangement. Pieris (1956) states that *kaiya* was a system of requested assistance in which a land operator or shareholder would go about the village offering betel leaves and informing recipients of the time, nature and place of work to be done. In turn, these helpers could expect the reciprocal labour services of their host at a later date (Pieris 1956). Villagers argued that the difference between *kaiya* and the system they termed *kiyanavaa* (telling) was the size of the work group and its level of formality. Contemporary exchange labour groups seemed to operate with three or four helpers whereas *kaiya* groups were at least double or treble the size. In the *kaiya* system more concern was attached to the form of reciprocation. *Kiyanavaa* was also based upon the issuing of an invitation to request assistance but any reciprocal obligations were less formally adhered to and often the host was someone who was quite unlikely to be able to reciprocate in labour terms due to off-farm commitments. Villagers claimed that this system of voluntary labour worked well for those who knew how to 'win over' others and depended upon having good social relations and certain powers of brokerage. If people respected the host they were unlikely to reject his request for assistance. In return they might expect to draw directly upon the host for financial assistance, advice or intervention, in a matter concerning some external authority. Alternatively, they might simply feel confident that, should the need arise, their association with the host would help to secure them in the future.

Forms of cooperative or exchange labour were less prevalent than in the past and elderly villagers expressed concern at the breakdown of communal working arrangements. Hired labour had not replaced exchange labour but to some extent competed with it in the total farming system. Interestingly, very little hired labour was needed for any of the harvesting operations since virtually all exchange arrangements took place at this time. The type of smallholder farming that existed in Karagahapitiya meant that farms could run for the most part on family labour. The introduction of modern farming techniques has necessitated the more widespread use of hired labour amongst all farmers, particularly in the peak seasons as farmers struggle to overcome the bottlenecks of the production cycle. This development has occurred alongside a gradual erosion in traditional patterns of cooperation, although hired labour has not replaced the use of exchange labour which has itself become less formalised. Contemporary exchange labour works in favour of those farmers with outside employment who have access to broader political and economic advantages dispensed through the State and the regional economy. Part time farmers, meanwhile, could secure exchange labour without the burden of direct reciprocal obligations. These exchange services were especially useful during the labour intensive operations of harvesting, where the observance of certain customary practices has meant the continued preference shown for more traditional harvesting labour arrangements. The use of hired labour in agriculture is similar to that found in Malaysia by Horii (1981) where the dominant economic rationality was not seen to be the maximisation of profit on the basis of a cost and return calculation.

Capital investment and the level of accumulation

The level of capital reproduction and its relation to the structure of the market plays a critical role in determining the overall pattern of capital accumulation and surplus appropriation. The purpose of this section, therefore, will be to examine the various forms of capital investment in Karagahapitiya village in relation to different farm size groups in order to highlight any monopoly over the effective use of such investment in the sphere of production or circulation and exchange. To this end it will be necessary to reveal the institutional characteristics of the distribution and marketing system over inputs, technology, credit, extension and output. Since expanded reproduction can be directly achieved through a combination of current and fixed capital expenditure in inputs and technology respectively, it will be useful to consider these investment strategies first. This will then be followed by an examination of different forms of credit, institutional support and a discussion of the operation of the market in paddy and trading activities.

The component of capital expenditure that has been most responsible for expanded reproduction in the form of increased productivity in the village has been investment in the various inputs associated with the green revolution technology. Here, it is considered correct to employ the term 'new technology' in relation to the introduction of agricultural developments in Karagahapitiya despite Rudra's (1971) claim in India that the widespread adoption of an input package does not in itself constitute a new technology. In Sri Lanka there has been a considerable advance in seed research, much of it pioneered in Kurunegala district at the Batalagoda Research Station. HYV seeds have been introduced into Karagahapitiya in three phases. The early HYVs, which had been cross-bred with certain improved traditional varieties, were released for cultivation during the 1950s and became widely established in the village by the early 1960s.

This first phase of adoption which included H series strains such as H.7 and the second phase, which introduced the new dwarf varieties developed from IR8 and TN1 such as the three month BG 34-8, all gradually led to the displacement of traditional strains. Prior to the rehabilitation of the tank in the late 1970s there was only one regular cropping per annum and it was still common for farmers to grow traditional varieties such as *hondarawala* during the dry season. Other traditional strains that were grown prior to the tank were *heenati* or *kalu heenati* and *kiri kurumba*. Farmers pointed out that by the early 1970s they had become 'addicted' to BG 34-8. The third phase of seed adoption came with the tank and an established regime of double cropping. This period has seen the triumph of BG 34-8 as the most popular variety grown in the village. Although a few farmers still cultivated a traditional variety known as *pachcha perumal* during the dry season, no farming household was observed to cultivate only a traditional variety. The adoption of new HYVs has been total.

In spite of this, farmers were still keen to point certain advantages of traditional cropping. They argued that the older varieties required little water and no artificial fertiliser. Farmers would obtain natural manure by encouraging buffalo and cattle to graze on the fallow land during the dry season. In this way their fields had time to regain natural fertility. Nevertheless, these qualities have been almost totally displaced by the new HYVs which allow for a much greater increase in productivity. Dias (1977) points to field trials that have shown that under favourable conditions the new three to three and a half month varieties can yield between 120-140 bushels per acre and that even the earlier H series could yield 80 bushels per acre, although somewhere between 40-80 bu per acre was probably more typical for these varieties.

The new HYVs that were well established in the village by 1983-84. They required a regular source of water and the application of fertiliser, weedicide and pesticide. Farmers argued that it was only since the construction of the tank that they have been able to apply a reasonable level of these inputs which had led to a marked increase in overall productivity. Without the assurance of water they had been reluctant to invest in the new technology package.

Fertiliser is perhaps the key input of this package. Long years of cultivation in the village have reduced the natural fertility of the land. Since the introduction of double cropping, cattle graze much less on the fields and the source of biotic fertiliser has been greatly reduced. Fertiliser is applied in three forms at three distinct stages of cultivation. The first application of a basal dressing takes place just prior to sowing at a recommended quantity of 75 kilos per acre. This application, commonly termed 'mud' fertiliser contains 30 percent super phosphate and 4 percent urea. Basal fertiliser is designed to benefit the structure and length of the root.

Table 4.11 Percentage adoption of basal by tenurial category and farm size (acres), maha 1983–84

Tenurial Category	% Adoption	% Incorrect Application
full tenant	78.5	71.4
part tenant	94.4	55.5
owner cultivator	88.8	38.8
landlord cultivator	84.6	46.1
Size		
< 1	90.3	61.2
< 2	87.5	66.6
> 2	100.0	66.6

Although basic data on input use was collected from all farming households, only sixty three farmers could reliably estimate the actual quantity used for the 1983–84 wet season. These farmers are represented in tables 4.11 and 4.12 for different tenurial and size categories respectively. The highest adoption rate of basal dressing amongst the tenurial categories was for part tenant cultivators followed by owners and landlord cultivators successively. Full tenants had the lowest adoption rate at just over 78 percent. Yields ultimately depend on the correct use of fertiliser and the tables 4.11 – 4.12 indicate that incorrect application is prevalent, especially among tenant farmers. There was little size to adoption correlation between the operational holding groups. The overall adoption of basal was over 90 percent. This compares to a figure of 30 percent found by Dias (1977) in a study in the southern part of the country more than ten years earlier.

The second application of fertiliser is urea which contains 46 percent nitrogen. Urea helps the plant to grow and the results are most obvious to the casual observer. It is applied around two weeks after planting and in two phases for broadcasted seed. The recommended quantity is around 37 kilos per acre. The percentage of incorrect adoption for urea represented over application whereas for basal dressing it was largely under adoption.

Table 4.12 Percentage adoption of urea by tenurial category and farm size (acres), maha 1983–84

Tenurial Category	% Adoption	% Incorrect Application
full tenants	92.8	7.1
part tenants	94.1	11.7
owner cultivators	100.0	nil
landlord cultivators	100.0	nil
Size		
< 1	96.7	3.2
< 2	95.8	8.3
> 2	100.0	11.1

Table 4.12 shows that urea was more widely applied and used in greater quantity than was recommended by the extension service. Farmers were strongly influenced by the immediate change in size and appearance of the plant following the application of urea. The overall adoption rate of urea was found to be nearly 97 percent which compares to 78 percent found by Dias 1977).

The third and final type of fertiliser consists of a top dressing and is usually applied between four to six weeks after planting or sowing depending on whether the seed has been transplanted or broadcast. The recommended quantity was around 50 kilos per acre. The top dressing contains 30 percent nitrogen and 20 percent potash designed to promote a large pod with an optimum weight that is disease resistant. Paradoxically, some farmers admitted not applying the top dressing for the very reason that they felt it tended to attract pests. On the whole there was a more consistent trend in the incorrect adoption of the top dressing which was higher among full tenants and smaller

126

farmers. The adoption rate of top dressing was 88 percent and, although it was the least adopted fertiliser component, its overall adoption was high.

All the evidence indicates that, as far as fertiliser adoption was concerned, there was a lower overall adoption level among full tenants than with other tenurial categories. Whereas small owner cultivators and part tenant cultivators had a higher average adoption rate than landlord cultivators. This suggests that small farmers, many of whom have external income, have a higher income to input ratio which has ultimately enabled them to adopt at levels sometimes exceeding larger farmers and to under utilise less often than larger farmers. An explanation for the lower levels observed among full tenants is the fact that their land tended to be at the tail end of the irrigation system and they often experienced insufficient water to allow for the adoption and correct use of fertiliser. Part tenants on the other hand often owned land further upstream and were thus less constrained by lack of water. In summary, it can be stated that adoption levels were very high although the quantities applied were rarely correct.

The application of chemical weedicides and insecticides was also widespread. Four popular types of weedicide were commonly used. The most popular being one that was used for controlling all annual grains, broadleafed weeds and sedges. Weedicide was less commonly applied, however, than fertiliser, since alternative forms of weed control such as flooding and hand weeding were still widely practised. The percentage adoption of weedicide from the total sample stood at just over 71 percent.

Table 4.13 Percentage adoption of chemicals by tenurial category and farm size (acres) 1983–84

Tenurial Category	% Adoption
full tenant	64.2
part tenant	82.3
owner cultivator	100.0
landlord cultivator	100.0
Size in Acres	
< 1	87.0
< 2	91.6
> 2	77.7

Over ten brands of insecticides were regularly applied in both liquid and powder form. The percentage adoption of insecticide from the total sample was 82 percent. Farmers rarely controlled insects by biotic methods such as maintaining high water levels, encouraging crabs, cranes and other birds into the fields, using night lanterns to attract insects, or by adhering to a strict cultivation timetable. Adoption of weedicide and insecticide was less for tenants than owner cultivators yet the adoption rate was inversely related to farm size reflecting the large proportion of owner cultivators and landlord cultivators who operated holdings of less than two acres. The use of chemical inputs was high although the figures above demonstrate the lower use of weedicide compared to insecticide.

All this has obviously contributed to raising productivity over the last few years. Elsewhere, agricultural economists have estimated that the absence of pesticides can reduce total output by as much as 30 percent (Weeraratne 1983). An indication of the high HYV adoption level for Sri Lanka as a whole has been noted in a study contrasting this situation with Tamil Nadu (see Farmer 1977). Here, as Harriss (1977) demonstrates, adoption levels among tenant farmers in Hambantota district were higher than for owner cultivators. Having broken down the adoption statistics for all inputs by farm size and tenurial category without revealing any significant concentration of productive current expenditure, it will now be useful to examine the nature of capital expenditure.

Capital expenditure

The widespread use of HYV seeds and associated inputs can be contrasted with a much lower introduction and use of capital equipment in the form of farm machinery. Rotary weeders and seeders were rarely used by farmers in the village and no household owned such equipment. Mechanised ploughing, threshing and winnowing were more commonly practised but for the most part ploughing was still undertaken with the aid of buffalo. The introduction of capital investment into the farming process in the form of increased tractorisation is a growing trend in Sri Lanka. Ahmed (1974) has shown the scale of this process by revealing the number of four wheel and two wheel tractors imported from the mid 1950s onwards. The use of tractors for farming is more widespread under dry zone farming conditions than under the intermediate conditions of the village where the average size of holding is smaller and the density of population higher.

In considering some of the broader implications of tractor use in Hambantota district, Harriss B (1977) draws attention to an earlier study by Carr in 1973 showing that more than 25 percent of tractors were not used for agricultural work and that 40 percent of tractor time was non agricultural. Of the one hundred and two farming households in the village, five were tractor owners. Only two of these tractors were predominantly used for agricultural purposes, one of which happened to be the only four wheeler. The remaining two wheel tractors were well occupied during the latter stages of the harvesting process, in particular for winnowing and transporting paddy, but other than this, and some use during land preparation, these tractors were mainly engaged for local haulage purposes relating to their owners' off-farm business activities. Tractors were used most frequently for threshing and winnowing. Of thirty cases where land preparation and harvesting practices were directly observed by the author, it was noted that tractors were used in twenty six and twenty one cases respectively for threshing and winnowing. They were only used in five cases for land preparation. Land preparation and winnowing was carried out almost exclusively by two wheeler while the four wheeler was mainly used for threshing. Harriss B (1977) has shown that a four wheeler has to be used roughly five times more frequently than a two wheeler in order to achieve relative profitability, with a slightly lower annual average rate of return on capital at 53.5 percent compared to 58 percent for a two wheeler.

Few households engaged in any form of mechanised land preparation, with 83 percent of farmers preferring to use buffaloes for two ploughings and a final puddling and levelling. This compares to an identical 83 percent found by the ARTI (1981a) pre project survey in Kurunegala district. Farmers pointed out that ploughing by buffalo allowed the subsoil to be compacted over time which improved the water retention capability of the soil. They also pointed to other related benefits such as a ready source of organic fertiliser which could be spread over the rice fields during fallow season grazing. These ecological and economic advantages have been emphasised by Senanayake (1983). He shows that tractorisation reduces the farm labour requirement by as much as nine man days per acre which is a severe disadvantage in a situation of high rural underemployment. Tractors are also subject to rapidly increasing operational costs of over four times that of buffalo ploughing. He also confirms the advantages of the 'hard pan' produced by buffalo trampling and mentions other ecological advantages associated with traditional ploughing techniques. There has, however, been a considerably higher level of mechanisation in the harvesting process. Winnowing is carried out with the aid of a fan attachment driven by the engine of a two wheeler. Few farmers claim to prefer traditional hand winnowing. Despite the levels of tractor use for threshing and winnowing there is still a high labour requirement during both processes.

Credit

An early survey conducted by Amunugama (1964) into the sociological aspects of rural credit reviewed the state of credit facilities and the role of indebtedness in Sri Lanka. He observed that institutional credit needed to be more flexible to deal with the twin problems of farmers' inability to raise collateral as security against high rates of defaulting and the timing of credit in relation to the farming cycle. Farmer (1957) had earlier noted that most rural debt in the dry zone revolved around direct consumption needs as opposed to agricultural requirements with a high percentage of villagers being in debt to the local *mudalali* (shopkeeper) or landlord.

The credit system has since evolved and expanded in line with national attempts to raise agricultural productivity and reduce external debt resulting from the high import cost of foodstuffs. As the agricultural system has moved away from a traditional pattern of reciprocal rights and duties with services being transformed into commodities within a highly fragmented smallholder environment, indebtedness has become an extreme problem. Based on the prevailing productivity levels of the early 1970s Jogaratnam and Schickele estimated that most farms were under sized and involved in a low debt low productivity technology cycle while Jayaweera (1973) pointed to the consequent need to improve the institutional credit system if farmers were to employ and exploit the new technology. Ironically, measures that were taken by the United Front Government in 1972 to eradicate merchant capital profiteering had disastrous results when non institutional lenders, deprived of the ability to engage in paddy marketing, and consequently to hold security over loans, were forced to reduce their lending activities. At the same time institutional sources cut lending due to high rates of defaulting.

A number of changes have taken place in the institutional credit sector since then. Under the Agricultural Credit Scheme of 1967 commercial banks entered the rural credit market. A refinancing scheme for agricultural loans provided low interest credit for production purposes at an interest rate of 9 percent. The ceiling on each loan was Rs 2,400 per acre per season (1984). Other loans for housing, construction and machinery were outside the refinancing scheme and charged at a rate of 23 percent with a ceiling of Rs 15,000 later increased to Rs 35,000 (1984). Loans for trading, redemption of debts or emergency loans were subject to a rate of 23 percent interest rising to 24 percent for consumption loans.

By 1984, around Rs 400,000 had been lent to 250 farmers in the form of production loans within the local electorate. This small number reflected past high rates of defaulting which had resulted in 65–75 percent of all potential borrowers in the electorate being categorised as defaulters or guarantors to defaulters and therefore not eligible to apply for further loans. Debt recovery on loans took place through the local committees of branch societies. Failing this, the Bank Services manager and Development Officer would visit farmers and demand payment within two weeks. If all this failed the parties were instructed to attend a Commissioner's inquiry before legal action was resorted to.

Once the village tank had been rehabilitated, the local Rural Bank Officer made a special effort to increase borrowing by publicising credit facilities and providing a special period to process applications. In spite of this, the bank received no applications during this period. By 1981 the village contained nine past defaulters on loans dating back to 1973. Table 4.14 outlines the main credit source for forty eight farming households, comprising twelve in each tenurial category over four cultivation seasons between 1982–84. The table represents just under 50 percent of all land operating households and encompasses only those debtors whose answers were checked with their respective creditors but does cover the spectrum of farming households from large farmers to small tenants.

Table 4.14 Distribution of credit sources by tenurial category over four seasons, 1984

Tenurial Category	Kin	Neighbour	Shop	Instit	None
full tenants	27.2	38.4	33.3		18.1
part tenants	36.3	38.4	16.6	14.2	9.O
owner cultivators	18.1	7.6	33.3	42.8	36.3
landlord cultivators	18.1	15.3	16.6	42.8	36.3

From this it is possible to see that tenants borrowed most often from kin and neighbours while landlords and owner cultivators appeared to depend on their own resources for financing agriculture, house building etc. The main points, however, are that among those surveyed, institutional credit was only used by 14.5 percent of households. This compares to a figure of 15 percent noted on a district wide basis by an ARTI survey (1981b). Kin ties and close contact with neighbours and friends were reported as a source of credit for nearly 50 percent of households. Twenty two percent of all households claimed to have no borrowing requirement. Most of the amounts borrowed were small (under Rs 500) but occasionally loans were much larger particularly, for house building, with one farmer claiming to have borrowed as much as Rs 25,000 from a relative working overseas. Institutional credit encompassed more than simply bank loans, which were only taken up by 6 percent of borrowers, since a further 6 percent arranged preferential low interest loans with their employers. Finance companies had few dealings with villagers although one resident purchased highland with a loan from a leading finance company. Over 20 percent of all borrowers claimed to be raising loans for agricultural purposes, 14.5 percent were borrowing for general consumption purposes, 10.4 percent for house building, and 8.3 percent for emergencies and 8 percent for other reasons.

Virtually all loans in the informal sector were private arrangements at zero interest including loans from local shopkeepers who were either related or well known to many of the villagers. The latter were usually only negotiated with a supplier of rice or coconuts who insisted that the loans be repaid in kind after the harvest when the prices were low. Institutional loans were perceived by many villagers to be too cumbersome and likely to involve the very real possibility of forced legal repayment. Farmers recalled a recent incident when two institutional borrowers in the village were summoned by the bank to repay a loan within a matter of weeks. These loans necessitate the kind of forward planning that farmers are unused to in order to ensure credit at the correct time. The ARTI (1981b) survey found that the two main reasons that made farmers reluctant to borrow from banks in Kurunegala district were, firstly, a lack of capacity to repay any outstanding loan and, secondly, little need for institutional credit in the first place. The bank manager concluded that the village was a very weak link in the formal credit chain. He argued that farmers did not take loans partly because they were able to cultivate without credit due to the small size of farm enterprises and access to off-farm or supplementary income and the low incidence of wage labour. He also pointed out that farmers credit needs were for small amounts which did not justify using institutional procedures.

As can be seen from the above, levels of expanded reproduction remain low as little investment in agriculture takes place beyond that needed for the highly divisible biochemical inputs. The landholding pattern demonstrates a continuing trend towards subdivision and fragmentation while the land tenure system serves to maintain traditional forms of tenancy without moving towards individual consolidation or forms of commercial contract. Meanwhile, the high level of adoption of biochemical inputs is consistent with developments in other rice growing economies where considerable investment has been made in providing the necessary agricultural infrastructure. This investment has not led to the development of agrarian capitalism reflected in an expanding large farm sector with increasing levels of accumulation and reinvestment but instead has served to reinforce the smallholder base upon which a diversified off-farm economy depends. Given that most employment in the off-farm sector in a typical South Asian setting is likely to be in local service related activities and that in these circumstances the growth potential of the rural industrial sector will not have been realised, total labour demand will rarely outstrip rural labour supply. Consequently, there has been little incentive to introduce labour saving machinery on a large scale. In this situation, credit demand has been largely met from informal or semi-formal sources and reflects the continuing smallholder character of the farm sector. Where credit has been obtained on any substantial scale it has mostly been for nonfarm purposes. Over 71 percent of the larger institutional loans, for example, were obtained for domestic house building purposes. At the same time rising levels of off-farm income represent an additional and important source of inward investment into the farm.

Finally, it may be useful to raise the question of the role of merchant capital in the agrarian economy. It is often assumed that surplus extracted from the merchant classes is reinvested in agriculture in a form that establishes large scale commercial farming. In Karagahapitiya, merchant capital has had an important influence on rural differentiation, partially through the operation of credit tied purchases of agricultural inputs and the milling of agricultural produce, but more crucially by divesting out of agriculture altogether. This can be illustrated by the fact that a number of leading merchants were pulling out of agriculture because of its lack of profitability resulting from the state manipulation of agricultural prices. Consequently there has been little capitalist restructuring of the agrarian economy dependent on merchant capital control of the production process. The direct investment of surplus value generated by merchant capital into agriculture was minimal. The leading village entrepreneurs were predominantly tenant farmers and where land had not been inherited there was an opposite trend to divestment out of agriculture. The largest entrepreneur claimed that he was seriously contemplating giving up farming altogether despite the fact that his tenanted land was held on a kin based sharecropping arrangement. He saw the opportunity cost of farming as being too high and not worth the labour investment. Exchange relations have not directly intervened over the production process but, on the contrary, could be seen to have initiated a process of disengagement from direct production.

5　The off-farm economy in rural Sri Lanka

Over the years Sri Lanka has experienced increasing pressure on land. Per capita land availability declined from 4.5 acres in 1901 to 1.1 acres by 1979 with an increase in population density from 55 persons per sq km in 1901 to 283 persons per sq km by 1983 (Arachchi 1985). Over 43 percent of all paddy holdings were found to be below one acre in size. In spite of a decline in the annual rate of rural population growth from 2.2 percent between 1953–63 to 1.8 percent between 1971–81, the economically active population almost doubled between 1946–81 (Arachchi 1985). The resulting pressure on land coupled to the strong seasonality of cultivation has encouraged extensive diversification into off–farm employment.

The trend towards off–farm employment and income in Sri Lanka has already been observed by one or two commentators. As long ago as 1962 the national census of Sri Lanka showed that 46 percent of agricultural smallholders were engaged in off–farm employment, 30 percent of whom claimed the majority of their income to be derived from off–farm sources compared to the remaining 16 percent who depended more upon agricultural earnings (Herath 1986). More recent evidence from Sri Lanka shows that off–farm employment continues to be an important source of rural income. Herath (1986) cites a number of examples that demonstrate its prevalence in the rural sector. Firstly, there are the findings of Jogaratnam in 1970 on the Elehera Colonisation Scheme where at least 15 percent of total income was seen to be generated outside agriculture despite the agricultural nature of the scheme. Secondly, a study by Herath (1980) in Kandy district revealed that

134

every farmer reported at least some off-farm earnings. A further study by Gunadasa, Wickramasekera and Herath (1980) on minor irrigation systems in nine dry zone districts found a universally high proportion of off-farm employment accounting for as much as 75 percent of total income in Trincomalee district. In Kurunegala and Hambantota, however, this figure was lower at 34 percent which still represents a substantial number of rural households.

The same pattern has been noted elsewhere in Asia as seen in chapter three. In West Malaysia, Horii (1981) argues that an important indicator of change can be found not only in the size of landholdings or agricultural productivity but in the changing employment pattern of agrarian households. He points out that in West Malaysia generally, the small size of farms coupled with relatively low productivity, have meant that farmers have sought other non agricultural sources of income. In a similar situation to that of Karagahapitiya village in Sri Lanka, he found that wage opportunities in the paddy sector were low and that forms of mutual assistance in rice farming such as voluntary and cooperative labour arrangements were still widely practised during harvesting between close kin and friends. Consequently, low wage opportunities in paddy reinforced by low wages in the cash crop sector have led, in West Malaysia, to a drift towards off-farm employment. In Indonesia White (1981) discusses a rather more complex response to rural employment from the local population in rural Java. He identifies that only a small proportion of working hours are actually spent in rice cultivation which is seen to have low returns to labour. Most people are therefore engaged in a multiplicity of activities, apart from rice cultivation, all with varying degrees of return. The maximisation of return to labour is achieved by the maintenance of a flexible response to current available opportunities.

In a rather similar finding to that of Horii (1981), Morrison et al (1979) note that a 50 percent increase in the population of the Kandyan area in Sri Lanka since the Kandyan Peasantry Report of 1951, has seriously intensified the pressure on land and forced villagers to seek alternative livelihoods. In Meegama village, Morrison demonstrates the declining size of landholdings between 1962–1976 to a point where the average holding size is three quarters of an acre, with an annual average yield of 75 bushels per acre.

Table 5.1 shows the distribution of the rural workforce by major economic activity. Agriculture still dominates rural sector employment but off-farm employment is nevertheless very substantial at just over 44 percent of total employment. As seen in the case of Kerala in chapter three, the bulk of off-farm activity is concentrated in the tertiary sector comprising a range of activities such as government service, health, transport, trading, retailing, banking etc. Of the 44 percent of the rural population engaged in off-farm employment, around 17 percent were classified as 'white collar' workers in the 1981 census.

Table 5.1   Percentage distribution of rural workforce by major economic activity

Sector		1963	1971	1981
primary	M	60.8	58.0	53.7
	F	72.4	70.2	63.1
	T	63.4	61.0	55.7
secondary	M	12.0	12.3	13.6
	F	9.9	12.4	10.1
	T	11.6	12.3	12.8
tertiary	M	27.2	29.7	32.7
	F	17.7	17.4	26.8
	T	25.0	26.7	31.5
total of-farm		36.6	39.0	44.3

Source from Arachchi (1985: 9)

Arachchi (1985) has examined the various components of the nonfarm sector in Sri Lanka in more detail. He shows that as far as small scale industry is concerned, the largest share of the 24,000 total units in 1971
was in the cottage sector which comprised over 46 percent of the total. The handloom sector stood at 25 percent and the factory sector at 20 percent of the total. A number of off-farm activities are concentrated in particular regions on account of the availability of raw materials or specialised skills. Examples of this include gem making, batik printing, cane and bamboo manufacturing etc. Coconut growing also provides a wide range of related off-farm work in copra, oil extraction, coir manufacturing (mats, ropes, brushes, rubberised coir etc), charcoal production and coconut trading.

A number of activities have expanded quite rapidly in recent years. Gems and batiks have grown in response to the tourist trade although the severe downturn in this business resulting from the ethnic and civil disturbances will have had a serious impact on many of these businesses. Carpentry and furniture making has expanded in response to domestic construction and the growth in public and private projects. Employment in transport has also expanded as a result of the influx of imported vehicles following the relaxation of import controls after 1977. Arachchi has drawn on census data to analyse employment in those activities associated with modern technology. The percentage change between 1971-81 for a variety of modern activities is presented in table 5.2. The table illustrates the growth of non traditional activities in the rural sector with the exception of machinery fitters etc. Most of this increase is in component, repairs and service type activity and much of it is based on the growth of consumer products in the rural economy. In this situation household survival strategies have become diverse with off-farm employment forming an important component of the village economy and class structure.

Table 5.2 Percentage change in employment in specific occupations (1971–81)

Occupation	% Change
machinery fitters, assemblers and precision instrument makers	– 8.2
electrical fitters, electrical and electronic workers	+ 103.7
plumbers, welders, sheet metal and structural metal workers	+ 27.0
transport operators	+ 25.8

Source from Arachchi (1985: 17)

Off-farm employment in Karagahapitiya village

An analysis of off-farm employment is central to an understanding of the nature of agrarian production relations and the emergence of a new class system at the local level. Both these issues will be discussed in relation to Karagahapitiya village in the remaining sections of this chapter. As Herath (1986) argues, agrarian economists and development analysts have largely ignored the role of off-farm employment in rural areas. Those households engaged in this sector have simply been categorised as a transitional group, either moving out of or into full time farming. He points out that off-farm employment is an integral part of the farming economy and is not a transitional labour system.

137

The importance of off-farm income in the village can be emphasised by drawing attention to the number of households reporting at least some off-farm earnings. A total of 114 households fell into this category, representing 74 percent of all households. The vast majority of village households had at least some links with the broader regional economy in direct employment terms, even if they did not depend upon these links as a main source of income. As seen below, however, off-farm income was more than a supplementary means of subsistence for 57 percent of all households in the village.

A large number of the total households in the village were predominantly engaged in off-farm employment. This group included those whose sole income was derived from regular off-farm employment and who possessed no paddy land and those cultivators who received more than 60 percent of their total income from off-farm sources. The number and percentage of households in the above category is represented in table 5.3 below.

Table 5.3 Household distribution of major income source by tenurial category

Tenurial Category	Farm		Off-Farm		Total	
	No	%	No	%	No	%
Landless	15	29.4	36	70.6	51	100
Tenant	31	60.8	20	39.2	51	100
Owner Cultivator	12	42.9	16	57.1	28	100
Landlord	8	34.8	15	65.2	23	100
Total	66	43.1	87	56.9	151	100

The proportion of off-farm to farm households is shown for each tenurial category including landless households which have been split into a regular waged and casual labouring category. Here, although casual labouring does not necessarily imply agricultural labouring, the majority of casual labourers generally found employment within the village. Table 5.3 shows that off-farm employment formed the central economic activity of all household categories except tenants, where it provided the main income for 39 percent of households. The group most fully engaged in off-farm employment was the landless agricultural category. This was due to the fact that there relatively few landless labouring households in the village. The majority of the landless households, constituting exactly one third of all households in the village, were not involved in farming at all. They were mostly newcomers to the village who had managed to buy non agricultural on which to reside, finding the village a convenient dormitory settlement for their work. The type of employment they were engaged in was fairly diverse and will be examined below. Among the remaining two thirds of households, all of whom retained access to paddy land either in the form of sharecropping or private ownership rights, the percentage of off-farm households rose through the tenurial categories from 39 percent for tenants to 65 percent for landlords. The total number of households predominantly engaged in off-farm earnings exceeded those dependent on farming by 57 percent to 43 percent respectively.

The availability of off-farm employment opportunities was partly due to the physical setting of the village in geographical terms and partly due to State policy. Being situated just under ten miles from the district capital which has become a thriving regional centre and less than two miles from many of the headquarters facilities for Hiriyala electorate, villagers have good access to regional employment opportunities. Being located at the junction of two main roads local transport facilities are also good. Successive governments in Sri Lanka have encouraged the regional decentralisation of services throughout the countryside and villagers have been able to secure outside jobs while remaining residents of the village. Since the majority of public and private sector employees are not part of a migratory workforce their social base remains very much in the village. The evidence of this decentralised employment programme coupled with the State's policy of promoting smallholder farming, which together form the basis of a diversified rural economy, can be seen in the low rates of urban migration for Sri Lanka.

The employment pattern and class structure in Karagahapitiya appears reasonably complex. There is, for example, no clear correlation between landholding size or indeed landlessness and the quality of employment, although job quality and security of income are related. Exactly one third of all households were strictly categorised as landless with no access to paddy land. Of the fifty-one landless households, 70 percent were employed in regular off-farm activities with a remaining 29 percent were engaged as casual farm and off-farm labourers. There was no landholding differential that determined which category a particular household was likely to fall into. Of the 70 percent group, although there was some difference between the quality of job each household was engaged in, there was no predetermined landholding status nor any prior agrarian class characteristic that governed access to particular jobs. There appears to be some correlation, however, between quality of job, employment sector and caste. Nearly all the 29 percent group were low caste with the exception of two households.

Of the farming group, consisting of those households with direct access to paddy cultivating land under private ownership and those households with tenancy rights secured by means of a share payment in kind, the highest percentage of those engaged in secure off-farm employment came from the group of smaller land operators. The fact that the level of off-farm employment is positively related to tenurial status, where it increases from tenant to owner operator to landlord, means that further account should be taken of the farm size to tenurial category data prior to examining the farm size to off-farm employment findings.

Table 5.4   Average operational holding size by tenurial category

Tenurial Category	Average Size (Acres)
full tenant	0.9
part tenant	1.9
total tenant	1.4
owner cultivator	0.9
landlord	2.5
total	1.6

Table 5.4 details the average operational holding size by tenurial category. Since full tenants are seen to operate the same size holdings as owner cultivators and part tenants operate more than twice the holding size of owner cultivators, it can be seen that in landholding terms the positive relationship between tenurial category and off-farm employment is less significant. When account is taken of the reduction in income from sharecropping on all tenanted land, the equivalent average landholding size for the tenant group is exactly one acre, resulting in a similar average farm income for both the tenant and owner cultivator groups. At the same time the income reduction for landlords on tenanted land results in an equivalent landholding size of 1.8 acres reduced from the 2.5 acres seen above. This broadly means that the majority of households at the bottom of the farm size scale were from the full tenant and owner cultivator groups rising through the part tenant and part owner groups to landlords.

In order to demonstrate the proportion of off-farm to farm income in relation to farm size given in table 5.5 below, a calculation based on average gross farm earnings over four seasons was compared to total off-farm income over the same period. An annual average figure was calculated over this extended period in order to reduce any anomalies arising from variable seasonal weather conditions. Table 5.5 lists the percentage of off-farm to farm income based on these calculations for four operational size groups ranging from less than one acre to over three acres.

Table 5.5 Percentage distribution of off-farm income by farm size

Farm Size (acres)	Off-Farm Income %
0 - 0.9	70.5
1 - 1.9	63.2
2 - 2.9	53.5
> 3	57.0

The table shows that from zero to three acres there is an inverse relationship between farm size and off-farm earnings. Although farm income may be positively related to farm size, if the quality of job and level of off-farm earnings were also positively related to farm size, it is unlikely that this inverse relationship would be observed. Another factor that appears to operate to produce a slight upward trend in the proportion of off-farm earnings in the over three acre category, is a small rise in the number of off-farm earners per household in this group. Although this can dramatically affect the overall outcome of any one household, it is a demographic characteristic that was seen to be fairly evenly spaced throughout all size groups with the exception of the largest. This is most likely due to the fact that there was less domestic pressure for adult income earners to leave the larger farming households once they had reached a certain age. The results in table 5.5 are somewhere between those found by Herath (1986) for Anuradhapura, where the total proportion of off-farm earnings was lower but the negative relationship to farm size was more marked, and for Kandy which showed a slightly higher proportion of off-farm earnings and a less inverse relationship to farm size.

Table 5.6 Household distribution of main sources of off-farm employment

Source	% of Households
Government Service	62.6
Private Sector	21.4
Skilled Labour	16.0

Hearth (1986) also notes that this inverse relationship 'appears to hold irrespective of the type of income examined after having analysed both gross and net income. The main sources of off-farm employment are listed in table 5.6 alongside the percentage distribution for all off-farm households. A sample of the more typical positions that villagers occupy within each of the three main categories above is given in the following list.

A sample of off-farm employment categories

Private Sector

Employees:
accountant, private gem merchant
dispenser, private dispensary
estate overseer
estate superintendent
factory worker, free trade zone Colombo
garage mechanic
proctors clerk
shop assistant
tourist hotel worker
construction project driver
shop assistant

Self-employed:
betel trader
carpenter
coconut trader
driver
shopkeeper
tailor
trader, miscellaneous
trader, vegetable produce
tobacco barn owner

Government Service

White collar:
Administrative Officer, State Mining and Mineral Development Corporation
Bank Clerk, Loans Department People's Bank
Bead Forest Officer, Forestry Department
Cooperative Inspector, Cooperative Department
Cooperative Manager, Cooperative Society, Textile Department
Cooperative Manager, Cooperative Society, Retail Branch
Department of Health Overseer, Malaria Eradication Office
Dispenser, Government Dispensary

Divisional Officer, Agrarian Service Centre
Farm Officer, Batalagoda Research Station
Clerk, Kachcheri Kurunegala
Technical Officer, Highways Department
Technical Officer, Irrigation Department
Lecturer, Education Department
Plan Implementation Officer, IRDP Kurunegala
Police Constable
Postmaster
Public Health Inspector, Department of Health
Revenue Inspector
School Principal
School Teacher
Technical Officer, Education Department

Blue collar:
bank security guard
bus conductor
bus driver
driver
postman
labourer, Cooperative Stores
labourer, Department of Health, Malaria Eradication Office
labourer, Highways Department
labourer, Survey Department

This sample list confirms the observations made by Herath (1986). He concludes that the main sources of off-farm employment are government service followed by self-employment. The majority of the 21 percent of households engaged in the private sector seen in table 5.4 were in fact self-employed as small traders. Interestingly, the form of employment that appeared to offer most potential in terms of total earnings was that of self-employment in trading and retailing. This represents a change from the past where government service was seen as the prime status occupation. Some government service employees such as the village school teacher, for example, were seriously considering leaving their profession and going into private business or working abroad in the Middle East. The new off-farm elite (entrepreneurs) who enjoyed substantial nonfarm earnings were mostly tenant farmers operating less than two acres of land in total. The structural position of households within the landholding and tenurial system does little to determine the level of off-farm earnings and type of off-farm employment which is the major source of income for just under 57 percent of total households.

Another factor that has served to modify access to off-farm employment in a rather unusual way but with significant implications in terms of an emerging class structure in the village is overseas work in the Gulf. A small but growing number of households were fully dependent on remittance earnings from one or more household members working in the Gulf. Each of the Muslim families had at least one member working overseas and in one case both a father and a mother had left their children under the effective guardianship of their fourteen year old son in order to work in the Gulf. Three Sinhalese families had received substantial earnings from work in Oman and in one case the returning householder has invested his savings in a new shop and trading business, while in the other two, a substantial investment had been made in the building and equipping of new family houses. This phenomenon has been analysed by Ahmed (1984) in relation to the ethnic problems encountered by guest workers into the Middle East from Pakistan. He highlights how the Urdu phrase 'Dubai chalo' literally 'let us go to Dubai' has become part of Pakistani popular culture along with its Punjabi counterpart 'Visa Duba da' or 'Visa for Dubai', signifying the possibility of accruing quick, legitimate and abundant wealth in the Arab States.

In the village, it appears to have become quite fashionable to discuss the possibility of temporary migration to the Middle East. This trend received wide coverage in many of the popular newspapers and its popularity was reinforced by the often elaborated accounts of returning guest workers to the village. One householder who returned with sufficient funds to invest in a small roadside shop, amused many of his customers with stories of his escapades in Oman whilst apparently working on the Sultan's private farm. Many villagers discussed the possibility of working overseas and even the schoolteacher rather unexpectedly expressed his desire to secure such work. In the past it was he who was instrumental in propagating traditional Sinhalese values in the village. He now felt that temporary migration would be a means to combat the erosion in his living standards caused by inflation and would allow him the chance to compete with some of his neighbours in the acquisition of certain material goods.

Since overseas incomes could be anything from three to ten times higher than from local employment, remittance earnings were an important factor in modifying social and economic alignments in the village. A new wealthy group had sprung up from a previously underprivileged section such as the Muslim community, most of whom lived at the tail end of the irrigation system occupying marginal paddy land. In other cases families had been able to reinforce their economic position by capitalising on their professional skills to obtain overseas work. One householder employed in a white collar occupation as a public health inspector was working in the Gulf for a US multinational oil company. His remittance earnings were spent on vastly improving the family house and equipping it with an array of consumer goods. His wife and daughter remained in their new house, aloof from the majority of villagers and demonstrated a quiet pride in the ownership of their new acquisitions which included high speed electric fans, a fridge–freezer, radio–cassette, television and video etc. The 1990 Gulf crisis following the Iraqi occupation of Kuwait may result in such work being seen as a less attractive proposition in the future, although it is unlikely that this will have a lasting effect among aspirant Asian migrants.

Class formation in an evolving farm to firm context

The significance of off–farm employment, both in terms of a locally based occupational diversification and a growing pattern of overseas earnings, lies in the important effect it has had on the overall pattern of stratification in the village. In a typical peasant society class categorisation is difficult to resolve since peasant farmers often own and control the means of production in the form of land. Surplus extraction which depends upon control over the means of production tends to operate at the level of exchange where farmers are subordinated to the market. In this context, internal differentiation depends upon the nature of both production and exchange relations often resulting in a specific alliance of more powerful producers able to engage in surplus extraction through the system of exchange and in turn consolidating their power over the production system itself.

The previous chapter has explored the concrete nature of agrarian production and exchange relations in Karagahapitiya. It has already been noted, for example, that tenurial relations have failed to transform themselves into a system of commercial surplus extraction. Meanwhile, the social and political basis of sharecropping which depends on differential access to the means of production has itself been undergoing considerable change. In the present context of full commodity exchange and monetary circulation, the form of surplus extraction in agriculture appears to retain certain pre capitalist features. These features are usually seen to be broken down over time at the level of exchange (Gunasinghe 1975). However, an examination of both the input and output markets in chapter four demonstrated that although levels of current expenditure on inputs remained high, there was little capital investment in agriculture and no significant collusion between particular landowners and merchants in a process of separating direct producers from the means of production.

The argument presented in this chapter rests upon the fact that dynamic production and exchange relations have now developed outside the agricultural system and that features of agrarian differentiation do not, in themselves, determine the nature of contemporary class formation. It is true that in the past, the monopoly of power had traditionally been the preserve of a small elite who held local bureaucratic office, but this power was used to consolidate a local production advantage in agriculture. Today, the scale of off–farm involvement and the reduced significance of agriculture as a repository for any advantage accrued off–farm has fundamentally altered the former class structure. Consequently, in order to explore the nature of emerging class relations it will be necessary to look beyond the agrarian economy in both a local and regional sense.

Contemporary class relations in the village will be explained with reference to local and regional developments up to the period of field research (1983–84). This explanation will rest upon a brief examination of broader national economic and political issues as a means of clarifying specific developments in the village. The explanation contrasts with that of Gunasinghe (1980) who argues that contemporary village production relations reflect certain archaic features of production, such as sharecropping and temple service, that have been adapted and modified under the particular form of colonial development. The present argument, however, is based on the assumption that smallholder relations are not directly determined by the particular historical development of the national economy but rather that the national economy has given rise to a specific regional market which, through its precarious dynamism, contributes to the survival of smallholder relations.

The development of a non agricultural petty bourgeoisie

Analysis of agrarian production and exchange relations in this study has revealed a number, of structural discontinuities with a system of agriculture based on a rigid hierarchy of production and exploitation. The dissolution of semi–feudal relations in agriculture in Sri Lanka has been widely documented. Silva (1982) argues that the influence and authority that landlords once exerted over tenants has disappeared. As land has become a scarce resource, the larger estates have been fragmented. Landlords have reacted to the legal protection offered to tenants in the 1958 Paddy Lands Act by treating tenants with some caution and instituting temporary tenancies. At the same time the lower caste groups were able to challenge the feudal landlord element in social and economic terms.

In Karagahapitiya a similar change has taken place in the dissolution of the former hierarchy. The same pressure on land has resulted in the fragmentation of estates and villagers have also benefitted from broader political initiatives associated with State policy. Karagahapitiya, however, is still predominantly a rice cultivating village. There has been no drastic agricultural transformation in response to new regional market opportunities. The main explanation for the challenges that have taken place to the old order and the development of contemporary class relations in the village, lies outside the village itself. The critical issue of off–farm employment forms the basis of this explanation. Meanwhile, rice cultivation has not been subjected to a level of commercial investment that has resulted in the employment of mass wage labour. There has been very little consolidation of farm units to form viable commercial enterprises. Although high levels of inputs were utilised and the productivity of land had increased, the family farm still prevailed. As demonstrated above, off–farm earnings were widespread and new off–farm activities were the subject of considerable investment. The specific challenges to the authority of the former aristocracy have been made by those who no longer rely on the village as their main source of income. These public servants, private sector employees and entrepreneurs now maintain contact with external sources of power and patronage. In so doing, these people's perceptions of the nature of authority has altered. Brokerage links that have been struck up in recent years between particular members of the village and external power sources have encouraged people to oppose the old aristocracy. Once these defiant initiatives are made public the loss of status experienced by the former village aristocracy becomes even greater. In order to understand the conditions that have brought this about and to examine more fully contemporary social and economic relations in the village, it will be useful to explore the development of wider regional, political and economic changes and the links between these changes and particular households in the village.

The rise of an educated elite

The early post independence period up to 1956 saw the continuation of the colonial legacy in terms of social and economic relations throughout the country. Wealth was generated largely from the changes that had come about in the transformation from mercantilism to a colonial production system based on plantation agriculture. Although the expansion of the estate sector resulted in the alienation of Crown land from the peasant sector, Roberts (1970b) argues that the impact of the plantation economy and the waste lands legislation on peasant cultivation was not as damaging as might be assumed. In this light it would be difficult, as Roberts points out, to equate the impact of Crown land alienation with the British enclosure movement as was done by Pieris in an earlier study.

The new Government inherited a system of expanded educational and social services largely underwritten by the plantation sector with tea providing the single largest contribution to state revenue (Uphoff and Wanigaratne 1982). During the first decade of independence there was a boom in the export sector with increased demand for plantation crops such as rubber in response to the Korean war and a significant rise in tea prices from 1954–1956. There were large increases in the productivity of the smallholder sector as the Government pursued a policy of striving for self sufficiency through the regeneration of peasant farming and the dry zone colonisation. Paddy production doubled from 16.7 million bushels in 1947 to 37.7 million bushels by 1955, largely due to the strength of institutional incentives such as a guaranteed purchase price for rice, representing a 50 percent subsidy over world market rates (de Silva 1981).

147

Wealth and power were still largely centred on land rather than capital and the dominant class lacked the power and purpose that greater investment in an industrial base would have created (Uphoff and Wanigaratne 1982). Educational expansion and growth in the administrative machinery meant that new sources of power and prestige grew up centred on bureaucracy and control of the administration rather than production. Uphoff and Wanigaratne further emphasise certain historical and political initiatives that have contributed to an increasingly aware and mobilised electorate. As far back as 1906 local councils had been authorised to open primary educational facilities for compulsory attendance. The Constitution of 1931 created a State Assembly providing for internal self government under universal franchise. These initiatives, alongside extra parliamentary representation through trade union activity, the Temperance Society and the Sinhala and Tamil Cultural Associations, all assisted in creating an effective and powerful demand for early welfare legislation, land and tenancy reforms (Uphoff and Wanigaratne 1982:485–487).

Karagahapitiya at this time fell within the Kurunegala electorate and villagers had a chance to exercise their democratic rights of political self determination. A prominent local figure in the district was Sir John Kotelawala who was the MP for Kurunegala. This large electorate was later subdivided to form a new electorate for Dodangaslanda (later split again to form the current electorate of Hiriyala within which the village now falls). Kotelawala, who owned extensive plumbago mine interests in Dodangaslanda, became the MP for the new electorate. By 1952 the early Korean war export boom had declined and the Prime Minister Dudley Senanayake attempted to reduce the burden of the rice subsidy, having campaigned on its popularity only months before. The ensuing price rises from 25 cents a measure to 72 cents (de Silva 1981) and the effects of a stringent economic policy provoked a massive protest from the left culminating in the hartal (general stoppage) of 1953 which led to Senanayake's resignation. His successor was his cousin Sir John Kotelawala who in de Silva's words had 'neither his political vision nor any substantial reserves of committed public support' (1981:499).

Despite widespread public dissatisfaction with Kotelawala's policy on cultural issues, particularly language and religion, which led to his defeat at the 1956 elections, villagers in Karagahapitiya remained generally loyal on account of his new power and authority as their MP. The older generation in the village still talked of how he was responsible for the building of forty six schools in the locality and numerous district roads. It was this early association that villagers had with their local MP and his party that has subsequently resulted in an almost unanimous support for the United National Party (UNP)in the village. It has helped to secure particular social and economic advantages such as good local educational and employment facilities that have been instrumental in providing wider opportunities for the local population. Although there were relatively few direct political challenges to the village power structure at this time, with the former village headman and irrigation headman monopolising authority at the local level, the wider regional changes brought about during this period were to undermine this monopoly of power and wealth.

The post 1956 coalition under Bandaranaike did little to increase private sector industrial capital. Investors preferred to focus on plantation agriculture or trade where returns were higher. This period did see a rise in Government sponsored industrial development however, although as de Silva points out, the State was unable to nationalise the 'commanding heights' of the economy and instead concentrated on the nationalisation of bus transport and the port of Colombo. Snodgrass (1966) regards one of the main industrial problems of this era as a much too high capital per worker ratio related to a low level of capital output. The majority of State investment at the time was designed to promote import substitution and further nationalisation of the petroleum, insurance and banking sectors while productivity in the agricultural sector slowed down considerably.

An important feature of the whole SLFP period was the Government's willingness to engage in expansionary financing that led to a series of budgetary deficits which went on to characterise the economy of the late 1960s and early 1970s. High taxes were levied on imports, particularly those of a consumer nature in order to contain the balance of payment problem and in turn this led to a rising local consumer industry. State intervention and ownership coupled with a substantial welfare programme meant that a large proportion of employment opportunities were created within the administrative machinery.

In spite of its posturing, the Bandaranaike Government brought about little change to the nature of top leadership in the country. The same patrician families dominated national politics and the government adopted a populist rather than a radicalist stance. Piyadasa (1984) argues that the Bandaranaike Government was successful in mobilising patriotic support and radical mass opinion but cleverly redefined the problem proposing a nationalist Sinhalese solution that undoubtedly benefitted the majority community at the expense of the Tamil minority. These policies did, however, bring about a number of direct challenges to traditional leadership at the local level. The Paddy Lands Act, for example, was designed to strengthen tenants' rights and new bureaucratic appointments were no longer the preserve of the old village elite.

Initially these challenges were not as sharply felt in Karagahapitiya as in some of the more favoured SLFP villages. Unlike other local political developments such as those described by Silva (1982) in Kandy district, where the mobilisation of the low caste vote initially by the UNP politician George E. de Silva and later by progressive SLFP legislation, crystallised low caste tenant solidarity under a Nakati (drummer) caste leader, in Karagahapitiya challenges to the aristocracy were less caste based and less prominent. In Welivita, Silva claims that the 'low caste share tenants, to their advantage, had a favourable political climate, long term possession and use of land, the strength of numbers and, above all, a remarkable degree of solidarity among themselves in their fight against the gentry' (1982: 17). In Karagahapitiya, the tenurial changes were less marked. Nevertheless, the early political initiatives of the SLFP revolving around programmes of nationalisation and tenurial reform, the latter at the initiative of Philip Gunawardena as Minister of Food and Agriculture, did herald a phase of increasing State intervention and control of the economy reaching down to the local level. Gradually the upper caste landlord group in the village were displaced from monopolising local bureaucratic authority while the ineffectual opposition stance of the local MP Arthur Senanayake failed to preserve the former status quo.

Under the provisions of the 1958 Paddy Lands Act a cultivation committee was set up to maintain a paddy lands register, to oversee minor irrigation facilities, to settle tenurial disputes and fix agricultural wages. Revenue was generated through an acreage tax of up to Rs 6 per acre. The committee consisted of twelve elected members for a three year term. In 1964, membership legislation required all members to be cultivators in an attempt to reduce the domination of the committee by landlord interests. Tenant farmers in the village felt that the committee had been an important means of breaking the power of the landed households although they argued that the committee never functioned according to the statutes. The *walawwa* (aristocratic) households no longer monopolised the management of agrarian affairs but since the majority of them were landlord cultivators they were able to protect their interests by remaining vociferous members of the cultivation committee. According to a number of the older tenant farmers, this often resulted in biased intervention in the area of water and tenurial disputes and the maintenance of a false paddy register, all favouring landlord interests.

After 1961 the office of the former headman was abolished. Newly appointed government officers took over the functions that had earlier been carried out by a number of the leading families in the village. The village became incorporated into the local government Grama Sevaka (GS) unit of Karagahapitiya which was itself a new level of bureaucracy within the local administration. The significance of this in terms of the village is the final replacement of the former land/office monopoly of the old elite by a bureaucratic stratum who were better disposed towards and influenced by their fellow employees in the village. An increasingly important feature of the rise of a new influential group in Karagahapitiya is associated with the gradual politicisation of local power and office which will be discussed below with reference to more recent changes since the SLFP dominated government of the early 1970s and the current UNP regime.

The UNP Government of 1965–1969 spent much energy on attempting to raise production in agriculture through its populist policy of smallholder development. The Green Revolution was introduced into the countryside through the Government's National Food Drive designed to offset rapid population increases and unemployment (de Silva 1981). This contrasted with the former left dominated policy of State capitalism through industrial development. The implementation of smallholder development and the introduction of agrarian technology and services which led to overall production increases, saw an expansion of the agricultural service sector under administrative control although direct benefits to smallholders and tenants were only marginal. During this phase of UNP Government the local MP representing Hiriyala electorate was S.B. Herath. He was regarded locally as a down to earth politician unlike Kotelawala and was seen as an important figure in directing agricultural improvements in the vicinity. His popularity was largely emotional and he was loved as a symbol of the aspirations of the ordinary villager. Many of the UNP supporters in the village, particularly the part time farming householders, regarded both him and UNP policy as helping to initiate important changes in the nature of village society. The emphasis on agricultural development was recognised as having contributed to the productivity of paddy land and the inevitable reluctance of many off-farm employees to give up cultivating and possibly migrate elsewhere.

A further change of government in 1970 brought the SLFP back into power in a United Front coalition with the LSSP and the CP representing a broad socialist front. There was a continued emphasis on the promotion of capital investment in the public sector although the rate of new public corporations declined, having previously doubled between 1958–70. An under utilisation of industrial capacity and inefficient management contributed to poor labour relations and poor economic performance. State controls over industry undoubtedly increased the opportunities for the Government to exercise considerable patronage and enabled it to more fully gain control over the reigns of economic as well as political power (Slater 1985). A rising rate of inflation and a growth in unemployment from 14 percent to 20 percent between 1969 and 1975 resulted in a decline in real wage levels for a large percentage of the electorate but at the same time the Government did succeed in dislodging the former landed class by implementing land reform legislation, rent restrictions and capital levies (Ponnambalam 1981). These assaults on the concentration of wealth, according to Ponnambalam, did result in a decline in income inequality. He demonstrates that the income share of the top decile fell from over 42 percent in 1953 to 29.9 percent by 1973 and draws on the Central Bank's Consumer Finance Survey of 1973 to highlight that the income share of all groups other than the top 20 percent increased over this period. Many of the economic problems of the day were disguised in the Government's pursuit of political and cultural objectives. These revolved around the issues of a national language and State religion both enshrined in the Republican Constitution of 1972, which tacitly allowed the Government a further two years in office and a total seven years of Emergency rule instituted after the youth insurrection of 1971. The social implications of the 1970–77 period have been analysed by Ponnambalam who argues that those who benefitted most were the middle income groups including business employees and government servants. After a drive to encourage exports by granting tax concessions and convertible Rupee accounts, which in turn allowed exporters the opportunity to import scarce luxury goods for sale on the domestic market at inflated prices, a new super wealthy group sprang up who were firmly rooted in import and export trading (Ponnambalam 1981).

In the village, the dissolution of the former landed elite and the rise of the new middle income groups meant that people's aspirations became centred on the opportunities offered by certain types of off-farm employment. After an initial lack of interest in agrarian development favouring industrial sector policies instead, the Government was forced to institute a redevelopment of the agricultural machinery and bureaucracy, aware of falling productivity rates and the problem of youth unemployment as seen by the insurrection of 1971. Many new vacancies therefore were associated with the agricultural bureaucratic machinery both in the locality and in the district headquarters in Kurunegala. It was, for example, during the mid 1970s that the offices of what later became the Agrarian Service Centre were built on the periphery of the village and just over a mile from the village centre. De Silva argues that it took nearly two years for the Government to rebuild the administrative structure and consolidate necessary levels of administrative and scientific personnel in agriculture.

By 1974–75 and 1975–76 the harvests had improved once again but were still below 1969–70 levels (de Silva 1981). Morrison has emphasised how the need for improved local coordination in agricultural development led to a reorganisation of local services and the creation of agricultural productivity committees and agrarian service centres. In many respects the Government's attempts to increase production in the countryside revolved around a number of legislative initiatives. The Agricultural Productivity Law of 1972 set up productivity committees with appointed agricultural officers; it also set up agricultural tribunals and extended the activities of the cooperatives. The Agricultural Lands Law of 1973 extended the powers of the cultivation committees and improved the status of settlers on colonisation schemes. The Government meanwhile extended its monopoly over paddy marketing through the guaranteed purchase price scheme. The Government also created Divisional Development Councils (DDC) to be responsible for a decentralised planning function at the local level with a particular focus on local and regional employment. The DDCs were staffed by official representatives of government departments at the divisional level and popular representatives consisting of the chairmen of local committees and societies such as the cultivation committee and the rural development society, the MP and local authority members. Few DDCs worked successfully or effectively due to the problems of vested interests, internal conflicts and institutional inefficiency (see Slater 1989). The DDCs have now been superseded by the Provincial Council system.

The consequence of these State initiatives on village society were fairly marked. A new well educated group had by this time emerged to challenge the position of members of the old *walawwa* (aristocratic) families. This new group did not rely on its landowning, nor even its land operating, status for its authority. It was rather the status and power they achieved in both a material and symbolic sense from their employment in the regional economy. This was directly connected to the local infrastructural network that had been set up by the successive Governments outlined above and, in particular, by the United Front coalition of 1970–77. Part of the key to this new group's success was their political astuteness and their political pragmatism. The core members of this group were capable of publicly expressing and confirming the new cultural ideals and objectives of the Government. Not only did these ideals include the dismantling of the power of the landed elite, partially achieved by means of successive SLFP agrarian legislation, but also the Government's stand on the Sinhalese language and the Buddhist religion. The latter issues centred around the creation of a Buddhist Sinhala hegemony as the national religion and language respectively, officially protected in the 1972 constitution. The arousal of inter communal tension, which these constitutional enactments created, could be seen as clear illustration of the process of political opportunism which dates back to SLFP policies of the late 1950s and has increased dramatically in recent years under the UNP. This in turn relates to worsening national economic conditions such as a massive foreign debt, a high level of inflation, a heavy dependence on short–term capital loans and reduced welfare expenditure, the ill effects of which could be partially defused by the pursuit of national cultural chauvinism.

The SLFP vanguard

The core members of the old SLFP group in the village comprised Tilekeratne – a schoolmaster, Ariyaratne – a proctor's clerk, Jayatileka – an extension worker and Wijeysinghe – a cooperative manager. In traditional landowning terms the group fell into a number of different subcategories. Tilekeratne and Ariyaratne each owned less than one acre of paddy. Wijeysinge owned roughly one acre and Jayatileka over two acres. Although all of the above were owner cultivators, Jayatileka was also a part tenant, cultivating temple lands, and part landlord renting out to his son–in–law on ande sharecropping. Since the abolition of the post of village headman and the loss of influence of the former aristocratic elite, many of the representative functions in the village were performed by this new group, often on a shared basis. These core members, especially the first three, were adept at propounding themes of national cultural importance such as the place of Buddhism, the Sinhalese language and tradition and the historical importance of rice cultivation in Sri Lankan society. These themes were reiterated at religious ceremonies in the temple and public meetings, as well as private functions such as weddings and funerals. Today, with an increase in communal tension and national identity, these same themes are repeated on similar occasions with a surprising degree of formality even at small private gatherings which can be occasions for airing misconceptions often inflamed by official propaganda. In addition to performing this ideological role the same group were closely linked to the temple for a number of years, providing the organisational capability for temple functions and meetings.

This same group had a monopoly over many of the office bearing posts of village societies and organisations. The rural development society was re-established by Tilekeratne after a long period of inactivity. Both Tilekeratne and Ariyaratne were instrumental in initiating a number of rural development society sponsored projects such as the construction of two or three roads and paths to the more isolated hamlets and neighbouring settlement. The society was also active in providing water for both domestic and cultivation purposes and the core members also played a key role in pressurising the MP and government officials to rehabilitate the village tank. Once successful, it was the rural development society that helped to organise the village labour contingent during the construction phase of the tank. The only members of the village who would never turn up to the society's shramadane (voluntary) activities were the *walawwa* families.

This core group came to reflect an increasingly important social division in the village between those who were able to secure salaried off-farm employment, often alongside the continued part time maintenance of the family farm, and those who solely relied on smallholder cultivation for the provision of all their family requirements. The latter could in turn be further divided along conventional landholding and operational categories.

By this time some of the basic characteristics of contemporary differentiation had already been established. Small tenant farmers, who supplemented their meagre farm incomes with casual labouring, and landless labourers constituted the poorest section of the village. The middle income group comprised those households operating larger farm units, totalling anything from one to two acres, which could be made up of a mixture of owner operated and tenanted land. The upper income group comprised the larger farmers owning or operating more than two acres of cultivable land and those households with regular off-farm incomes. Within this group there was a marked income differential between some households that obtained more than one regular off-farm income and also a marked difference between those with a large supplementary landholding compared to the majority of part time farming households holding between half and three quarters of an acre.

Although no single person any longer commanded the same level of authority that the former headman had done previously, the core group monopolised most positions of public power. In addition, by not openly abusing their positions of influence for personal gain, they maintained the respect of most villagers. A feature of this new power alignment within the restructured

154

economic categories above, no longer drawn solely around agricultural differentials, was a process of increasing politicisation at the local level. This is a particularly significant feature in that it will be seen to play an increasingly important role in determining the contemporary character of rural social and economic differentiation. Throughout the early 1970s the Government gradually replaced the democratically elected agricultural and bureaucratic officers or representatives with State appointees. Uphoff and Wanigaratne (1982) show how the reorganisation of the cooperative movement led to nine of the fifteen board members becoming Government appointees, and how the evolution of cultivation committees, agricultural productivity committees and divisional development councils all became subject to State interference, leading to a direct increase in political favouritism and corruption. Increased state intervention, which manifested itself in the local power structure was, in turn ,linked to a faltering national economy and stagnant growth.

All the members of the core group mentioned above were, to a greater or lesser extent, supporters of the SLFP in a village that was predominantly UNP. It is not difficult to see why they might have constituted a 'favoured group'. The case of Wijeysinghe clearly illustrates this point. Like the other SLFP supporters Wijeysinghe had made a conscious decision, which was to some extent ideological, to support the party and be seen to be different from the rest of the village. The SLFP had no grass roots party organisation in the village but had simply relied on these few enroled members for support, all of whom were well educated. Like the other SLFP supporters, Wijeysinghe has a high level of political awareness and understanding. He defended the SLFP on the grounds that it had been responsible for improving the life of the ordinary villager and particularly for reducing the inequality between the old officials and the common man. He claimed that in the past, for example, 'if one ever encountered the Assistant Government Agent he would have been treated with enormous respect but thanks to Bandaranaike's social revolution, this was no longer the case'. In addition, he regarded as positive the policies of the 1970–77 Government which emphasised the closed economy, the promotion of local production and the curtailment of private investment to make way for public sector expansion. He accepted that the obvious negative effects of the policy particularly noticeable for the consumer, did contribute to the SLFP's defeat in 1977. He identified the Government's handling of the 1971 insurrection and the extension of the parliamentary term by two years as helping to bring about the Government's eventual downfall in 1977.

Wijeysinghe flourished throughout the SLFP period of the early 1970s. He was reinstated as a cooperative manager having been earlier suspended during the UNP term of office. At the time of his suspension a group of UNP supporters in the locality had complained about him to the MP who, being influential, had him suspended on grounds of misconduct. After his reinstatement he became a significant personality in the village and, although he never played the same public role as some of his SLFP colleagues, he was nevertheless a powerful broker. It was through him that a number of UNP householders were recruited into the Cooperative Department.

As Perera (1982) has shown, control over rural organisations and party political links became an increasingly important agent of social stratification in rural Sri Lanka, especially after 1970 when these organisations became the only channel for distributing scarce resources, agricultural equipment and credit. He goes on to demonstrate how the shift away from land as an important source of power to the control over resources, finally sealed the fate of the landed gentry.

The power and influence of the new educated elite undoubtedly grew during the early 1970s as State involvement in the rural economy through the proliferation of rural organisations increased. Growing politicisation of the bureaucracy favoured the core SLFP members in the village. Wijeysinghe, for example, was able to convert his political links into material gain. He built one of the first modern houses in the village. Another was built by Jayatileka the former extension officer who had been employed as a food production overseer. Both houses had brick walls, tiled roofs and a number of bedrooms. Wijeysinghe was also one of the few householders to run a private motorcar and his daughter was sufficiently well educated to be a university candidate. Wijeysinghe felt, however, that the benefits would have been even greater had the MP at the time not been a UNP politician. He was keen to point out that the MP has been a potential source of patronage but that the full benefits of government office had not accrued, on account of the MP being a member of the opposition party. At the same time, many of the local SLFP organisations suffered from lack of direct support from the MP.

Like many villagers, Wijeysinghe argued that to get significant extra legal benefits there needed to be a link between local and national politics so that one could use the MP as an effective means of patronage. These developments can be seen to represent the beginning of what has subsequently become the rampant politicisation of many walks of life. Meanwhile MPs' families and proteges manipulated State patronage for their own benefit. As Piyadasa claims 'At the expense of the whole people they enriched themselves, travelled abroad at public expense, grabbed lucrative posts, promoted their business interests and persecuted those whom they disliked. Jobs were at the disposal of this privileged elite, regardless of qualifications or merit....' (Piyadasa 1984: 39).

Emerging class relations and the politicisation of power

After the change of government in 1977 it became increasingly possible to exploit the patronage links in the village as loyal UNP householders inherited public office. At the same time broader national economic objectives served

156

to propel a new hybrid class of rural entrepreneurs into positions of economic supremacy at the local level. The new economic strategy of the UNP Government centred upon trade, aid and capital investment, and has played a decisive role in the process of contemporary rural class formation. The links between national economic strategy, regional economic and political developments and production relations in the village, will be more clearly elucidated in due course.

The liberal growth oriented economic policy of the UNP government has had a very different effect on the various sections of both the rural and urban population. While the poor in both sectors continue to suffer hardship and deprivation and many professional and public servants complain of deteriorating living standards, a new upwardly mobile group of entrepreneurs and political opportunists had begun to emerge as the main beneficiaries of State policy. One means of protest initially adopted by the organised labour section of the urban poor was that of mass unrest. This was dealt with harshly by the State, highlighted by the Government's response to the general strike call of July 1980. Having declared temporary Emergency rule, the Government then dismissed all public servants on strike and froze trade union funds in an attempt to defeat mass protest. Unorganised agricultural labour, particularly landless labourers, suffered in silence. In the village, it was this small group of landless labourers and the larger group of tenant farmers without access to off-farm income who experienced the most difficulty in the face of rising inflation and welfare cuts. This same category have also benefitted least from productivity increases in agriculture. This problem was further accentuated by the higher than average productivity increases in paddy production since the rehabilitation of the irrigation tank.

In the liberal economic climate of the 1980s an off-farm income began to be more highly valued than ever as a means of acquiring newly available material advantages. As rural unemployment levels remained high and land was subject to increasing subdivision, many villagers, particularly the younger generation, began to value the opportunity provided by public service employment. This was so in spite of the fact that many public sector employees claimed to be experiencing a decline in real living standards as wages failed to keep abreast of prices. Two young men whose fathers had set aside land for them to cultivate, decided that in order to increase their chances of obtaining a regular job they must seek employment elsewhere. Two friends of theirs, in turn, had decided to commute daily to Kandy rather than face the prospect of being confined to the family farm. Those who had benefitted most, however, were closely involved in the expanding regional economy, either in the trading of agricultural or consumer products or other entrepreneurial activity.

At the regional level, a new entrepreneurial class sprang up centred on the provision of imported consumer and agricultural goods. Kurunegala city a thriving regional centre with an emphasis on expanding retail activities. A

157

number of large shopping complexes were constructed in the heart of the city during the 1983-84 period. The same pattern was expressed in the vicinity of the village. The nearby town of Madagamuwa was well supplied with televisions, radios, record players and cassettes. One local shop which previously stocked a wide range of general provisions had been turned over to electrical goods and consumer durables. While the shop window displayed an enticing world of electronic gadgetry the former hoardings still advertised a service 'for all one's daily needs'. One of the largest local merchants expanded his retailing operations into Kurunegala itself. The local periodical market also supplied imported goods and the newer maha pola (large market) concept which had been actively encouraged by government ministers appeared to be specifically designed to promote consumerism. A number of the more affluent villagers talked with great excitement of the maha pola at the nearby town of Mawatagama. As a 'one-stop' shopping concept they pointed out that it provided local consumers with the opportunity of purchasing anything from a tractor to a television set.

Although the nature of the social formation in the village is seen as a direct result of the popular experience of these economic developments, it is also closely linked to the local articulation of a national political response to these same developments. The importance of the MP in assisting public material advancement has long been understood in the village. Villagers were keen to see the restoration of a UNP Government in accord with their own MP S.B. Herath, especially in view of the long tradition of local political intervention on behalf of the community in the provision of public services and utilities dating back to Sir John Kotelawala. Herath was granted ministerial responsibility in the UNP Government of 1977 as Minister of Food and Cooperatives, a post that related to his earlier career in the rural administration. He was seen in the elitist circles of Colombo as a middling politician of mediocre intelligence and breeding. However in his mediocrity he found his strength. He is often described as having a certain 'earthy' quality and was popular in the village. He had a capacity to assess useful local development initiatives in the manner of a true village politician. Consequently, direct approaches were made on behalf of the whole village to the MP for the rehabilitation of the tank. With the introduction of a district wide IRDP scheme in Kurunegala in 1979, funded by the World Bank, there arose the very real possibility of financing the village project. The MP not only managed to push through this local project but the village tank ended up being the very first in the country to be restored under the IRDP minor tanks programme resulting in a State ceremonial opening.

Political involvement in the village has not always centred on community issues and projects. Access to off-farm employment has been increasingly subject to political scrutiny and the maintenance of a secure off-farm income has depended upon political loyalty. It is perhaps not surprising, therefore, to discover that Wijeysinghe subsequently lost his job as a cooperative manager and no longer owned a private car. Ariyaratne was reputed to have switched allegiance to the UNP and had consequently improved his career prospects. In the past he had supported one of two local SLFP candidates. His candidate lost against the competitor and he failed to obtain the posting he had hoped for. Having switched support to the UNP he was able to secure this post. Unlike Wijeysinghe who was inspired by a notion of political idealism, Ariyaratne's actions reflected the dominant trend of political pragmatism where party allegiance and commitment were seen purely in terms of individual opportunism. Both men agreed that strong political support was vital for career mobility and Wijeysinghe accepted that the most effective strategy in this area was to support the UNP during a period of UNP Government, with the distinct possibility of the local MP becoming a Minister with more patronage to disburse.

Grass roots support for the Government came mainly from the UNP branch society, there being no single party organiser in the village. At the 1977 elections two key individuals formed one such society. Interestingly, neither was a prominent member of village society, one being a low country *goyigama* (farmer caste) owning no productive agricultural land, the other a Muslim who again had no cultivable land. Once the campaigning and elections were over and the UNP achieved its landslide victory, both men were offered much sought after jobs. The former took up employment in a bank and the latter the position of a special service officer in the Assistant Government Agent's Office in the nearby town of Madagamuwa. The new beneficiaries of local political patronage did not constitute a group of leaders or brokers over local affairs. A number of villagers pointed out that, theoretically, the officers of branch societies could wield considerable power and influence over others especially in preventing access to off-farm employment and channelling patronage. This was seen to be the case because they were the ones who would prepare a list of party applicants to send to the MP which would be consulted during any recruitment programme. However, in this case, once the aspirations of the two office bearers were fulfilled and they obtained their employment, they were no longer interested in remaining active. The branch society then collapsed and ceased to exist.

In the new context of a diversified regional economy political patronage can be seen as a stabilising factor in national terms. Everyone depends on favours from above in the form of direct assistance or support. This limits opposition and the display of public dissent. It is curiously akin to the old Kandyan form of king's rule under local chiefs (*ratemahattayaa*) who enjoyed office on a non tenured basis, as their contracts were renewed depending on their behaviour and level of support to the king. Villagers were aware of the importance of political intervention in the regulation of the regional economy and the more ambitious competed for office in the branch society as a means of assisting their upward economic mobility.

Consequently, a new UNP branch society was formed prior to the 1982 Referendum. The office bearers were from among a group of aspirant residents interested in diversifying their source of income from their traditional agricultural base. They represented those who were keen to activate political links in order to ensure they could achieve this objective. The secretary of the branch society was Ranbanda the most successful emerging entrepreneur in the village. He only owned three quarters of an acre of farmland but had been cultivating a further one and a quarter acres on a sharecropping basis from his wife's mother. As a part tenant cultivator he claimed that he had little interest in farming. His efforts were concentrated on developing his business activities in coconut trading, rice milling and general retailing instead. He operated from a new brick and tiled shop attached to his newly constructed roadside house. The treasurer of the society was Dassanayake described as one of the few villagers to have got rich through farming. He owned less than half an acre of farmland but cultivated a further one and a half acres as a sharecropper. Since the rehabilitation of the tank he had taken farming very seriously and was elected to the post of Assistant Cultivation Officer (ACO) for Karagahapitiya. Dassanayake expressed a keen desire to pursue an off-farm role within the agricultural bureaucracy at local level. He submitted his application for the vacant post of Cultivation Officer (CO) for Karagahapitiya GS division and was fairly active in soliciting the support of the MP for this post. He built a new house at a cost of Rs 70,000 which he shared with his sister and brother-in-law who had started up a carpentry business profiting from the new boom in house construction.

One of the former key SLFP supporters was Tilekeratne the schoolteacher. Since 1977 he appeared less openly partisan and was still respected by most of the villagers. He bitterly complained, however, of the problems of career mobility in his present job and demonstrated that as others in the village now prospered and openly displayed their newly acquired wealth he was unable to complete the building of his house. Unlike many others who owned a house with plastered walls, concrete floors and electricity he and his family were surrounded by bare bricks, a temporary cow dung floor and no internal doors. Despite his idealism and loyalty to the village and local tradition, he was considering the possibility of employment in the Middle East to boost his off-farm income. Tilekeratne expressed great concern over the rise of local political thugs, a phenomenon which has been documented on a national scale by the Civil Rights Movement of Sri Lanka. They form part of a pattern of growing political intimidation and interference which, during the run up to the Referendum, led to the calling of a general emergency, the banning of opposition newspapers and the sealing of presses, mass detentions, the illegal display of official propaganda, intimidation, harassment and impersonation. It was well known that a prominent local UNP voter who was disciplined by the Police managed to obtain the assistance of the MP to secure his release. This anti–democratic trend has contributed to the institutionalisation of lawlessness which has been so apparent in the ethnic and civil disturbances after 1987.

Within the context of official illegality there is a growing sense of frustration among some political activists in the village. Since the death in 1983 of S.B. Herath, the former MP who had been responsible for the rehabilitation of the tank, and the succession of his brother, Dr S.B.S.Y. Herath, the channels of patronage became less clear. This new MP was described by some villagers as 'the chit MP who doesn't even know the four ends of his own electorate'. Benefits only accrued to those who were able to seek him out and gain his personal favour. A few younger villagers who founded a youth group, for example, felt frustrated that in spite of their campaign efforts, they remained unpatronised. These political developments have meant that within the context of a solid UNP village, beneficiaries have to be increasingly competitive to retain economic and political power. The Muslim special service officer who benefitted from branch society office after 1977 was rumoured to have temporarily blocked Dassanayake's candidature for the post of CO by falsely informing the MP that Dassanayake had been an opposition supporter in the past.

The twin objectives of the post 1977 UNP Government centred around the manipulation of widespread political support and the promotion of economic growth based on greater economic liberalism. This was designed to revolve largely around direct foreign investment, joint equity participation and increased privatisation. Foreign aid and investment depended upon the Government's commitment to an open economic policy, the pursuit of which led to a consumer boom in imported goods disproportionately catering to the needs of a new elite. In turn this has been made possible by the implementation of a comprehensive programme of welfare cuts and savings all the more necessary in view of the accelerating defence budget in the face of continuing ethnic violence. With rising consumer aspirations and an increase in political intervention and authoritarianism, a new and competitive group of beneficiaries emerged at the local level, some of whom constituted a dynamising force in their own right within the village, rather than simply being the agents of state exploitation, manipulating local factor markets in the system of exchange.

This small group of expanding local entrepreneurs were beginning to employ wage labourers on a fairly regular basis. Ranbanda already employed one regular labourer and a number of casual labourers on a daily basis. Two or three retailers have also engaged a handful of employees from the village. Dassanayake's brother–in–law had contracted a waged apprentice carpenter to work under him and was thinking of increasing his staff. Many of the off–farm employees were investing income in home improvements or complete reconstruction. All house building was undertaken locally and casual labourers were engaged from among those in the village who supplemented their meagre agricultural income from farming small plots or from agricultural labouring

161

with casual non agricultural work. This labouring group regularly talked of the new social divide in the village which they express in terms of 'those with tiled roofs and those with *cadjun* (coconut frond thatching) roofs'. The implication behind the term 'tiled roofs' being plastered brick walls, cement floors, new furniture and electrical goods. Almost 60 percent of houses in the village were either modern or of a previous design that incorporated a tiled roof and cement floor, while 41 percent were of the traditional mud and cadjun. Nearly all those households with a regular off–farm income, amounting to just under 60 percent of total households, resided in such a 'tiled roof' house. There were of course one or two exceptions such as that of Tilekeratne the schoolteacher who had only managed to half complete his present house and lacked a new roof or cement floors.

Welfare cuts and rising consumer prices, with inflation averaging 15 percent p.a. between 1977 and 1982 (Piyadasa 1984), hit the group of poorer families quite noticeably. One tenant farmer stated that 'these days some villagers were getting wealthy without growing the food their families required, while others might grow all their food yet fall further behind the rich'. Villagers appeared to perceive social and economic divisions in a fairly complex manner. Often they would group households according to more specific criteria than simply the material the family house is built of, where subtle combinations of mud walls and a corrugated roof or brick walls and a thatched roof may confuse categorisation. The criteria tended to be associated with material manifestations of the level of a household's income. The appearance and contents of the dwelling place were still seen as central to the description. An additional point may well be the size of the domestic estate or compound which is directly related to the amount of coconut highland owned. One of the wealthiest villagers who was working in the Middle East lived in a secluded house in a large compound. Old style (*purana*) settlements with clustered housing were no longer considered prestigious. An exception to this was the fact that some of the very poorest families mostly of low caste or low country origins lived in isolated huts on the edge of the village. These families made up the bulk of the 10 percent of households at the very bottom of the economic ladder.

Other criteria on which perceptions of poverty were based concerned the nature of one's employment. Those who owned no land and who were forced to seek labouring work in and around the village were generally perceived to be among the poorer sections of the community. Other poor households included tenant and owner cultivators who were forced to supplement their farm income with casual labouring work. These constituted a further 14 percent of all households. One source of casual labouring activity was in the formal plantation sector but with daily wage rates at around half that of an agricultural labourer, Rs 13 per day was not an attractive full time incentive. Other features of status included the ownership of some means of transport in the form of car, motorcycle, tractor, cart or bicycle, a private well and status electrical goods such as a television, radio–cassette, electric fan or refrigerator. Poorer families owned none of these items while the richest families either owned or had access to almost all of them.

The rather limited success of economic liberalisation coupled to mounting defence expenditure as a result of continuing violence in the north and east as well as terrorist activity in the south, has all meant that, at the local level, those who are unable to take advantage of political patronage, which serves to direct access to restricted spoils, have not fared well in the contemporary economic and political climate. Those, of course, who have been hardest hit are the families that have no direct links with the regional economy. These poorer households, which depend partly on agricultural work and partly on casual labouring, are the victims of current State policy. These families with little or no land and no alternative regular income found it difficult to operate in the new environment. Certain public services have declined in quality and availability for those who cannot afford to pay. In the town of Madagamuwa, for example, two new private dispensaries opened up in 1983–84. One was operated by the same dispenser who worked in the government clinic. Many of the wealthier villagers claimed that it was no longer worthwhile going to the Government clinic. The service for a private consultation was quicker and more efficient. Indeed some villagers preferred to use the private hospital in Kurunegala rather than the general hospital. Private travel had also become a preferred means of transport in competition with the State Transport Board. Those who benefit from any level of improved efficiency in such services are those with a job to commute to or those who place a premium on their time such as local traders and entrepreneurs. In other words, households with direct links to the wider regional economy.

Expressions of economic and social differentiation

Considerable variation in the level of income exists between village households. It is, of course, income which ultimately determines a household's place in the new economic and social hierarchy. Unlike former times when income related more directly to the extent of total agricultural land owned or operated by a particular household, the relationship now appeared less constant. This reflects the high level of diversification in employment already noted above.

An account of income distribution and average earnings is presented in tables 5.7 and 5.8 for one hundred households representing around 65 percent of all households in the village. Gross paddy farm earnings were calculated over two seasons during 1983–84. Earnings were derived from total yields allowing for any deductions or receipts depending upon the household's tenurial status over specific plots. A monetary equivalent for any subsistence crop was calculated at post harvest prices whereas the sale crop was calculated on the basis of prevailing market prices. Net farm income was then arrived at by deducting all major farm costs from gross farm income. Costs were broken down to cover labour, farm power in the form of tractor or buffalo

163

hire, farm inputs, equipment, debt servicing and miscellaneous expenditure etc. Net paddy farm income was then aggregated with any income generated from the cultivation of coconut, tobacco or subsidiary highland crops after having deducted related agricultural costs.

All off-farm earnings for each household were then added to total farm income. The most significant off-farm earnings came from household members who were either in regular waged employment in the regional economy or who were local self-employed traders and businessmen. Although account was taken of all household members with off-farm earnings only those earnings which regularly contributed to the family income 'pool' were aggregated into the household budget. Members who did not regularly contribute to the 'pool' were normally the younger single family members who spent or saved the majority of their earnings on their own account.

Table 5.7 reflects the significant level of household diversification with relatively high annual earnings in relation to the small size of agricultural holdings. The very extensive range in household income which varied from just over Rs 1,000 per annum to Rs 120,000 per annum resulted in a disproportionately high annual average household income of Rs 16,800. Both the median and modal points, however, stood at around Rs 12,500 per annum. This compares to an annual average household income of Rs 5,654 and Rs 5,492 for Kurunegala district and the intermediate zone respectively, found six years earlier in an ARTI study (1981a). Over the same period, the poverty line remained at Rs 3,600 per annum but was subsequently revised upwards to Rs 7,200 in 1984-85.

Table 5.7 Household distribution by income

Income band earnings p.a (Rs 000)	%households
<5	16
5-10	19
10-15	25
15-20	8
20-25	9
25-30	8
30-35	7
35-40	2
>40	6
Total	100

Despite the relatively high average annual income per household, the extensive variation does indicate that household differentiation in terms of income was extreme. Adaptation and diversification which enabled certain households to benefit from a combination of farm and off-farm earnings, still resulted in over 28 percent of all households falling below the 1984–85 poverty line. The previous poverty line resulted in less than 9 percent of households being categorised as severely underprivileged and obviously did not represent the full extent of poverty in the village. High earners at the top end of the scale who benefitted from overseas earnings tended to be a temporary phenomenon in terms of any particular household. What these disparities have brought about is a tendency for members of poorer households to be even more eager to seek ways of securing diversified earnings channels and new income opportunities.

At the same time there appeared to be an absence of any organisational representation or radical group consciousness among the poorer households. This lack of class identification, which was emphasised by certain poorer household members arguing that they would 'chase away' local voluntary workers committed to improving the plight of the underprivileged, was partly the result of the opening up of sources of income to a wider section of the population in a new political climate. As lucrative off-farm employment was no longer restricted to a particular landed class but became increasingly focused on political favouritism, a large number of villagers began to identify

Table 5.8 Average earnings per household by size of operational holding

Size in Acres	Average Income (Rs 000)
<1	15.6
1–2	16.5
2–3	25.7
3–4	29.7
>4	27.0

with these ideals. Consequently, there was a high turnover of activists in the village branch office of the ruling UNP party.

Table 5.8 shows the annual average income for 69 households representing the subset of land operating households reviewed in table 5.7. Table 5.8 reveals that the arithmetical progression of income does not rise evenly with the operation of increased paddy land. There appears to be a reduction of growth in total income with increased land size. The drastic inverse relationship of land size to growth in income amounts to a factor of three per acre. What is emphasised here is the fact that returns to scale for efficiency and input use on farm land are not constant (Herath 1986) and consequently, off-farm income has become a key factor in determining household wealth and social status. A further illustration of this point can be made with reference to the earnings of landless households. Of those with regular off-farm employment, the average earnings amounted to Rs 23,200 while the average figure for other landless households was a mere Rs 3,200. Indeed, the majority of households in the village that had a relatively high total income also enjoyed a higher degree of household diversification through a larger number of income receivers. In a number of cases where both husband and wife held regular off-farm jobs, the wife's income actually exceeded that of the husband's.

The pattern of stratification in the village up to 1984 has evolved in line with the changing political climate at the district and national level. What has been seen above is the decline of bureaucratic power which formed the basis of most early off-farm positions of any significance and the growth of political control over the administration and aspects of the regional economy under the direction of the MP. An examination of the evolution of the village power structure up to 1984 in both economic and political terms has revealed the emergence of a new 'ascendant group' in a situation where economic power stems from the nature of individual and household links to the wider regional economy. In turn, these links had become increasingly politicised and were not simply dependent on a household's standing in the agricultural system itself.

A study conducted by Gunasekera (1984) into social change and stratification in a village community during 1979 to 1980 revealed a similar increase in the power of the local MP. She points out that no longer is the MP restricted to dispensing collective goods and favours such as wells and roads but has recently extended patronage over individually attributable benefits such as jobs and land grants. In a subsequent paper on 'the politicisation of the power structure and the death of leadership in a highland community', Gunasekera terms as 'henchmen' those who, with the support of the MP, most effectively manipulate the distribution of patronage. It is these 'henchmen' who constitute the new village elite (1984b:8). In the same way Karagahapitiya had its own political 'henchmen'. Once the power of such people is extended over a wider area in the electorate these 'henchmen' become transformed into regional party bosses and as such are the recipients of greater patronage and wider authority. At this point it may be useful to consider briefly the case of Premeratne, a particular individual in the locality who enjoyed the reputation of being seen as a regional party boss. The patronage mechanism at work in this case was linked to the disbursement of State funds from the Ministry of Housing and Local Government to the gramodaya mandalaya, a local level organisation set up as an umbrella organisation representing village level institutions and societies. One gramodaya mandalaya (GM) was set up for each Grama Sevaka (GS) division and its membership comprised the presidents of key village societies who, in turn, elected a chairman. The secretary was the special service officer of the AGA's office who as noted above (in the case of the Muslim beneficiary) was a political appointee.

Karagahapitiya GS division's gramodaya mandalaya was made up of thirteen members from surrounding villages with only one office bearer from Karagahapitiya village itself, representing the credit society. The GM under the chairmanship of Premeratne received around Rs 25,000 through the Government's decentralised budget scheme for local development work and was also responsible for administering the State's 'million housing programme' with a budget of Rs 42,000 p.a. The chairman had ultimate responsibility for the planning and execution of all expenditure.

A number of villagers complained that very little was done with the money for local development work and that funds appeared to go astray. Ariyaratne, the village representative, confirmed that little effective work had been done by the GM and he pointed out that it was incapable of acting as an efficient pressure group on account of its own political links. This was the direct result of the nature of the membership system. Members were drawn from recognised village societies at the discretion of the special services officer at the AGA (a political appointee) in consultation with the MP. Members of village societies themselves were not necessarily elected and many had few loyalties to a wider village constituency. The records of the local GM illustrated that inadequate funds had been received by the organisation and that little or no pressure had been brought to bear on the MP and District Minister who managed the decentralised budget. Ariyaratne who became vociferous over the issue of budget anomalies was cunningly disqualified as a member of the GM. He failed to attend the requisite number of meetings having first received false information as to their dates and whereabouts.

Premeratne, the Chairman of the gramodaya mandalaya, was widely recognised among villagers to be a powerful and rich beneficiary of the regional political system. He was responsible for the GM's budget and had authority to award local contracts. In order to reap the benefits from his own budgetary management and be in a position to manipulate local contracts, the chairman had to defer to the regional party machine and key political representatives.

The political and economic links that determine the new power structure at the local and regional level are, as Gunasekere (1984) has pointed out inherently unstable and impermanent. This is so because the relationship between the MP and a particular 'henchman' is never secure. The recent history of the evolution of economic and political power in the village illustrates the impermanence of this relationship. Under the SLFP Government, Wijeysinghe had occupied an influential position although he could not depend on the support of his MP who was in the opposition party at the time. During this period the local party organiser was a powerful regional figure. It was the SLFP party organiser who, for example, in 1975 officially opened the newly built Agrarian Service Centre near the village. After the change of government in 1977 new beneficiaries emerged and the level of increased instability resulting from ethnic and civil disturbance has served to make the system even more unstable.

The individualised nature of patronage appeared to limit the constituency of its beneficiaries and although they succeeded in achieving their immediate objectives, their prominence may well be short lived. This helps to explain the high turnover of beneficiaries up to 1983–84.. The death of the former MP and the succession by his brother in 1983, further highlighted the tenuous nature of patronage links. The post 1983 incumbent was seen as more inaccessible than his brother. Consequently, it became a harder struggle for an aspiring householders to gain the MP's favour. In this situation leadership no longer stemmed from within the community. 'The power exercised by the contemporary power elite is quite different from that of their predecessors... because they lack any independent resources of their own they cannot be considered 'brokers' in the conventional sense' (Gunasekera 1984b: 14). The ascendant group in the village was, quite noticeably, a vulnerable elite. In recognition of their precarious position they were forced to remain competitive and distant in economic and social terms and unlike the petty office holders of the past, they no longer consolidated their power in the agrarian economy by invoking complex obligatory duties and ties with fellow villagers.

What has been amply demonstrated in the above micro analysis of emerging power relations at village level, is that those who can manipulate resources disproportionately to their own benefit, are those who have exploited local political links in order to enhance their position in the off–farm economy. This has simultaneously enabled such beneficiaries to improve their bargaining and negotiating powers within the village itself. Those able to incur political favours prior to 1977 were from among the more educated members of an upwardly mobile SLFP group in the village. This group, often in alliance with the Buddhist

sangha (clergy), comprised those most able to articulate a national ideology which emphasised the place of Buddhism and the small rice farmer within the planned economy. After 1977 this group was superseded by a new breed of political opportunists. These beneficiaries displayed an altogether different skill of entrepreneurial cunning. With an eye for the main chance they were prepared to compromise where necessary on certain politically sensitive issues of a public nature, such as lobbying for improved irrigation facilities, in order to optimise on their chances of individual patronage. On more than one occasion villagers scornfully remarked that 'some of us have no shame in bending with the trees' when referring to the tactics of these opportunists.

Rural differentiation now largely depends upon the level of household diversification and is further refined by the network of political patronage. Some households enjoy neither patronage nor regular off–farm income. Those who have access to larger units of land as owner cultivators or part tenants, survive as smallholder farmers. The remainder struggle as poor peasants and landless labourers. This latter category have ended up being those who have benefitted least from State sponsored development schemes such as the IRDP funded tank rehabilitation project in the village, the very group to which IRDP was originally targeted. This group has little or no regular off-farm earnings, limited land to cultivate and engages in casual labouring work around the village. Conscious of their low status in comparison to the majority of diversified households they do not hesitate to draw attention to the widening gap in relative terms between themselves and others. Their main argument revolves around the fact that the rich are getting visibly richer all the time. They talk of those with tiled roofs and new electronic gadgets indicating a level of awareness that implies an incipient notion of class consciousness.

From the above, it is obvious that the twin processes of national economic development and the growth in party politics brought about significant change to the economy and society of Karagahapitiya village up to 1984. An examination of the impact of this change has revealed an emerging pattern of stratification. Since the early 1970s this has become increasingly dependent on direct political patronage and growing diversification at the village level. The was seen to result in the emergence of a new elite that occupied a precarious economic position that paradoxically required the reaffirmation of particular aspects of traditional smallholder relations. The escalation of ethnic violence and the climate of general lawlessness following the rise of the outlawed JVP movement, which was active in the Kurunegala region in 1987-90, has undoubtedly threatened the existing political patronage network. However, the sharp repression of this movement by the Government has ensured, temporarily at least, that former political influence is likely to survive albeit in a less secure and hence predictable form.

In the context of a South Asian rice economy where agricultural intensification is accompanied by increasing pressure on land and the fragmentation of holdings, it is not surprising to find that local political links act as a mechanism which controls access to scarce organised sector (formal) employment. In so doing, these links have become one of the major factors which can explain the emerging pattern of stratification. The intermediate nature of the typical South Asian rice economy, where growing levels of off-farm employment have not been accompanied by the same 'pull' factors as seen in the case of rapid secondary sector expansion in Japan and Taiwan, means that much off-farm activity is still low wage/low productivity oriented and consequently associated with household survival rather than household success.

6 Conclusion: promoting off-farm enterprise

In much of monsoon Asia, where there is a severe constraint on the physical extension of paddy land, intensification of production is the only alternative to large scale capital investment in agriculture. This strategy has been widely adopted throughout Asia and has contributed to maintaining the viability of individual smallholdings so that few farming households are prepared to consider selling paddy land. Thus we can see that the whole system of the provision of services to agriculture helps both to maintain smallholder farming, a fact reflected in production and input increases noted earlier, while at the same time underwriting the importance of economic diversification and off–farm employment. In this latter regard, not only does the whole spectrum of government service offer a direct source of rural employment in many developing economies but it often becomes the major mechanism by which the particular nature of the off–farm economy is perpetuated.

As intensification increases as a result of the development of the forces of production and the greater application of divisible inputs, there is a concomitant increase in support services and infrastructure and a rise in total family earnings. Where this has led to the parallel development of agriculture and rural industry as in the case of Japan and Taiwan, the demand for labour in the off–farm sector will result in a further rise in real family wages and an increasing shift out of the family farm and into the rural firm.

However, where increasing pressure on land has led to the rapid diminution of the family farm without the parallel development of a dynamic off–farm sector, the shift from farm to firm is less a question of maximising opportunities and more a question of necessity. In this situation a growing number of households may well engage in off–farm employment but this may not result in equalising the distribution of income or fostering a growth oriented economy, since the gulf between employment in the organised sector and casual off–farm employment or petty self–employment may be substantial. As Islam (1986) points out, in much of South Asia off–farm employment is confined to traditional cottage based activities where returns to labour are so low there is little prospect of improving rural income distribution. This is quite unlike the situation in the more advanced monsoon economies where an increase in the share of labour income (in the modern sector) to farm income has led to an improvement in overall income distribution. Islam goes on to argue from data drawn from 15 villages in 6 Asian countries that in quantitative terms off–farm employment is very substantial and that its importance varies inversely with farm size. Yet, the low returns associated with much of this employment has reduced its income equalising effect (Islam 1986).

Nevertheless, for the majority of villagers in the contemporary Asian context, access to different sources of diversification has improved with regional economic development and the growth in rural services. Improved access has simultaneously resulted in the breakdown of the former hierarchical monopoly over external resources and brought about a fundamental change in the character of village social relations and ideology. In some cases this has been accompanied by an incipient trend towards politicisation and political patronage which serves to regulate access to regional employment and services, thus contributing to the process of contemporary economic differentiation. The growing complexity of any socio–economic structure which is partly located in agriculture and partly outside reflects a certain degree of change at the local level which will vary under different local and national conditions. In those economies experiencing strong 'push' factors related to the increasing pressure on land, as seen in the case of Kerala in chapter three and in Sri Lanka in chapters four and five, off–farm employment in the tertiary sector has become substantial. This employment reflects different things for different actors. At the higher end of the income scale are entrepreneurs and those in the organised waged/salaried sector, while at the lower end are those in petty employment or self–employment and casual off–farm work. Yet, access to these different forms of employment and hence returns to labour is not necessarily governed by the agricultural asset base of the household concerned and often has more to do with local political linkages than with landholding status, as clearly illustrated in the case of Sri Lanka in the previous chapter.

The specific form of rural diversification and related differentiation that will be expressed in any national or regional context is likely to depend, amongst other things, on a combination of the particular technological requirements of economic activity and the nature of development policy that has been pursued in that context. As already seen in chapters one to three, what characterises

171

much of rural Asia is smallholder based rice farming which is responsive to high levels of intensification and labour absorbtion leading to increased land productivity and output. The degree of intensification, however, is by no means uniform and can vary widely as shown in chapter three in the case of the relatively poor performance of the rice economy of Kerala.

The importance of State policy in determining the character of the rural economy in the Sri Lankan context has been examined by Moore (1984 and 1985). He argues that many of the agrarian features of Sri Lanka have evolved out of a long tradition of the State promotion of smallholder farming. He goes on to point out that although in the past there has been a high level of political awareness amongst the Sri Lankan peasantry they have, by force of circumstance, been unable to make any radical demands on the State in respect of improving the profitability of agriculture. He sees this as stemming from the nature of the political system itself, where the State, irrespective of party political differences, can be characterised as an elite dominated entity which is not committed to transferring sufficient resources to the smallholder sector. In a similar way, Manor (1979) has examined the failure of successive governments in Sri Lanka since the Donoughmore Constitution of 1931 to build a participatory political system at the regional and local level. He perceives this problem as a function of poor political integration resulting in an elite/mass discontinuity which he regards as the principal cleavage in society. An examination of the various attempts at decentralisation in Sri Lanka, from the District Political Authority system and the Decentralised Budget of 1973-74 to the District Minister system of 1978 and the District Development Councils of 1980 through to Provincial Councils (first round of elections being held in April 1988), reinforces the view that genuine participation has been subordinated to administrative deconcentration (Slater 1989).

In a situation such as that of Sri Lanka, the result has largely been one of meeting 'mixed cultivator demands' through the State delivery of subsidies on farm inputs and irrigation facilities. Yet, this has not always been accompanied by high levels of institutional efficiency and high crop prices so vital to the farming community. The evolution of this type agricultural development policy in Sri Lanka has consequently resulted in the maintenance of a smallholder sector which has suffered from insufficient incentives and institutional inefficiency. Rice prices have increased, however, as market forces have been allowed to dominate in recent years, and between 1977-78 and 1882-83 production rose by an average of 5.8 percent per annum according to some government estimates. Nevertheless, there have been certain aspects of national economic policy and legislative neglect which have served to maintain smallholder farming rather than promote commercial agriculture. Trade and exchange rate policies coupled with domestic rationing have traditionally facilitated the cheap importation of basic foodstuffs and the depression of output prices for domestic cultivators. Resulting low rates of profit have blocked capital investment in agriculture. In recent years State policy has begun to address some of these issues. Artificial trade restrictions were lifted in the post 1977 liberalisation of the economy and the exchange rate floated while the State monopoly over agricultural marketing was abolished with the result that private traders became more actively involved in the process.

The very nature of rice cultivation, often reinforced by State policies designed to conserve a smallholder tradition, either through fiscal management or land reforms, has meant that in many parts of Asia there has been no major transition to agrarian capitalism in a conventional sense. Rather it has been argued that the smallholder farming sector can only be adequately understood in terms of individual household diversification into the off-farm economy. In this sense, developments within the rural community cannot be isolated from the urban or semi-urban sectors but have to be seen as a complex relation of agricultural and non-agricultural activity.

It is only when account is taken of the total activity of the rural household, that the survival of contemporary smallholder relations within a socio-economic structure that is not undifferentiated or homogeneous, can be adequately understood. As Harriss (1982) has pointed out with reference to South India, family reproduction now depends on a mix of petty commodity production and marginal activity in a wider and more generally accessible economy. The evidence presented in chapter five bears out Harriss's proposition for the Sri Lankan case. As noted in chapter five, many villagers are involved in a wide range of diversified activities, both within the village and to a greater extent in the regional economy, which often represent a far more profitable investment than farming itself. At the same time off-farm income serves to sustain many small farmers and tenants who continue to value their plot of land without having to face the problem of indebtedness and the possible threat of becoming fully appropriated by a larger farmer. In this situation the productivity of tenants remains high as they are able to cultivate with modern techniques and inputs.

It is this process that helps to explain why, in the absence of agrarian capitalism, the former power structure is no longer dominant although aspects of traditional agrarian relations have been preserved. The examination of agrarian transition and off-farm diversification at village level in Sri Lanka during 1983-84 showed that emerging forms of social and economic differentiation do not necessarily revolve around the persistence of traditional hierarchical social relations at village level, as noted by Gunasinghe (1979) and Moore (1985); nor do they represent a more conventional transition towards agrarian capitalism; instead they may reflect the complex process of politicised diversification in a smallholder farming context. The critical factor in determining contemporary social and economic differentiation is the level of household diversification within the regional economy. Any analysis of this process at village level must include all households within the community whether or not they are predominantly engaged in rural activities.

As seen in chapters four and five, one third of all households in Karagahapitiya village in Sri Lanka during 1983-84 had no involvement in active farming and received no income from paddy cultivation, while half the total number of households engaged in cultivation were in fact predominantly employed in the off-farm economy which accounted for their main source of income. This figure rose to include two thirds of all households if diversification away from agriculture as the sole traditional source of rural livelihood was taken into account. In this case, economic diversification began as early as in the middle of the last century when household members would work on neighbouring coconut estates in off peak periods of the paddy cycle. Over the years, as regional economic activities and services expanded, so too did the level of off-farm employment amongst household members. In more recent years as the demand for new opportunities has grown the level of political control over these opportunities has increased. This may seem paradoxical in the face of greater economic liberalisation and the increasing call for privatisation but the nature of contemporary political control has more to do with informal political networks than formal systems of public intervention and has doubtless been strengthened in response to the rise of violent opposition. A journalist reporting on Sri Lanka in 1985 noted that 'political cowardice continues to inflate the civil service. Politicians are expected to get government jobs for their constituents, and civil servants are expected to get them for friends and relatives – much as the president is expected to provide ministries for as many members of parliament as possible'. The correspondent also witnessed a job applicant at an interview being told that he needed a letter of reference from his member of parliament, the justification that there were 'all sorts of terrorist and Marxist fellows around these days' was perhaps an early forewarning of what was to come.

This analysis of the farm to firm transition in the contemporary Asian countryside has attempted to demonstrate that rural production relations have evolved in such a way as to sustain a particular form of differentiation within the community. Despite the relatively advanced development of the forces of production in wet rice cultivation, many features of small farming remain. As seen in chapter four in relation to village Sri Lanka, these include the survival of a traditional landholding pattern, the continued operation of an egalitarian inheritance system and the maintenance of a labour system based on the family and mutual cooperation, low interest credit and traditional tenurial arrangements. Even new forms of cooperation between cultivators have grown up as a result of bureaucratic intervention in seasonal cultivation meetings and water management policy. Although these features have been subject to adaptation in response to contemporary social and economic change, they have not become transformed into relations of capitalist production. This point is further emphasised by the low level of capital investment in land and equipment in spite of high current expenditure on inputs.

In such cases, the reformulated nature of smallholder farming now revolves around the links that particular households maintain between the village and the regional economy and, in so doing, has created a new pattern of social and economic differentiation. This has become further influenced by the pattern of local political manipulation. Agriculture remains an important source of livelihood for most families yet the key to the nature of contemporary social and economic relations lies outside agriculture. Aspects of former agrarian relations still function but rather than supporting an undifferentiated mass of smallholders within an hierarchical total system dominated by landlords, they are part of a reformulated set of social relations.

Today, these relations are geared towards individual advancement through household diversification. Where cooperation exists it helps to perpetuate these adaptations in a situation in which, on the whole, villagers claim that the maintenance of social distance between households is a more common feature than traditional cooperative relations. Although cooperation may still be an important feature of the labour system and the credit system as noted in chapter four, in many respects it contributes to a degree of household independence within a smallholder system of agriculture which in turn facilitates complex household diversification. In an attempt to explain the ultimate logic behind contemporary inter household relations in Sri Lanka, a group of farmers on one occasion seemed to agree that these days 'it is better to keep arms length relations with neighbours, friends or even kin'. This phrase was often repeated by household members in discussion concerning their relation with other families in the village.

In this situation social and economic relations cannot be theorised in terms of the survival of a peasant mode of production, in spite of the continuing operation of the family farm. Nor can they be theorised in terms of a gradual transition towards agrarian capitalism. The use of family and exchange labour still far outweighs the incidence of wage labour in many rice farming communities and reinvestment appears to be limited to optimising smallholder yields with little or no accumulation of land as the primary means of production. The majority of output is consumed locally and merchant capital has little control over the means of production. Here, merchants cannot be seen as mediators in a process of surplus extraction under national capital despite an increasing involvement on the part of the cultivator with the market. Harriss (1982), for example, has shown with evidence from Tamil Nadu, that the application of the concept of formal subsumption is somewhat problematic in a situation in which merchant capital does not exercise such complete control over the producer as to bring about the separation of the means of production from the producer.

This fact is perhaps not surprising when one considers more generally the unique dynamic of wet rice culture. Bray (1986) has emphasised a number of historical examples ranging from Java to China where the trend has been to smaller units of production to underline this very point. In many contemporary Asian rice economies, modified cultivation practices have combined through extensive household diversification with certain aspects of the regional economic system to produce a 'hybrid' class of off-farm smallholders and urban employees supported by cultural institutions and adaptations that assist in bridging the rural-urban divide. The multifarious character of the occupational structure found within many rice villages reflects an emerging pattern of differentiation which has its roots both in the cultivation system itself as well as in the mechanisms governing access to the wider off-farm economy.

In this context smallholder rice farming can be seen as an integral part of a broader economic strategy that, through a process of individual household diversification, depends on a particular system of links between the village and regional economy. In this way the organisational and ideological influences acting upon the local and regional economic system are seen to be capable of dynamising particular sections within it (see Long and Robert 1984). This dynamism is generally dependent upon the functioning of a particular ideological commitment of the contemporary nation State which serves to coopt the majority of households by offering them the hope of increased future participation in the wider economy. This process is not predetermined and, as the analysis of changing beneficiaries in chapter five has shown, it is neither constant nor stable. Yet at the same time it has produced a particular economic and social system in which the former agrarian hierarchy is no longer perpetuated and a new form of economic differentiation has been created.

The policy implications of off-farm diversification

Smallholder diversification is thus becoming an increasingly important element of the rural economy in many countries especially where there are severe constraints on the physical expansion of farming activity and increases in output are largely dependent on agricultural intensification. The development of the typical monsoon rice economy demonstrates the strong relationship between agricultural intensification leading to rises in output and yield and the resulting increased pressure on land leading to the diminution in holding size. Both factors have contributed to the growth in off-farm activity; the first by increasing the general level of development of the rural economy and the demand for nonfarm goods and services, the supply of which may exert a pull effect into the off-farm sector; the second by a steady decrease in holding size which will exert a push effect into the off-farm sector in response to a growing demand for alternative employment of a seasonal and permanent nature which may not conflict with the continuing viability of the family farm.

An immediate issue of policy relevance is the question of the long term impact of off-farm diversification on agricultural production. It is quite likely that diversification will have an adverse effect on farming if off–farm activities compete with agriculture for scarce inputs (Ho 1986). This assumes that labour, as the major input, is diverted away from farming in a manner that reduces optimal intensity and skill. Ho (1986) has examined the impact of off–farm activity on agricultural production showing that yields decline as participation in non agricultural activity increases. Having first isolated the farm size variable in relation to productivity, since the smaller the farm the greater the level of off–farm employment, he shows that households that earn around 80 percent of total income from off–farm sources have an average yield that is only 57 percent of those households with an off–farm income of less than 20 percent of total income. He concludes that the inverse relationship between yield and off–farm activity is the result of a per hectare decline in labour and material inputs for those households with greater off–farm participation. This relationship is bound to be more marked where the demand for labour is higher as a result of the rapid growth in rural industry as in the case of Japan or Taiwan. Where surplus labour and under–employment exist the impact of diversification on farm productivity may be negligible.

A further point of interest is that if a total productivity measure, such as the return to fixed assets, is used in place of yield, no such inverse relationship is observed (Ho 1986). If it is assumed that there is an adverse impact on farming in terms of yield in those economies where demand for off–farm labour is high, the question then becomes one of whether or not the potential gains in total net productivity outweigh the loss in potential agricultural yield. What is certain is that substantial off–farm diversification of a productive nature is only likely to follow substantial agricultural intensification. Once agricultural development policy has helped to achieve this, it may then be instructive to examine to what extent the trade–off in yield decline can be minimised.

The small farm structure of monsoon Asia has proven to be capable of securing impressive rises in land productivity and total output through farm intensification while simultaneously maintaining high levels of employment through off–farm diversification. The policy implications for those countries which have nearly completed the transition from farm to firm (Japan & Taiwan) are different from those which are still in the early stages of transition. As small farms reach the limits of productivity, the farm pressure groups lobby hard for protection and subsidies. As farm size decreases farms become non viable and can only survive with injections of off–farm income. Oshima argues that here 'the time has come for the conversion of these small farms into larger units which can utilise larger–scale mechanised technologies... which can sharply raise productivity per worker and release more workers for full–time urban employment' (1986: 53–54). The consolidation of farm holdings into specialised, commercial units of production might thus complete the development of monsoon paddy agriculture by sustaining output and reducing costs in the face of rising wages in the off-farm economy.

The consolidation and growth in size and scale of operation may offer one means of escaping existing dependency on protection and subsidy but is not necessarily the only means. Assuming there is a baseline of acceptable productivity that can be achieved without a major transformation of the agricultural system, existing smallholder units might more profitably focus on food quality rather than quantity, especially given the increasing evidence of the harmful health and environmental effects of conventional large scale farming. If traditional small farm practices prove to be a better means of meeting these objectives by concentrating on expanding niche markets then they should not be discouraged. This is all the more relevant when considering the deeply entrenched resistance amongst part time farmers to move out of farming altogether.

A useful conceptual framework of the various stages of off-farm development has been outlined by Shand (1986). In this model the rural economy is seen to pass through four stages of development based on different farm to firm linkages. The first stage is represented by generally low agricultural productivity, although rising population may stimulate land productivity through higher labour investments. Off-farm employment is supply led and supplementary in nature. The second stage is brought about by higher agricultural productivity based on the adoption of new technology with supporting infrastructure. Off-farm activity generally remains less productive than agriculture but there is a tendency for off-farm productivity to rise. The third stage represents a more fundamental transformation of the rural economy with rising agricultural productivity generating a rise in demand for agricultural and non agricultural goods and services. As the opportunity cost of labour in agriculture rises, labour saving technologies are gradually introduced. The fourth and final stage represents the transition to a mature off-farm economy where labour intensity in agriculture declines as off-farm activity develops a powerful self-sustaining dynamic (Shand 1986: 235–238).

The majority of monsoon economies in Asia, and indeed a number of economies in Africa and Latin America, have already reached stage three in their transition from farm to firm. In many of these economies the expansion in off-farm activity has been substantial although much of this expansion to date has been associated with the deconcentration of public administration and the decentralisation of public services coupled to the growth of petty tertiary activity. The task now facing policy makers is that of expanding off-farm enterprise more generally and promoting productive activity in particular so as to meet the challenge of generating full employment in a self-sustaining and dynamic manner.

Evidence of the need for a coherent strategy on the promotion of productive off-farm activity can be seen from the rapid growth in rural demand. Even in the least developed regions of Asia, rural markets for non agricultural products have been growing at an astonishing rate. The rural market for packaged consumer goods in India more than doubled between 1983–88. The product wise breakdown of sales in this market shows that toilet soaps have been growing at an enormous 60 percent per annum, while nearly 50 percent of all mono cassette players and mopeds and 20 percent of colour televisions are sold to rural consumers. 'From the remote hamlets in eastern Bihar to the prosperous sugar belt of western Uttar Pradesh, from the wheat fields of Punjab to the rice paddies of Kerala, from marginal farmers to rich landlords, villagers are flocking to buy consumer goods – and buying them with a vengeance' (India Today, July 1990: 66). This particular press feature on the rapid expansion of rural markets in India goes on to explain that it is a myth that only cheaper products sell in rural markets and that once consumer taste has been properly researched, the considerable purchasing capacity of the rural middle class can be effectively mobilised.

In order to meet this demand it is necessary to explore ways of increasing the growth rate of output from rural producers. It is not sufficient simply to concentrate on developing a range of high labour intensity activities to meet this objective, since high labour intensity may not, in itself, lead to long term growth in employment but merely reflect the cheapness of labour. As Anderson and Leiserson (1980) point out, simultaneous growth in rural employment and income can only come about from an expansion of productive activity. They argue that many of the inherent characteristics of rural industry are conducive to such an expansion for the following reasons: the type of goods and services produced and the techniques allow for a high degree of substitutability between capital and labour; the labour supply situation and the absence of formal wage setting tends to ensure that wage increases are moderate and in line with supply and demand; as the labour force gains experience one could expect substantial improvements in the efficiency of use in capital and labour; it is generally believed that the price elasticity of demand for many non agricultural goods is quite high. There is, therefore, considerable scope for expanding off–farm employment and income by raising the growth of output through increases in the efficiency of production and the introduction of some capital investment without a sharp rise in prices (Anderson and Leiserson 1980).

The promotion of off–farm activity has not always been looked upon in a favourable light. There have been many critics in the past who have seen rural small enterprise as being instrumental in lowering the reproduction costs of labour via the production of cheap wage goods and services. These critics have argued that such forms of enterprise are highly exploitative and that policies designed to promote exploitation can not succeed in either alleviating poverty or generating growth for the masses. This question of the low level of remuneration of rural petty enterprise requires careful consideration and can only be properly examined in relation to the total household employment pattern and the prevailing characteristics of family labour. It is quite likely

179

that low remuneration levels, particularly in the early stages of farm to firm transition, are a means of compensating for low productivity where a good deal of off–farm labour may be simultaneously engaged in agricultural activity. As Schmitz (1981) points out, even where there is evidence of exploitation in the sense that the returns to labour are less than the equivalent hours worked multiplied by the prevailing wage rate, the opportunity costs of engaging in poorly remunerated off–farm activity should be closely examined. In any case, the real issue is not so much whether any particular form of off–farm activity at a given time is more or less exploitative but whether or not off–farm activity is capable of generating wealth for the rural community as a whole. The evidence presented in chapter two in relation to the small firm economy of Northeast and Central Italy shows that there is no necessary link between small family firms and low levels of remuneration. Although low remuneration may be one means by which small firms attempt to remain competitive, those which have been successful in innovating within the context of small scale production are able to raise remuneration levels to those prevailing in the economy at large. A crucial point, here, relates to the medium term growth potential of off–farm enterprise and, as mentioned above, its ability to retain capital in a manner capable of raising the growth rate of output and hence the expansion of overall employment and income in the countryside. Off–farm employment has already been seen to be a critical source of income for the smaller farmers and landless labourers while simultaneously acting as an important source of goods and services for the local community and a source of secondary and seasonal employment for those whose primary income remains in agriculture.

For all these reasons it is highly desirable to consider a policy of active promotion of off–farm enterprise. In the absence of any strategic direction in this area it is quite possible that off–farm activity will be confined to a permanent supplementary role within the rural economy based on stagnating production in the secondary sector and the artificial cushion of an inflated government administration alongside a multitude of precarious private service businesses in the tertiary sector. It is essential, therefore, that policy makers begin to address themselves to the task of establishing a policy framework capable of stimulating the growth of productive off–farm enterprise.

The promotion of off–farm enterprise

The expansion of off–farm activity arising from increases in the growth rate of output is only likely to come about if there is sufficient commitment to a strong supportive policy, designed to create the right external environment in which off–farm enterprise can flourish and, at the same time, improve the internal operating environment by helping such enterprises to overcome existing constraints and to harness new opportunities. In the external arena, which is by definition beyond the control of the rural firm, there are many factors that will effect the viability of the off-farm economy. However, in this case the off-farm economy should not be seen as a unique sector requiring special macro policies but 'should be the norm on the basis of which everything is ordered – the stability of the currency, the liberalisation of trade (including external trade), tax incentives, interest rates, etc' (Lassort and Clavier 1989: 60). In this sense, what is seen as good for rural enterprise is good for the economy as a whole and many of the necessary macro economic reforms have been proposed as part of structural adjustment programmes in a variety of countries in the developing world. The detrimental effect of over valued exchange rates on both domestic manufacturing and agriculture is now all too familiar where domestic producers are unable to compete with artificially cheap imported goods. Similarly, the negative impact of extensive bureaucratic control over domestic production, through direct public ownership, licences and production quotas, has been considerable.

Since there is already an extensive literature on structural adjustment which examines both the need for and impact of such programmes in the developing world, what might be emphasised at this point is that the creation of an enabling environment in many of the low income countries of South Asia and Africa, with deep structural constraints arising from their dependence on commodity exports, is only likely to happen if there is an increase in net capital flows to these countries from the industrialised world and the removal of discriminatory restrictions against exports of manufactured and processed products from low income countries. At the same time as governments trim expenditure to reduce budget deficits and interest payments on borrowings they should ensure that there is sufficient support for rural enterprise initiatives particularly in the form of small and micro industry, women's activities etc (see Persaud 1989). The policy implications of the creation of a more enabling small enterprise environment are quite clear. As Persaud contends, the answer does not lie in a laissez faire approach but sensible economic direction and strategic support for employment and income generating activities of a productive nature. This must be reflected in fiscal, sectoral, technological and educational policies designed with this in mind where the primary role of government is one of supporting rather than directly controlling local enterprise.

Much can be done in the external arena to improve the way macro economic policies impact on rural enterprise. While the general liberalisation of many parts of the economy will provide greater incentives to local producers, government intervention will still be required if the rural off-farm economy is to expand in a productive manner. The creation of a general policy environment that is at least neutral with respect to the size of small enterprises is crucial for their long term survival (Haggblade, Leidholm and Mead 1986). Tariffs on tools and equipment, raw materials and spare parts should not be higher for small firms. Government support may take the form of intervention in the area foreign exchange supply, customs and excise duty and trade regulations to assist small enterprise overcome their lack of access to foreign exchange and imported raw materials, equipment and technology. Tax holidays and excise duty concessions linked to investment in plant and machinery or the value of output can act as useful incentives to newly established enterprises. In some cases sales rebates have been introduced to assist particular small enterprise sectors. For example, the khadi and village industries sector in India has enjoyed substantial sales rebates at certain times of the year varying from 10 to 35 percent. Finally, the strong linkages between agriculture and off-farm enterprise (see Kilby and Leidholm 1986; Haggblade, Hazell and Brown 1989) means that every effort must be made to increase agricultural output through sensitive farm pricing and direct service provision in the form of agricultural credit, research, extension and marketing.

Concessionary finance

Anderson (1982) has drawn on Kilby's definition of entrepreneurship to isolate the key attributes of efficient enterprise as the central issue relating to the growth of employment and income in small enterprise. He analyses efficiency in terms of the investment behaviour and operating behaviour of the enterprise. Both sets of behaviour can be significantly affected by different forms of intervention and these will be considered in relation to a variety of financial and operational support options outlined below. Another major problem experienced by many off-farm enterprises is the shortage of domestic capital. Although a good number of off-farm activities are funded by family savings or out of cash flow, the promotion of self-employment for the poorest groups (as in the Indian IRDP scheme) and the promotion of process and product innovation for small scale industry will require improved access to investment capital. This need for capital may be met by governments seeking greater injections of loan capital from regional development banks and other multi-lateral and bi-lateral sources. It may also be met by governments making adjustments to their existing loan portfolios to improve the balance of spending on productive enterprise and, as Persaud (1989) argues, moving away from public financing and towards private investment.

One of the main factors which has exacerbated the problem of the lack of domestic capital for small enterprise and has thus limited the further expansion of the off-farm sector, has been the reluctance of commercial banks to provide term loans for (rural) small enterprise. Steel and Webster have identified five factors responsible for this inadequacy: commercial bank's funds come mainly from short-term deposits; inflation rates are generally high; credit rationing and fixed interest rates favour large loans with lower administrative costs; small enterprises are perceived as being highly risky with associated high default rates; small enterprises often lack necessary collateral and accounting systems (1989:65).

182

Many of these problems could be overcome with the introduction of a sufficiently flexible finance and banking policy. This may require a drastic revision of existing financial systems and procedures so that the cost of finance would be reduced and access widened as far as possible. The introduction of differential rates of interest would ensure that the cost of loans could be more closely related to ability to pay and that specific location, size and wealth criteria could be targeted for special loan assistance. A common shortcoming in many credit schemes is the restriction on the use of credit for capital investment. A large number of off-farm enterprises, however, suffer from insufficient working capital resulting in a failure to manage cash flow. This problem is one of the commonest causes of small firm failure and could be eased if working capital requirements were more adequately met.

Repayment schedules could be made more flexible in line with different client's circumstances and loan procedures simplified to improve customer access. Default rates can be dramatically reduced by introducing a range of repayment rewards and controls. In Italy, for example, a special fund offering low interest loans to artisans and small producers operates through the commercial banking system and incorporates a discounting scheme against prompt repayment. The Grameen Bank scheme in Bangladesh offers a different form of control over loan repayment. The scheme, which began in 1976, now covers over 500 rural bank branches servicing over 10,500 villages. Like the Indian IRDP programme, the scheme aims to provide finance to the assetless poor especially women and the landless. Unlike the Indian programme, however, the scheme is based on group saving and lending where groups of five people constitute the primary mechanism through which credit is disbursed. Loan eligibility is dependent on the repayment record of other members of the group thus mobilising peer pressure to minimise default rates. The scheme also involves compulsory regular savings where all members of the group contribute to a group fund and an emergency fund on the basis of regular weekly contributions and a percentage contribution of loans received. As Rahman (1989) points out, savings components have now been introduced into many rural credit schemes and are a notable feature of the Small Farmers Development Project in Nepal, the Smallholder Agricultural Development Project in Malawi, the Income generating Project for the Rural Poor in Indonesia and the Village Development Fund Project in Mali. The latter involving an entire village as the primary group and drawing on the combined savings and resources of 160 villages (Rahman 1989: 71). In some cases it may be useful to pool resources by establishing a revolving fund for an association or group of enterprises. This has been the guiding principle in the Malawi Mudzi Fund pilot scheme for small rural income generating activities in Chiradzulu and Mangochi districts. This kind of financing initiative can act as the catalyst for a greater concentration of activity around specific product areas as a means of enhancing the survival opportunities and improving the competitiveness of small enterprise. This will be discussed in more detail in the following section.

Improved credit disbursal and monitoring procedures can also make a substantial contribution to loan repayments and overall business management. Loan disbursal and monitoring requires assistance at all stages of project planning and implementation. Procedures need to be developed in conjunction with the local administration to enhance current planning and monitoring process. A common practice in both banks and local administration is to sponsor loans for schemes that are capable of being widely replicated hence minimising the extent of supporting infrastructure and the level of overall administrative complexity. The first years of the Indian IRDP scheme were characterised by a huge concentration of loans for animal husbandry schemes in general and the acquisition of milch cows in particular. This not only had the effect of saturating local markets but distorted the price of essential inputs to stall fed cattle in the form of animal feeds and supplementary nutrients as well as the price of the primary assets themselves (see Jain et al 1985).

Local level planning must be more accurately tailored to supply and demand factors where physical, material and human resources should be matched against local demand for goods and services. This is only likely to happen if a rapid method of assessing such factors can be devised in a form that is accessible to administrative staff without adding to existing work burdens . This also raises questions about the kind of institutional structures that might be adopted to facilitate local level planning which will simultaneously involve local communities in the planning and implementation process. This may be of a formal nature in the context of local government reform as seen in Karnataka in India (see Slater and Watson 1989), or part of a community based/locally managed process (see Curtis 1991). Loan selection and asset procurement mechanisms should ensure that lending criteria are translated into an operational form with minimum leakage and misidentification. Selection mechanisms could be designed to give priority to enterprises with reasonable employment potential and loan instalments could be linked to the number of verified workers per enterprise. An interesting variation on this theme has been proposed by Pradhan (1989) who advocates the disbursal of low interest loan entitlements to individual beneficiaries who can then offer their services to potential employers who will, in turn, be able to realise the loan against the provision of secure employment to the original beneficiary.

The functioning of loan selection, verification and asset procurement procedures may require the active participation of local community organisations and bank/administrative extension officers. The Indian IRDP programme which provides loans for the assetless poor has a well developed system of coping with such tasks. Beneficiary selection is undertaken by representatives of the local community within the village panchayat (council) structure. Assets for which the loan is taken are acquired on behalf of the beneficiary by a local procurement committee to ensure loans are used for the intended (productive) purpose. Monitoring is undertaken by extension workers who periodically examine the current status of the asset, the level of incremental income generated from the asset and loan repayments which are recorded in a bank pass book kept by the individual beneficiary.

A number of small enterprise promotion and rural employment schemes include the provision of grants for capital assets such as premises, plant and machinery. These often vary according to the status of the beneficiary and are conditional on total investment not exceeding specific ceilings. The small scale industries (SSI) programme in India provides a 25 percent subsidy on investment in plant and machinery in industrially backward districts and between 10 and 15 percent in other districts. A special assistance component within the same programme designed to promote women's enterprise includes a 50 percent subsidy on plant and machinery up to a maximum of Rs 50,000 and graduated rent subsidies over a four year period declining from 100 percent to 75 percent to 50 percent and finally 25 percent in the fourth year. Likewise, the Indian IRDP programme provides varying grants/subsidies depending on the social and economic status of the individual beneficiaries. The standard rate of subsidy (grant) is 25 percent of the total financial package for small farmers. This increases to 33.3 percent for marginal farmers, agricultural labourers and rural artisans and rises to 50 percent for tribal beneficiaries. The subsidy ceiling also varies depending on the area in which the beneficiary lives (higher in drought prone areas) and his or her socio-economic status.

Legal and institutional procedures governing the establishment and operation of non agricultural enterprise should be streamlined thus rendering them more comprehensible and effective as forms of regulation and incentive. Effective financing from commercial banking sources may not be possible without a lead role being performed by an apex refinancing institution. The exact responsibility and function of such an institution will differ according to the existing level of activity in the commercial sector. Where commercial lending is well developed the apex institution may act as a central project accountant but where it is not, the apex unit may have to adopt a more active role in training and supervising commercial operations (Steel and Webster 1989). This may have to be accompanied by a loan guarantee system if commercial banks are to increase lending in a substantial manner to a new rural clientele.

Operational support initiatives

A number of the critical operational or managerial functions of small enterprise have been discussed by Anderson (1982). He identifies these functions within the context of materials procurement, production and marketing and highlights key aspects of these functions which affect overall efficiency and productivity. The main concerns relate to the time spent on dealing with public bureaucracies over licences, taxes and regulations; materials procurement problems and poor levels of stock control; inadequate production management and supervision resulting in low productivity and high levels of wastage, damage and pilferage; poor use of technology and negligible maintenance; inadequate accounting procedures resulting in a lack of financial control; sales and marketing deficiencies based on poor customer contact and market intelligence.

Many of these problems, in turn, relate to questions of access as pointed by Schmitz (82) in an analysis of the main growth constraints on small scale manufacturing in developing countries. Schmitz argues that small firms suffer serious disadvantages in access to raw materials, credit, technology and markets. The main obstacles in regard to raw material supply are to do with insufficient bargaining capability, lack of working capital and existing allocation preferences. The technology gap between large and small firms is a serious problem where alternative production techniques show significant differences in initial investment per unit of output. As far as markets are concerned, the lack of a powerful brand name tends to limit market exposure while insufficient capital means that little is spent on promotional activity (Schmitz 1982). Although many of the problems affecting the small firm, relating both to the external operating environment and the internal operating efficiency of the enterprise, appear almost insuperable, there are a host of enabling measures which could be introduced to overcome a number of these problems.

Initial start up procedures could be streamlined so that they did not act as a disincentive to potential entrepreneurs. In most cases this would require some modification to the existing administrative structure so that all services and official support could be provided by a single agency at district level. Such an agency would be responsible for the registration of eligible units as a means of ensuring that they could gain access to concessionary finance and raw materials where applicable. This agency might also engage in the preparation of market studies, feasibility studies and project reports covering a range of potential activities which could be developed in the locality identifying likely public/private investment contributions. The agency could also act as the central point of contact for banks and assist clients in the development of a rudimentary business plan for loan applications etc.

The District Industries Centre (DIC) concept in India functions on these lines with the General Manager of the DIC responsible for the implementation of all Central and State protection and promotion initiatives as well as liaison with banks and other departments. The main functions of the DIC are as follows: the provision of basic information on district growth potential; assistance in the identification and provision of necessary infrastructure; the preparation of techno-feasibility reports to identify materials and equipment needs, organising local training courses; the provision of consultancy services and market surveys. Although the basic concept is sound, the actual performance of individual DIC's is often variable. There tends to be a great deal of discrepancy in the time taken to process different applications and little communication between the agency and the client on standard procedures. Most of the performance targets are expressed in quantitative terms on the basis of start ups rather than in qualitative terms reflecting business performance and employment generated etc. These targets could also be more closely related to individual officer's performance and tied into a system of rewards for accurate targeting, responsive processing and good consultancy. At present, functional managers do not have adequate credit limits and much decision making has to be passed on to the general manager. The DIC itself could be further professionalised by introducing technically qualified staff to work at district level as part of a small enterprise extension and training programme.

Adequate premises are often in short supply and can act as a constraint on business start up and expansion. Although access to land and low cost building materials will be less of a problem in the rural off-farm sector, premium sites with good communication facilities and within close proximity to a reasonable market are likely to be scarce. The provision of land and worksheds at subsidised rents can act as a considerable incentive to local producers. Small enterprise estates could be especially attractive for infant industry development and constructed as part of a public works employment generation programme along the lines of existing rural housing schemes. Rents could be adjusted according to space occupied as well as production and employment criteria and should be capable of being flexibly divided to accommodate a certain amount of expansion from nursery unit to larger enterprise. Rents should be of short duration so as to minimise the financial problem of being bound into long rental periods. The most successful attempts at providing low cost, flexible premises have been based on a shared common structure where the smallest and cheapest unit may be demarcated with nothing more than a single white line painted on the floor. The main facility will be sub-divided into component units in such a way as to gain the maximum benefit from shared physical facilities such as electricity and water and access to shared services in production and administration.

The technology gap could be bridged by operating common production facilities on the estate, which could be rented by individual operators on an hourly basis and maintained regularly. In some cases shared equipment may be restricted for testing and design purposes with suitable low to medium technology equipment being supplied to individual units for production purposes. As Morgan has stated, 'there is every indication that the use of carefully designed modular systems could achieve significant reductions in its cost to the entrepreneur (1989: 79).

Small rural industries have generally experienced little or no mechanisation over the years. This is often the result of the misplaced apprehension that technological innovation is likely to displace labour. The experience of successful small enterprise economies such as those of Japan and Northeast and Central Italy shows that the reverse is true. It is only by maintaining a competitive edge in the market with the emphasis on product quality and productivity that small enterprises can compete with large firms and retain or expand their market share. In Japan, small units have been able to survive and prosper by introducing a ceratin amount of technology which has allowed them to continue to supply larger industries with high quality components. In Italy, much of the flourishing small enterprise economy has depended on technical innovation. In the Veneto and Emilia Romagna regions, craft based technology has been replaced by more advanced flexible technologies where small firms at the apex of a production network use a wide range of advanced machine tools, micro processing equipment and computer aided design equipment. High levels of inter firm cooperation and the fragmentation of the production process tends to facilitate the introduction and use of new equipment by defraying the cost and encouraging collaboration (see Slater and Watson 1990). This point will be discussed in more detail below. The research and development function can be as crucial for small enterprise as it is for large firms. Given the resource constraints of small enterprise, research and development could be provided by an integrated small enterprise support and extension service. One of the important research and technology functions that could be provided by this service would be the testing of product quality and consistency to provide a guaranteed minimum standard which would help small firms sell into larger firms and penetrate export markets.

Training is another area which can make a significant contribution towards the success of a small enterprise economy. The supply of a skilled workforce, in both technical and managerial terms, is essential if small and micro enterprise is to develop an internal dynamic capable of ensuring that it is more than a residual employer. Morgan (1989) argues that training is a long term activity and has to anticipate the demand for skills likely to be required by micro enterprises at least five to ten years ahead. Basic technical training can easily be incorporated into school curricula feeding into specialist technical training colleges for those pupils most suited to follow a vocational rather than academic education. This practice has been adopted in the Italian case where training institutes play a major role in supporting small enterprise. The Instituto Technico Industriale in Bologna is one of the oldest and largest in Emilia Romagna catering to the needs of local artisan production. The institute offers a variety of courses to pupils aged over fourteen including mechanical, chemical and electrical engineering and graphic design etc. The institute also doubles up to offer vocational training to workers employed in industrial units, many of whom go on to become self-employed artisans having first obtained both on and off the job training. Students use a variety of equipment ranging from the most up to date computer aided devices to relatively simple low cost machinery providing them with an excellent grounding in much of the equipment they are likely to encounter in the small and micro industry sector. Vocational training is an especially important ingredient in any self-employment programme where beneficiaries of concessionary finance are first provided with technical and/or managerial training to enhance existing skills. This is the principle behind the TRYSEM training programme in India which is designed to link into the IRDP self–employment programme. A common deficiency in this initiative, however, is the lack of integration between the programmes so that finance is not always received for the activity that a particular beneficiary has been trained in.

Entrepreneurial development programmes are also a possible means of encouraging greater participation in self–employment. These programmes which tend to concentrate on developing commercial skills could be usefully aimed at employees in the private or public sector who would be eligible for early retirement and interested in a period of self–employment. This practice has been adopted in Japan in a modified form where employees retiring from large private companies are encouraged to work in a subcontracting capacity where they can continue to use their experience and skills for their own benefit as well as that of the parent company. A special incentive scheme could be tied into this programme to attract budding entrepreneurs into new small enterprise ventures.

Marketing support can be of immense value to the small entrepreneur who typically lacks the resources to engage in effective market promotion and the scale of operation to generate a product image. In many developing countries this role, if it exists, is most often performed by a variety of State marketing boards. While these boards can facilitate the marketing effort of small firms by providing them with direct sales outlets through State run emporia and exhibiting in national and international trade fairs, they are often insufficiently entrepreneurial themselves to allow the full sales potential of the product to be realised. Furthermore, these institutions are often confined to a few product areas such as handicrafts, textiles and other traditional items. The consortia concept has been adopted in a number of cases as an alternative to bureaucratic marketing. Some of the best developed examples of this can be found among small enterprises in Italy. On the one hand, these consortia may consist of around 20 to 30 firms in a common product area which agree to pool resources and expertise in order to extend their marketing effort. On the other hand, they may consist of a much larger network of small firms, organised into a national confederation with sufficient resources to assist member firms with market intelligence, brand formation, domestic and export marketing, including participation in local, regional and national trade fairs and export missions.

The right kind of institutional support is the key to the successful delivery of much small enterprise assistance (see Harper and Hailey 1989 on NGO assistance). Gibb and Manuh (1989) have emphasised the importance of managerial autonomy within any small enterprise extension service where the management would be responsible for a substantial part of strategic as well as operational decision making. He argues that staff should be encouraged to develop a broad personal business network and play an active role in supporting a variety of small business initiatives. He concludes that flexible service delivery lies at the heart of effective small enterprise extension and support which should integrate research and technology with finance, training, consultancy and marketing. In order to achieve these objectives a support service should be established with the aim of becoming wholly or partially self-financed either from a flat rate contribution from member firms or through a system of user charging. The latter would have the advantage that any research, extension or consultancy services would have to be highly responsive to client needs and attempt to ensure that technical solutions were within the context of the resource constraints of the individual small enterprise.

One institutional support initiative which is unique in terms of the scale and range of small business support that is provided is the Confederazionale Nazionale dell' Artigianato (CNA) in Italy (see Slater and Watson 1990). This organisation is specifically designed to support small enterprise in a broadly defined handicraft sector, most of which are firms or workshops with less than 20 employees (10 employees and 10 apprentices) defined under Italian law as 'artisan shops'. The CNA has become the largest business service organisation in Italy with a staff of 7,000 working in 2,300 offices throughout the country and in its headquarters in Rome and in its European liaison office in Brussels. The sector that it serves has become one of the more significant sectors of the national economy characterised by the widespread use of new technologies, productivity, flexibility and an export orientation. This sector contains over 1.5 million enterprises employing around 4 million people.

The organisation of the CNA extends from national to regional, provincial and local level, influencing policy and programme execution at each level, as well as providing specific support to member firms. The range of services includes legal, financial, technical, marketing and administrative support. The CNA is also active in negotiating with trade unions, lobbying government on behalf of members and organising a variety of training initiatives. The CNA has also created local advisory panels of experienced proprietors who are able to evaluate prospective business plans, render technical and managerial advice and identify linkages and networks for new businesses. The CNA has its own credit division which works closely with regional and national banks and has created two units in partnership with local banks to provide specialist financing and leasing (Artigianfin and Artigianfin leasing). In order to access these services firms are expected to organise themselves into guarantee cooperatives, pooling contributions to create an insurance fund as collateral for loans and equipment leases. One of the more innovative forms of direct support is offered by the CNA in Emilia Romagna region. Here, the organisation has identified business administration as one of the major unproductive activities of the small firm and has consequently devised a system which releases members from the arduous task of paperwork and allows them to concentrate on producing and selling goods. As part of this service, the CNA will undertake many of the administrative functions of its member firms such as the maintenance of accounts and payroll, including the issuing of all weekly and monthly payslips, internal audit, insurance etc. To complement these services, the CNA in Emilia Romagna is in the process of introducing desktop banking by issuing member firms with microcomputer hardware and software which will allow them direct access to on-line banking facilities. The organisation is also considering acquiring a major shareholding in one of the region's largest banks which would give its small enterprise members an unusually influential role in local and regional financial policy.

Structural innovation for small enterprise expansion

Much of the success of a small enterprise economy will depend on the kind of industrial structure within which it will function. Certain kinds of structure have proven to be more conducive to the needs and constraints of small enterprise than others. Once again, evidence from Italy has shown the importance of industrial districts in developing the optimum level of industrial concentration encouraging high levels of inter firm linkage and industrial networks. This phenomenon has been examined in detail by Goodman (1989) who emphasises that the significance of industrial growth in Italy in the 1980s is that it has been largely led by the small firm. Moreover, the small firm is no longer confined to traditional product areas but is found in all types of modern and high technology sectors. Goodman sees technology as the key factor behind the expansion of the small enterprise economy in Italy. Modern numerically controlled machine tools and microcomputer equipment have enabled the small firm to meet demand quickly and efficiently catering to the growing personalised, limited and specialised market at relatively low cost.

Goodman has summarised the main characteristics and advantages of the typical Italian small firm as comprising: adaptability; competitive tendency; freedom from legislative controls and trade union pressure; collaboration and inter firm linkage; family domination coupled to inbuilt resistance to takeover and lack of owner/worker divide. A number of these attributes also characterise the typical small enterprise found in developing countries. What needs to be stressed at this point, however, is the importance of those attributes that are missing in many developing countries and how they might be fostered to produce the same advantages.

In many cases the modern industrial district has emerged out of a long history of product specialisation often based on the local availability of raw materials or specialised skills. It is the re-emergence of these districts in recent years that has been partially responsible for the impressive expansion of the small enterprise economy in Italy. The development of the industrial district concept has allowed firms to exploit the inherent, complex balance between cooperation and competition displayed within each district and to expand inter firm linkages in the most productive manner. The concentration

191

of industrial units specialising in a particular product area helps to generate competition between firms while at the same time providing them with a basis for cooperation and collaboration. For example, units can achieve near full capacity utilisation by trading workload with each other. If one unit cannot meet production targets due to under capacity, it will look for under utilised capacity in a neighbouring firm. This kind of arrangement can be enhanced by the mediation of a support institution such as the CNA described above and more fully exploited within the context of an industrial consortium.

In many developing countries, areas of product specialisation already exist and could form the basis of a modern industrial district. In India, for example, certain types of specialist wood carving exist in Uttar Pradesh and Karnataka, handicrafts in Rajasthan, sericulture in Karnataka and Tamil Nadu, leather in Uttar Pradesh and West Bengal, coir in Kerala etc. Where areas of traditional concentration do not exist, the small enterprise estate could act as the focal point of a local growth centre drawing on a multitude of independent suppliers working in close proximity to the family farm. Certain types of infrastructural, technical and financial support could be channelled to these areas of concentration relatively easily. Furthermore, special incentives in the form of tax concessions, tariff on power and raw materials and low interest loans could be granted to activities within a district designated as industrially backward. The advantages of this type of concentration have been noted in India, where the promotion of sustainable self-employment under IRDP has been limited due to the scattering of loan assistance to numerous beneficiaries without any attempt to develop scale economies by clustering assistance on a product/activity basis. The current service area concept which has been adopted by rural banks in India, where an individual bank has been allocated a specific area of operations, may help to solve this problem by ensuring that any one branch has a comprehensive view of the existing lending pattern and is thus able to formulate a strategic plan for future lending which could include the clustering of loan assistance along product/activity lines.

Another advantage arising out of industrial concentration and inter firm linkage is the possibility of fragmenting the production process so that small units, instead of manufacturing the whole product, can specialise in the production of a part of the total process. High levels of specialisation in a part of the production process is one way of ensuring that there is constant innovation at every point in the total process coupled to the use of more advanced technology within the limit of the small firm's investment capacity. This kind of intense specialisation based on a highly fragmented production system has meant that there is maximum flexibility within the production system which is not tied down to a single, high fixed cost production process. This, in turn, has enabled small firms to respond rapidly to shifts in consumer demand and accommodate the growing diversity in consumer taste which is expressed in the expanding 'niche' markets.

This type of fragmentation of the production process is equivalent to subcontracting although relations between the various units of production may be different since it does not suppose the existence of a formal contract but rather a series of informal, mutual profit linked arrangements. In a number of cases, small firms in developing countries are already resorting to the informal 'job contract' as a means of economising on the ownership of machinery and equipment or overcoming problems of machine acquisition. This kind of relationship could be developed by a small enterprise extension service which could assist with the modification of machinery to speed up production and the provision of research and development facilities providing heat treatment, materials testing and quality control.

An alternative structural model is provided by the Japanese small enterprise economy, much of which is based on a formal subcontracting system operating between large firms and small enterprise and, in turn, extending down to micro enterprise at the household level. This system has already been described in chapter three but it will be useful to highlight one or two of the major features and consider how this system might be modified and adopted elsewhere. Modern forms of subcontracting have been favoured by large firms since it has allowed them to economise on fixed capital while taking advantage of cheap labour both of which have allowed them to avoid the instability of the business cycle. The impact of reduced costs and enhanced competition has resulted in considerable success in the export market and the further expansion of the parent firm and its subcontracting chain. This has only been possible with the introduction of a highly integrated system of subcontracting where the parent company provides technological guidance and controls product quality. The typical package of support that will be received by a small subcontracting firm may include: the establishment of financial and accounting systems; the introduction of advanced management principles; grounding in efficient production engineering techniques etc (Annavjhula 1989). The contract will specify the unit price of products, production targets and standards. Annavjhula shows that close cooperation between parent and subcontractor during the production process helped identify parts defects and reduce rejection rates by 50 percent within a single year.

He goes on to point out that the relationship is bound in a symbolic way where the parent company is involved in sponsoring training courses and seminars for workers in subcontracting units as well as providing second career opportunities for its own personnel in subcontracting firms. This relationship is often further cemented through share ownership by the parent in the subcontracting unit and the secondment of advisers and technical personnel to help overcome operating difficulties. The relations of production between parent and subcontractor are by no means equal and many would point to an inherent exploitative tendency underlying the system. Undoubtedly, wage differentials are marked, although in the high growth Japanese economy labour shortages have eroded these differentials. Subcontractors also tend to operate

193

with poor labour conditions, longer working hours where employee relations are based on patron-client ties, labour insecurity and coercion from the parent company particularly on price and production levels (Annavjhula 1989). Despite these problems, small subcontractors have not diminished in Japan but are gradually being transformed into a new generation of highly innovative, flexible small enterprises. These enterprises now tend to use more sophisticated technology as larger firms begin to decentralise manufacturing operations to maintain the competitive advantages that Japanese industry has long enjoyed.

Drawing on the experience of a variety of countries from the above it is clear that there is no single policy approach to small enterprise promotion. What is clear, however, is that a mix of policies relating to the general economic environment and specific support measures will have to be adopted if employment in the rural off-farm sector is to be increased. An initial attempt at this might include the kind of complementary packages that have been described above. However, empirical evidence from Asia suggests that a dynamic off-farm sector in the first instance depends on an expanding smallholder farm economy with rising farm income and demand. The high levels of intensification associated with rice farming provide a sound basis for this transition.

Bibliography

Ahmed, A.S., (1984), 'Dubai Chalo: Problems in the Ethnic Encounter Between Middle East and South Asian Muslim Societies, *Asian Affairs*, vol. 15. no. 3.

Ahmed, I., (1974), 'Green Revolution With or Without Tractors: The Case of Sri Lanka', *Marga Quarterly Journal*, vol. 2, no. 2.

Alavi, H., (1975), 'India and the Colonial Mode of Production', *Economic and Political Weekly*, vol. 10, nos. 33, 34 & 35.

Alavi, H., (1980), 'India: Transition from Feudalism to Colonial Capitalism *Journal of Contemporary Asia*, vol. 10, no. 4.

Alavi, H., (1989), 'Formation of the Social Structure of South Asia Under the Impact of Colonialism', in Alavi, H., and Harriss, J., (eds.), *South Asia*, Macmillan, London.

Amerasinghe, N., (1974), 'Efficiency of Resource Utilisation in Paddy Production on Settlement Farms in Sri Lanka', *Modern Ceylon Studies*, vol. 5, no. 1.

Amerasinghe, N., (1977), 'The Minipe Colonization Scheme' in Hameed, N. et al, *Rice Revolution in Sri Lanka*, UNRISD, Geneva.

Amunugama, S., (1964), 'Rural Credit in Ceylon – Some Sociological Observations', *Ceylon Journal of Historical and Social Studies*, vol. 7, no. 2.

Anderson, D., (1982), 'Small Industry in Developing Countries: A Discussion of Issues', *World Development*, vol. 10, no. 11.

Anderson, D., and Leiserson, M.W., (1980), 'Rural Nonfarm Employment in Developing Countries', *Economic Development and Cultural Change*, vol. 28, no. 2.

Annavjhula, J.C.B., (1989), 'Japanese Subcontracting Systems', *Economic and Political Weekly*, Feb 25.

Arachchi, R.B.S., (1985) 'Non-Farm Employment in the Rural Sector of Sri Lanka: Trends and Prospects', Seminar paper no. 4/85, Agrarian Research and Training Institute, Colombo.

Arrighi, G., (1971), *The Relationship Between the Colonial and the Class Structures: A Critique of A.G. Frank's Theory of the Development of Underdevelopment*, IDEP, Dakar.

Arrighi, G., and Saul, J.S., (1973), *Essays on the Political Economy of Africa*, Monthly Review Press, New York.

ARTI, (1980), 'Hired Labourers in Peasant Agriculture in Sri Lanka', Agrarian Research and Training Institute, Research Study 40, Colombo.

ARTI, (1981a), 'Kurunegala District Development Project: An Analysis of the Pre-Project Situation', Agrarian Research and Training Institute, Research Study 45, Colombo.

ARTI, (1981b), 'Agricultural Credit Schemes Under the Kurunegala Rural Development Project: An Evaluation', Agrarian Research and Training Institute, Research Study 49, Colombo.

Banaji, J., (1977a), 'Modes of Production in a Materialist Theory of History', *Capital and Class*, vol. 3.

Banaji, J., (1977b), 'Capitalist Domination and the Small Peasantry: Deccan Districts in the Late Nineteenth Century', *Economic and Political Weekly*, special number, August.

Bansil, P.C., (1971), *Ceylon Agriculture – A Perspective*, Dhanpat Rai, New Delhi.

Baran, P., (1957), *The Political Economy of Growth*, Monthly Review Press, New York.

Bayliss-Smith, T.P., and Wanmali, S., (eds.), (1984), *Understanding Green Revolutions*, Cambridge University Press, Cambridge.

Beneria, L., (1982), *Women and Development*, Praeger, New York.

Berger, S., and Piore, M., (1980), *Dualism and Discontinuity in Industrial Societies*, Cambridge University Press, Cambridge and New York.

Bernstein, H., (ed), (1976), *Underdevelopment and Development*, Penguin, London.

Bernstein, H., (1979), 'African Peasantries: A Theoretical Framework', *The Journal of Peasant Studies*, vol. 6, no. 4.

Black-Michaud, J., (1981), 'Review of J. Brow 1978 Vedda Villages of Anuradhapura: The Historical Anthropology of a Community in Sri Lanka' *Sri Lanka Journal of Agrarian Studies*, vol. 2, no. 2.

Booth, A., (1989), 'Indonesian Agricultural Development', *World Development*, vol. 17, no. 8.

Bray, F., (1983), 'Patterns of Evolution in Rice-Growing Societies, *Journal of Peasant Studies*, vol. 2, no. 1.

Bray, F., (1986), *The Rice Economies*, Blackwells, Oxford.

Browett, J., (1982), 'Out of the Dependency Perspectives', *Journal of Contemporary Asia*, vol. 12, no. 2.

British Refugee Council, (1990), *The Sri Lanka Monitor*, no.34, Nov.

Byres, T.J., (1979), 'Of Neo-Populist Pipe Dreams: Deadalus in the Third World and the Myth of Urban Bias', *Journal of Peasant Studies*, vol. 6, no. 2.

Byres, T.J., (1984), 'Historical Perspectives on Sharecropping' in T.J. Byres (ed.), *Sharecropping and Sharecroppers*, Frank Cass, London.

Byres, T.J., (1989), 'Agrarian Structure, the New Technology and Class Action in India', in Alavi, H., and Harriss, J., (eds.), *South Asia*, Macmillan, London.

Corner, L., (1986), 'The Prospects for Off-Farm Employment as an Anti-Poverty Strategy Among Malaysian Paddy Farm Households: Macro and Micro Views', in Shand, R.T., (ed.), *Off-Farm Employment in the Development of Rural Asia*, vol. 2, Australian National University, Canberra.

Chadha, G.K., (1986) 'The Off-Farm Economic Structure of Agriculturally Growing Regions: A Study of Indian Punjab', in Shand, R.T., (ed.), *Off-Farm Employment in the Development of Rural Asia*, vol. 2, Australian National University, Canberra.

Chattopadhyay, P., (1972), 'On the Question of the Mode of Production in Indian Agriculture', *Economic and Political Weekly*, vol. 7, no. 13.

Child, F., and Kaneda, H., (1975), 'Links to the Green Revolution: A Study of Small-Scale, Agriculturally Related Industry in the Pakistan Punjab', *Economic Development and Cultural Change*, vol. 23, no. 2.

Chinn, D.L., (1979), 'Rural Poverty and the Structure of Farm Household Income in Developing Countries: Evidence from Taiwan', *Economic Development and Cultural Change*, vol. 27, no. 2.

Chinnappa, B.N., and Silva, W.P.T., (1977), 'Impact of the Cultivation of High Yielding Varieties of Paddy on Income and Employment' in Farmer, B.H., (ed.), *Green Revolution?*, Macmillan, London.

Chuta, E., and Leidholm, C., (1979), 'Rural Nonfarm Employment: A Review of the State of the Art', MSU Rural Development Paper no. 1, Michigan State University.

Cliffe, L., (1977), 'Rural Class Formation in East Africa', *The Journal of Peasant Studies*, vol. 4.

Collier, P., and Lal, D., (1984), 'Why Poor People Get Rich in Kenya 1960-1979', *World Development*, vol. 12, no. 10.

Collier, W.L., (1981), 'Agricultural Evolution in Java' in Hansen, G.E.,(ed.), *Agriculture and Rural Development in Indonesia*, West View Press, Colorado.

Curtis, D.C., (1991), *Beyond Government, Organisation for Common Benefit*, Macmillan, London

De Silva, K.M., (1981), *A History of Sri Lanka*, Hurst, London.

Department of Economics and Statistics, (1986), *'Statistics for Planning'*, Government of Kerala, Trivandrum.

Department of Economics and Statistics, (1987), 'Report of the Survey on the Utilization of Gulf Remittances in Kerala', Government of Kerala, Trivandrum.

Dias, H.D., (1977), 'Selective Adoption as a Strategy for Agricultural Development: Lessons from Adoption in S.E. Sri Lanka', in Farmer, B.H., (ed.), *Green Revolution ?*, Macmillan, London.

Economist, (1985), 'Sri Lanka, Special Survey', *Economist*, August.

Economist, (1990), 'The Hindu Rate of Growth', *Economist*, January.

Eisenstadt, S.N., (1961), *Essays on Sociological Aspects of Political and Economic Development*, Mouton, The Hague.

Ekholm, K., (1981), 'On the Structure and Dynamics of Global Systems', in Kahn, J.S., and Llobera, J.R., (eds.), *The Anthropology of Pre-Capitalist Societies*, Macmillan, London.

Evers, H.D., (1978), 'From Subsistence to Generalized Commodity Production: A Study of South Indian Moneylenders and the Expansion of the Colonial Mode of Production', Paper Presented at the Seminar on Underdevelopment and Subsistence Reproduction in Southeast Asia, University of Bielefeld.

Fabella, R.V., (1986) 'Rural Nonfarm Employment in the Philippines: Composition Growth and Seasonality', in Shand, R.T., (ed.), *Off-Farm Employment in the Development of Rural Asia*, vol. 2, Australian National University, Canberra.

Farm Guide, (1987), *Farm Guide*, Farm Information Bureau, Government of Kerala, Trivandrum.

Farmer, B.H., (1957), *Pioneer Peasant Colonization in Ceylon*, Oxford University Press, London.

Farmer, B.H., (ed.), (1977), *Green Revolution ?*, Macmillan, London.

Francks, P., (1984), *Technology and Agricultural Development in Pre-War Japan*, Yale University Press, New Haven.

Frank, A.G., (1967), *Capitalism and Underdevelopment in Latin America*, Monthly Review Press, New York.

Friedman, H., (1980), 'Household Production and the National Economy: Concepts for the Analysis of Agrarian Transformations', *The Journal of Peasant Studies*, vol. 7, no. 2.

Friedman, J., (1976), 'Marxist Theory and Systems of Total Reproduction', *Critique of Anthropology*, vol. 2, no. 7.

Geertz, C., (1963), *Agricultural Involution*, University of California Press, Berkeley.

George, P.S., (1986), 'Emerging Trends in the Size Distribution of Operational Holdings in Kerala', *Economic and Political Weekly, vol. 29, no. 2.*

Gibb, A., and Manuh, H., (1989), 'Design of Extension Related Support Services and Institutions for Small-Scale Enterprise Development in Developing Countries', Paper Presented at the Symposia on Human Resource Development in the Non State Sector, IDPM, University of Manchester.

Glavanis, K.R.G., (1984), 'Aspects of Non-Capitalist Social Relations in Rural Egypt: the Small Peasant Household in an Egyptian Delta Village', in Long, N., (ed.), *Family and Work in Rural Societies*, Tavistock Publications, London.

Gold, M.E., (1977), *Law and Social Change – A Study of Land Reform in Sri Lanka*, Nellen, New York.

Goodman, E., (1989), *Small Firms and Industrial Districts in Italy*, Routledge, London.

Goodman, D., and Redclift, M., (1981), *From Peasant to Proletarian: Capitalist Development and Agrarian Transitions*, Blackwell, Oxford.

Gordon, A., (1982), 'Indonesia, Plantations and the 'Post-Colonial' Mode of Production', *Journal of Contemporary Asia*, vol. 12, no. 2.

Government of India, (1981), *Census*, Department of Census and Statistics, Delhi.

Grown, C.A., and Sebstad, J., (1989), 'Introduction: Toward a Wider Perspective on Women's Employment', *World Development*, vol. 17 No. 7.

Gunadesa, J.M., Wickramasekera, P., and Herath, H.M.G., (1980), 'A Socio-Economic Survey of Minor Irrigation in the Dry Zone of Sri Lanka', Research Paper, Univeristy of Peradeniya.

Gunasekera, T., (1984a), 'Stratification and Social Change in a Sinhalese Peasant Society', PhD Thesis, Cornell University.

Gunasekera, T., (1984b), 'The Politicisation of the Power Structure and the Death of Leadership in a Highland Community', Paper Presented at the International Conference on the Symbolic and Material Dimensions of Agrarian Change in Sri Lanka, Anuradhapura.

Gunasinghe, N., (1975), 'Production Relations and Classes in a Kandyan Village', *Modern Ceylon Studies*, vol. 6, no. 2.

Gunasinghe, N., (1980), 'Changing Socio-Economic Relations in the Kandyan Countryside', PhD Thesis, University of Sussex.

Gunawardena, R.A.L.H., (1971), 'Irrigation and Hydraulic Society in Medieval Ceylon', *Past and Present*, no. 53.

Haggblade, S., Hazell, P., and Brown, J., (1989), 'Farm-Nonfarm Linkages in Rural Sub-Saharan Africa', *World Development*, vol. 17, no. 8.

Haggblade, S., Leidholm, C., and Mead, D.C., (1986), 'The Effect of Policy and Policy Reform on Non-Agricultural Enterprises and Employment in Developing Countries: A Review of Past Experiences', MSU International Development Working Paper, no. 27, Michigan State University.

Hameed, N.D.A., et al, (1977), *Rice Revolution in Sri Lanka*, UNRISD, Geneva.

Hansen, G.,(ed.), (1981), *Agriculture and Rural Development in Indonesia*, Westview Press, Colorado.

Hanumantha Rayappa, P., (1986), 'Some Dimensions of Off-Farm Employment in Rural Karnataka', in Shand, R.T., (ed.), *Off-Farm Employment in the Development of Rural Asia*, vol. 2, Australian National University, Canberra.

Harper, M., (1989), 'Management Development for Enterprise Promotion: NGOs and the Development of Income Generating Enterprise', Paper Presented at the Symposia on Human Resource Development in the Non State Sector, IDPM, University of Manchester.

Harriss, B., (1977), Tractors, 'Profits and Debt in Hambantota District, Sri Lanka', in Farmer, B.H., (ed.), *Green Revolution ?*, Macmillan, London.

Harriss, J.C., (1977), 'Pahalagama: A Case Study of Agricultural Change in a Frontier Environment', and 'Social Implications of Change in Agriculture in Hambantota', in Farmer, B.H., (ed.), *Green Revolution ?*, Macmillan, London.

Harriss, J.C., (ed.), (1982), *Rural Development. Theories of Peasant Economy and Agrarian Change*, Hutchinson University Library, London.

Harriss, J.C., (1982), *Capitalism and Peasant Farming. Agrarian Structure and Ideology in Northern Tamil Nadu*, Oxford University Press, Bombay.

Harriss, J.C., (1989), 'Indian Industrialisation and the State', in Alavi, H., and Harriss, J., (eds.), *South Asia*, Macmillan, London.

Harriss, J.C., and Moore, M.P., (1984), *Development and the Rural-Urban Divide*, Frank Cass, London.

Hayami, Y., and Kikuchi, M., (1985), 'Agricultural Technology and Income Distribution: Two Indonesian Villages Viewed from the Japanese Experience', in Ohkawa, K., and Ranis, G., (eds.), *Japan and the Developing Countries*, Blackwell, Oxford.

Herath, H.M.G., (1983), 'The Role of Rural Institutions in the Diffusion of Agricultural Innovations in Sri Lanka' World Employment Programme Research Working Paper, 2-22, Geneva.

Herath, H.M.G., (1986), 'An Exploratory Study of Off-Farm Employment and Incomes in Sri Lanka', in Shand, R.T., (ed.), *Off-Farm Employment in the Development of Rural Asia*, vol. 2, Australian National University, Canberra.

Hirschmeier, J., (1964), *The Origins of Entrepreneurship in Meji Japan*, Harvard University Press, Harvard.

Ho, S. (1979), 'Decentralised Industrialisation and Rural Development: Evidence from Taiwan', *Economic Development and Cultural Change*, vol. 27, no. 2.

Ho, S., (1982), 'Economic Development and Rural Industry in South Korea and Taiwan', *World Development* vol. 10, no. 11.

Ho, S., (1986), 'Off-farm Employment and Farm Households in Taiwan', in Shand, R.T., (ed.), *Off-Farm Employment in the Development of Rural Asia*, vol. 1, Australian National University, Canberra.

Horii, K., (1981), *Rice Economy and Land Tenure in West Malaysia*, Institute of Developing Economics, Tokyo.

Hoselitz, B.F., (1960), *Sociological Factors in Economic Development*, Free Press, Chicago.

Ibrahim, Z., (1982), 'Perspectives on Capitalist Penetration and the Reconstitution of the Malay Peasantry' *Jurnal Ekonomi*, no. 5.

India Today, (Jan 1990), 'Getting into Stride', *India Today*, January 15.

India Today, (July 1990), 'Rural Markets, the Call of Consumerism', *India Today*, July 15.

India Today, (Sept 1990), 'Kerala Welcome the Capitalists', *India Today*, September 30.

Islam, N., (1986), 'Non–Farm Employment in Rural Asia Issues and Evidence', in Shand, R.T., (ed.), *Off–Farm Employment in the Development of Rural Asia*, vol. 1, Australian National University, Canberra.

Jain, L.C., et al, (1985), *Grass Without Roots: Rural Development Under Government Auspices*, Sage, New Delhi.

Jayaweera, N., (1973), 'Credit Support for High Yielding Varieties in Sri Lanka', *Marga Quarterly Journal*, vol. 2, no. 2.

Jogaratnam, T., (1971), 'Report of the Re–Survey of Elahera Colonization Scheme in Ceylon', Peradeniya University, Peradeniya.

Kada, R., (1986), 'Off–Farm Employment and the Rural–Urban Interface in Japanese Economic Development', in Shand, R.T., (ed.), *Off–Farm Employment in the Development of Rural Asia*, vol. 1, Australian National University, Canberra.

Kahn, J.S., (1980), *Minangkabau Social Formations*, Cambridge University Press, Cambridge.

Kahn, J.S., (1981), 'Mercantilism and the Emergence of Service Labour in Colonial Indonesia', in Kahn, J.S., and Llobera, J.R., (eds.), *The Anthropology of Pre–Capitalist Societies*, Macmillan, London.

Kahn, J.S., and Llobera, J.R., (1981), (eds.), *The Anthropology of Pre–Capitalist Societies*, Macmillan, London.

Kikuchi, M., (1986), 'Growing Impact of Off–farm Employment on a Rural Economy: Changes in Labour Utilisation and Income Earning Structure in a Philippine Rice Village', in Shand, R.T., (ed.), *Off–Farm Employment in the Development of Rural Asia*, vol. 2, Australian National University, Canberra.

Kikuchi, M. and Hayami, Y., (1985), 'Agricultural Growth Against a Land–Resource Constraint: Japan, Taiwan, Korea and the Philippines', in Ohkawa, K. and Ranis, G., (eds.), *Japan and the Developing Countries*, Blackwell, Oxford.

Kilby, P., and Leidholm, C., (1986), 'The Role of Nonfarm Activities in the Rural Economy', Employment and Enterprise Policy Analysis Discussion Paper Series, USAID, Washington.

201

KIRDP, (1981), 'Scheme Completion Report – Pallama Tank', Kurunegala Integrated Rural Development Project Report.

Kurian, N.J., (1989), 'Anti–Poverty Programme: A Reappraisal', *economic and Political Weekly*, March 25.

Laclau, E., (1971), 'Feudalism and Capitalism in Latin America', *New Left Review*, vol. 67.

Lassort, J., and Clavier, J.L., (1989), 'SMEs in the ACPs', *The Courier*, no. 115.

Leach, E.R., (1959), 'Hydraulic Society in Ceylon' *Past and Present*, no. 15.

Leach, E.R., (1961), *Pul Eliya a Village in Ceylon*, Cambridge University Press, London.

Leurs, R., (1989), 'Technology for Rural Development in India', Phd Thesis, University of Manchester.

Lipton, M., (1977), *Why Poor People Stay Poor: Urban Bias in World Development*, Temple Smith, London.

Lipton, M., (1989), 'Agriculture, Rural People, the State and the Surplus in Some Asian Countries: Thoughts on Some Implications of Three Recent Approaches in Social Science', *World Development*, vol, 17, no. 10.

Long, N., (ed.), (1984), *Family and Work in Rural Societies*, Tavistock Publications, London.

Long, N., and Roberts, B.R., (eds.), (1978), *Peasant Cooperation and Capitalist Expansion in Central Peru*, University of Texas Press, Austin.

Long, N., and Roberts, B.R., (eds.), (1984), *Miners, Peasants and Entrepreneurs: Regional Development in the Central Highlands of Peru*, Cambridge University Press, Cambridge.

Low, A.R.C., (1981), 'The Effect of Off–Farm Employment on Farm Incomes and Production: Taiwan Contrasted with Southern Africa', *Economic Development and Cultural Change*, vol. 29, no. 4.

Madduma Bandara, C.M., (1984), 'Green Revolution and Water Demand: Irrigation and Ground Water in Sri Lanka and Tamil Nadu', in Bayliss–Smith T.P., and Wanmali, S., (eds.), *Understanding Green Revolutions*, Cambridge University Press, Cambridge.

Manor, J., (1979), 'The Failure of Political Integration in Sri Lanka', *Journal of Commonwealth and Comparative Politics*, vol. 17.

Manor, J., (ed.), (1984a), *Sri Lanka in Change and Crisis*, Croom Helm, London.

Manor, J., (1984b), 'Blurring the Line Between Parties and Social Bases. Gundu Rao and the Emergence of a Janata Government in Karnataka', *Economic and Political Weekly*, special article Sept.

McClelland, D.C., (1961), *The Achieving Society*, Von Nostrand, Princeton.

Meillasoux, C., (1972), 'From Reproduction to Production', *Economy and Society*, vol. 1, no. 1.

Middleton, A., (1989), 'The Changing Structure of Petty Production in Ecuador', *World Development*, vol. 17, no. 1.

Mies, M., (1982), *The Lace Makers of Narsapur*, ILO, Geneva.

Misawa, T., (1969), 'An Analysis of Part–Time Farming in the Postwar Period', in Ohkawa, K., Johnston, B., and Kaneda, H., (eds.), (1969), *Agriculture and Economic Growth: Japan's Experience*, Princeton University Press, Princeton.

Morgan, D., (1989), 'Micro–Enterprises and their Role in the Development Process', *The Courier*, no. 115.

Moore, M.P., (1984), 'Categorising Space: Urban–Rural or Core–Periphery in Sri Lanka', in Harriss, J.C., and Moore, M.P., (eds.), *Development and the Rural–Urban Divide*, Frank Cass, London.

Moore, M.P., (1985), *The State and Peasant Politics in Sri Lanka*, Cambridge University Press, Cambridge.

Morrison, B.M., Moore, M.P., and Lebbe, M.U.I., (eds.), (1979), *The Disintegrating Village*, Lake House, Colombo.

Mukhopadhyay, S., and Chee Peng Lim (eds.), (1985) *Development and Diversification of Rural Industries in Asia*, Asia and Pacific Development Centre, Kuala Lumpur.

Nair, P.R.G., (1986), 'Report of a Survey of Returned Migrants', Centre for Development Studies, Trivandrum.

Nossiter, T.J., (1988), *Marxist State Governments in India*, Pinter, London

Obeyesekere, G., (1967), *Land Tenure in Village Ceylon*, Cambridge University Press, Cambridge.

Ohkawa, K., (1969), 'Phases of Agricultural Development and Economic Growth', in Ohkawa, K., Johnston, B., and Kaneda, H., (eds.), *Agriculture and Economic Growth: Japan's Experience*, Princeton University Press, Princeton.

Onchan, T., and Chalamwong, Y., (1986), 'Rural Off–Farm Income and Employment in Thailand: Current Evidence, Future Trends and Implications', in Shand, R.T., (ed.), *Off–Farm Employment in the Development of Rural Asia*, vol. 1, Australian National University, Canberra.

Oshima, H., (1986a), 'The Transition from an Agrarian Economy to an Industrial Economy in East Asia', *Economic Development and Cultural Change*, vol. 34, no. 4.

Oshima, H,. (1986b), 'Off–farm Employment and Incomes in Postwar East Asian Growth', in Shand, R.T., (ed.), *Off–Farm Employment in the Development of Rural Asia*, vol. 1, Australian National University, Canberra.

Otto–Walter, R., (1978), 'Subsistence Reproduction and Mode of Production: the Indian Contribution' Paper Presented at the Seminar on Underdevelopment and Subsistence Reproduction in Southeast Asia, University of Bielefeld.

Paci, M, (1982), *La Struttura Sociale Italiana*, Il Mulino, Bologna.

Panditharatne, B.L., and Gunasekera, G.D.A., (1977), 'Ussapitiya Village', in Hameed, N.D.A., et al, *Rice Revolution in Sri Lanka*, UNRISD, Geneva.

Patnaik, U., (1971), 'Capitalist Development in Agriculture: A Note', *Economic and Political Weekly*, vol. 6, no. 39.

Patnaik, U., (1972), 'On the Mode of Production in Indian Agriculture: A Reply', *Economic and Political Weekly*, A 145–151.

Patnaik, U., et al, (1978), *Studies in the Development of Capitalism in India*, Vanguard Books: Lahore.

Pearse, A., (1981), *Seeds of Plenty Seeds of Want*, Clarendon Press, Oxford.

Perera, J., (1982), 'Social Change and Class Relations in Sri Lanka', PhD Thesis, University of Sussex.

Perera, J., (1984), 'Trends in Agrarian Change: Past and Present in Wewagama, A Village in the Mahaweli Development Project', Paper Presented at the International Conference on the Symbolic and Material Aspects of Agrarian Change in Sri Lanka, Anuradhapura.

Perera, J., (1985), *New Dimensions of Social Stratification in Rural Sri Lanka*, Lake House, Colombo.

Persaud, V., (1989), 'Entrepreneurship Need Not Be A Problem in Africa', *The Courier*, no. 115.

Pieris, G.H., (1976), 'Share Tenancy and Tenurial Reform in Sri Lanka', *Ceylon Journal of Historical and Social Studies*, vol. 6, no 1.

Pieris, R., (1956), *Sinhalese Social Organisations*, Ceylon University Press Board, Colombo.

Piore, M., and Sabel, C., (1985), 'Italian Small Business Development: Lessons for US Industrial Policy', in Zysman, J., and Tyson, J., (eds.), *American Industry in International Competition*, Cornell University Press, Ithaca.

Piyadasa, L., (1984), *Sri Lanka: The Holocaust and After*, Marram books, London.

Ponnambalam, S., (1981), *Dependent Capitalism in Crisis*, Zed Press, London.

Pradhan, R.K., (1989), 'On Helping Small Enterprises in Developing Countries', *World Development*, vol. 17. no. 1.

Rahman, F.H., (1989), ' Rural Savings: A Neglected Dimension of Rural Development', *The Courier* no. 115.

Ram, N., (1972), 'Development of Capitalism in Agriculture.', *Social Scientist*, vol. 1, no. 5.

Roberts, M., (1970a), 'Grain Taxes in British Ceylon, 1832–1878: Theories, Prejudices and Contoversies', *Modern Ceylon Studies*, vol.1, no. 1.

Roberts, M., (1970b), 'The Impact of the Waste Lands Legislation and the Growth of Plantations on the Techniques of Paddy Cultivation in British Ceylon: A Critique', *Modern Ceylon Studies*, vol. 1, no. 2.

Robinson, M.S., (1975), *Political Structure in a Changing Sinhalese Village*, Cambridge University Press , Cambridge.

Roseberry, W., (1978), 'Peasants as Proletarians', *Critique of Anthropology*, vol. 3, no. 11.

Rudra, A., et al, (1969), 'Big Farmers of Punjab', *Economic and Political Weekly*, vol. 4, no. 39.

Rudra, A., (1971), 'The Green and Greedy Revolution', *South Asian Review*, vol. 4, no. 4.

Sabel. C., and Zeitlin, J., (1985), 'Historical Alternatives to Mass Production: Politics, Markets and Technology in Nineteenth-Century Industrialization', *Past and Present*, vol. 108.

Sandesara, J.C., (1988), 'Small-Scale Industrialisation – The Indian Experience', *Economic and Political Weekly*, March 26.

Schikele, R., (1969), 'Economic and Social Problems of Peasant Agriculture in Ceylon', in Schickele, R., Ceylon Papers on Agricultural Development and Economic Progress 1967-1970.

Selvadurai, J., (1977), 'Palannoruwa Village (Western Province)', in Hameed, N.D.A., et al, *Rice Revolution in Sri Lanka*, UNRISD, Geneva.

Senanayake, R., (1983), 'The Ecological, Energetic and Agronomic Systems of Ancient and Modern Sri Lanka', *The Ecologist*, vol. 13, no. 4.

Schmitz, H., (1982), 'Growth Constraints on Small-Scale Manufacturing in Developing Countries', *World Development*, vol. 10, no. 6.

Shand, (1986), 'Off-farm Employment in the Development of Rural Asia: Issues', in Shand, R.T., (ed.), *Off-farm Employment in the Development of Rural Asia*, vol. 1, Australian National University, Canberra.

Shand, and Chew, (1986), 'Off-farm Employment in the Kemubu Project in Kelantan, Malaysia', in Shand, R.T., (ed.), *Off-Farm Employment in the Development of Rural Asia*, vol. 2, Australian National University, Canberra.

Shinohara, M., (1970), *Structural Change in Japan's Economic Development*, Kinokuniya Bookstore, Tokyo.

Silva, K.T., (1979), 'Welivita: The Demise of Kandyan Feudalism', in Morrison, B.M., Moore, M.P., and Lebbe, M.U.I., (eds.), *The Disintegrating Village*, Lake House, Colombo.

Silva, K.T., (1982), 'Caste, Class and Capitalist Transformation in Highland Sri Lanka: Continuity and Change in a Low Caste Village', PhD Thesis, Monash University, Melbourne.

Siriwardena, S., (1990) 'From Planned Intervention to Negotiated Development: The Struggles of Bureaucrats, Farmers and Traders in the Mahaweli Irrigation Scheme in Sri Lanka, PhD Thesis, The Agricultural University of Wageningen, Netherlands.

Slater, R.P., (1985), 'Ethnic Crisis and Political Opportunism: A Background to the Communal Violence of Sri Lanka', *Groniek*, no. 92.

Slater, R.P., (1989), 'Central Control or Local Reform: The Case of Decentralisation in Sri Lanka', *Planning and Administration*, vol. 16, no. 2.

Slater, R.P., and Watson, J.R., (1989), 'Democratic Decentralization or Political Consolidation: the Case of Local Government Reform in Karnataka', *Public Administration and Development*, vol. 9.

Slater, R.P., and Watson J.R., (eds.), (1990), 'Small Enterprise Development in Italy', PAMORD Field Report, Development Administration Group, University of Birmingham.

Slater, R.P., Watson J.R., and Tripathy, R.N., (eds.), (1989), *In the Shadow of the Gulf. Case Studies in Poverty Alleviation in Kerala*, National Institute of Rural Development Press, Hyderabad.

Slater, R.P., Watson, J.R., and Srivastava, O.N., (eds.), (1991), *Participation and Development: Case Studies in Poverty Alleviation in West Bengal*, National Institute of Rural Development Press, Hyderabad.

Smith, T., (1969), 'Farm Family By-Employment in Pre-Industrial Japan', *Journal of Economic History*, vol. 29, no. 4.

Snodgrass, D., (1974), *Ceylon: An Export Economy in Transition*, Richard Irwin, Illinois.

Steel, W.F., and Webster, L.M., (1989), 'Building the Role of SMEs: Lessons Learned from Credit Programmes', *The Courier, no. 115*.

Stirrat, R.L., (1977), 'Dravidian and Non-Dravidian Kinship Terminologies in Sri Lanka', *Contributions to Indian Sociology*, vol. 11, no 2.

Subrahmanian, K.K., and Pillai, P.M., (1986), 'Kerala's Industrial Backwardness', *Economic and Political Weekly*, April 5.

Sudhakar Rao, B., (1985), 'Rural Industrialisation and Rural Non-Farm Employment in India', in Mukhopadhyay, S., and Chee Peng Lim (eds.), *Development and Diversification of Rural Industries in Asia*, Asia and Pacific Development Centre, Kuala Lumpur.

Sweezy, P., (1942), *The Theory of Capitalist Development*, Monthly Review Press, New York.

Taylor,J.G., (1979), *From Modernization to Modes of Production*, Macmillan, London.

Terray, E., (1972), *Marxism and 'Primitive' Societies*, Monthly Review Press, New York.

Tussing, A., (1969), 'The Labour Force in Meji Economic Growth: A Quantitative Study of Yamanashi Prefecture', in Ohkawa, K., Johnston, B., and Kaneda, H., (eds.), *Agriculture and Economic Growth: Japan's Experience*, Princeton University Press, Princeton.

Uphoff, N., (ed.), *Rural Development and Local Organisation in Asia*, Macmillan, New Delhi.

Uphoff, N., and Wanigaratne, R., (1982), 'Local Organisation and Rural Development in Sri Lanka', in Uphoff, N., (ed.), *Rural Development and Local Organisation in Asia*, Macmillan, New Delhi.

Wallerstein, I., (1974), *The Modern World System*, Academic Press, New York.

Wallerstein, I., (1976) 'The Three Stages of African Involvement in the World Economy' in Gutkind, P., and Wallerstein, I., (eds.), *The Political Economy of Contemporary Africa*, Sage Publications, Beverly Hills.

Watanabe, S., (1978), 'Technological Linkages Between Formal and Informal Sectors of Manufacturing Industry', Working Paper no. 34, ILO, Geneva.

Weeraratne, C.S., (1983), 'Pesticides - An Overview with Particular Reference to Sri Lanka', *Economic Review*, vol. 8, no. 10.

Weiss, L., (1988), *Creating Capitalism*, Blackwell, Oxford.

White, B., (1981), 'Population, Involution and Employment in Rural Java', in Hansen, G.E., (ed.), *Agriculture and Rural Development in Indonesia*, Westview Press, Colorado.

Wittfogel, K., (1957), *Oriental Despotism: A Comparative Study of Total Power*, Yale University Press, New Haven.

Williams, J., (1988), 'Vulnerability and Change in Taiwan's Agriculture', *Pacific Review*, vol. 29, no. 1.

World Bank, (1979), 'Sri Lanka Staff Appraisal Report, Kurunegala Rural Development Project', Report no. 2292–CE, Washington.

World Bank, (1986), *World Development Report*, World Bank, Washington.

Yalman, N., (1962) 'The Structure of the Sinhalese Kindred: A Re–Examination of the Dravidian Terminology', *American Anthropologist* vol. 64, no. 3.

Yalman, N., (1967), *Under the Bo Tree*, University of California Press, Berkeley.